Governance in Family Enterprises

*Maximizing Economic and Emotional Success*

# Governance in Family Enterprises

Alexander Koeberle-Schmid
Denise Kenyon-Rouvinez
Ernesto J. Poza

Softcover reprint of the hardcover 1st edition 2014 978-1-137-29389-3

First published 2014 by
PALGRAVE MACMILLAN

Palgrave Macmillan in the UK is an imprint of Macmillan Publishers Limited, registered in England, company number 785998, of Houndmills, Basingstoke, Hampshire RG21 6XS.

Palgrave Macmillan in the US is a division of St Martin's Press LLC, 175 Fifth Avenue, New York, NY 10010.

Palgrave Macmillan is the global academic imprint of the above companies and has companies and representatives throughout the world.

Palgrave® and Macmillan® are registered trademarks in the United States, the United Kingdom, Europe and other countries

ISBN 978-1-349-45139-5    ISBN 978-1-137-29390-9 (eBook)
DOI 10.1057/9781137293909

A catalogue record for this book is available from the British Library.

A catalog record for this book is available from the Library of Congress.

# Contents

# List of Figures

## Chapter 7

## Chapter 8

## Chapter 9

## Chapter 10

## Chapter 11

## Chapter 12

## Chapter 13

# Preface

The need for a comprehensive, global book on family business governance has become increasingly evident in recent years. There is a lack of recent work that provides families with a good and rigorous resource on family business governance covering both the family and the business aspects. The aim of *Governance in Family Enterprises – Maximizing Economic and Emotional Success* is to offer a general and exhaustive view of governance in a family enterprises context. It is very "hands-on," providing family owners not only with definitions and context, but also tools and ideas to put in place to help both the family and the family firm thrive and improve their economic and emotional value. This is the goal of family business governance.

Perhaps you are part of a business-owning family, concerned about which of the founder's children is suitable to be a chief executive officer (CEO). Or you are worried that there is too much power in one individual's hands, and no formal decision-making processes in the enterprise. Or you may be a nonfamily executive trying to understand the family culture. *Governance in Family Enterprises* will deepen your understanding and guide your approach, based on the accumulated wisdom of experience and research from successful family enterprises.

In 2010, 2012, and 2013 some of us were involved in writing similar books published in German, which have been received extremely warmly. The three of us felt that an international version was needed. With the agreement of the German publisher Erich Schmidt and the support of Palgrave Macmillan, we used the structure of the original book to develop

*Governance in Family Enterprises* for a global audience. Most of the material is completely new, and includes up-to-date case studies of family enterprises in North America, Latin America, Europe, the Middle East, and Asia.

The range of issues to be addressed is considerable, and we have felt frustration at times, as it can feel impossible to cover all of the subject areas in great depth. Nonetheless, in our daily work with families, we realize how much the global view is needed and we know that families who need to go deeper into the topics of family office, family councils, family philanthropy, or business boards, for instance, can grab any of the dozens of books written on any of these specialist topics.

Several families have helped us to prepare this book. Their stories each illustrate a specific aspect of the governance and management of family enterprises. They were very willing to share their experiences: great learning comes from great examples and we are forever indebted to them for their contribution.

We are also thankful to Philip Whiteley, who excelled at the difficult task of aligning three different writing styles, keeping us on our toes, and doing wonders at editing our work.

Working on this book has been a pleasure. We would like publicly to state our respect and admiration for families; for what family businesses represent; for their struggle and their genius; and for the jobs and stability they bring to our economies. We hope you will enjoy reading this book just as much as we have enjoyed writing it. Our aim is to provide deep insights into how you can maximize the economic and emotional value through developing strong family business governance.

Alexander Koeberle-Schmid    fbg@koeberle-schmid.de
Denise Kenyon-Rouvinez     kenyon@span.ch
Ernesto J. Poza               ErnestoPoza@aol.com

Germany, Switzerland, United States of America, January 2014

# part 1

# Structures for Family and Business: Family Business Governance

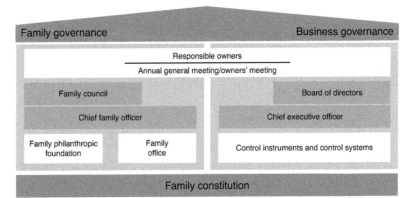

This figure illustrates the family business governance model and acts as a navigational tool for the reader.

## chapter 1

# Maximizing Success through Professional Family Business Governance*

"Family-owned businesses need to align their governance with that of public companies to some extent."

Interview with Dr. Jürgen Heraeus, Chairman of Heraeus Holding, Hanau, Germany

Dr. Jürgen Heraeus, chairman of the board of directors at Heraeus Holding, gives an account here of how the most important aspects of leadership, control, and family structures are implemented in his company. Heraeus is a globally active precious metal and technology group based in Hanau, near Frankfurt in Germany. The company has been family-owned for more than 160 years. With more than 12,200 employees, Heraeus generated product

revenues of €4.2 billion and precious metals trading revenue of €16 billion in 2012.**

---

* Alexander Koeberle-Schmid would like to thank Peter May, Peter Witt, Karsten Schween, Hans-Jürgen Fahrion, and Bernd Grottel for their support in developing this chapter from prior work on which they collaborated.
** This interview is translated into English and has already been published in the book Führung von Familienunternehmen (Leading the Family Enterprise) by Alexander Koeberle-Schmid and Bernd Grottel, published by Erich Schmidt, Germany.

*Alexander Koeberle-Schmid*: **Dr. Heraeus, governance in family-owned businesses differs from that in publicly-held companies. In your opinion, what is the most significant difference?**

*Jürgen Heraeus*: The most important difference is the time factor, really. Owners usually have a planning horizon that is measured in generations, whereas to managers and shareholders of listed companies quarters and quarter figures matter the most. This fundamentally different perspective of family-owned businesses has a major impact on the requirements for and the development of governance.

**A family enterprise that has reached a certain size needs to have its own family business governance. To what extent is this true for your company?**

We first established a family governance code within our company in 2006, on the basis of which we then adopted the Heraeus family code in June 2011. In its function as the code of the shareholder families, it forms a common basis for all shareholders and furthermore provides a knowledge base to all young and new shareholders.

**The board of directors takes a special position within the governance system. What significance does this board have in your company?**

True to our motto, "Good governance at Heraeus," we think it is important that the board is as professionally staffed as it would be in a public company. Also, we decided that owners must play an active part in our company's boards, thus taking on a great deal of responsibility for the company. In order to be eligible, candidates must comply with a range of criteria such as suitability and qualifications as well as commitment and acceptance within the ranks of owners. You see, we have set the bar very high.

**You have about 200 shareholders. This results in some shareholders becoming less attached to the company as well as an increase**

**in heterogeneity. How do you handle this situation?**

Our dividend payout corresponds to our system of values and is most appropriately characterized by the term "modest." Therefore, the links that bind shareholders to the company are more emotional than monetary. There is a considerable vested interest in the company and its development. In addition to our annual shareholders' meeting, we organize special activities such as young shareholders' meetings, family weekends, and education days.

**How do you proceed if a shareholder wants to drop out?**

Our share price, a so-called ceiling price, is determined annually. This price is announced at our shareholders' meeting. If a shareholder wants to sell his shares, he has the option of choosing a buyer from within the family or otherwise the shares are tendered. Should no shareholder be able to buy the shares, our asset-managing holding company will need to buy them.

**It is your wish that family members be represented within management. How do you**

**ensure that the managing director in your family enterprise is suitably qualified?**

Before they can hold a position in the family company, family members must have proven themselves in other companies. They can then apply for a position two levels below group management level. The shareholder committee will determine whether that family member is a good match for the company in terms of character and experience. They must be capable of leading the company *They must be capable of leading the company* but also of communicating with the family.

**What can be done if there is more than one candidate from within the family for a certain position in management?**

It is obviously easier if only one family member is applying than if there are several applicants for a position in the company. If there is more than one it might be preferable not to allow any of those family members to join the management team, in order to avoid conflicts. So far we haven't had this situation.

**Especially in times of crisis, a family enterprise needs to be able to rely on its management. We have seen family businesses overcome numerous crises over time. Do family enterprises cope with crisis situations more successfully?**

The best prerequisites for overcoming a crisis are sufficient liquidity, a sound equity basis, a broad, globally competitive business portfolio, and tailor-made governance. Speaking on behalf of Heraeus, I'm confident that, being an internationally operating family-owned group, we meet the most important requirements for coping with future crises.

**What kind of advice would you give to an entrepreneurial family wishing to further develop their governance?**

Family-owned businesses need to align their governance with that of public companies to some extent; that is, complying with those regulations stipulated by the German Corporate Governance Code that make sense. That being said, some of those regulations don't make sense for family businesses, in my opinion. For example, a retiring managing director should not have to take a two-year cool-off period before joining the supervisory board. If he is a family member, he should be allowed to join the supervisory board immediately to ensure the same standards continue because, after all, it is his own or his family's money that is at stake.

## Family enterprises are special

Three brothers jointly run their businesses.[1] They form a unit; a powerful team. They have divided up the tasks among themselves. One is responsible for finance, controlling, and human resources. The other runs the internet companies. The third takes care of the manufacturing businesses. The situation today is clear. But in the next generation, six cousins – the children of the three brothers – take up roles in the business. The brothers ask the following governance questions: Will all children inherit the shares equally? Which of the six cousins will manage the enterprise in the next generation? What happens when conflicts arise? How should the children be best prepared for their future role as owners? How can we ensure cohesion between the cousins?

Here is another example. An entrepreneur has five children from two marriages. He plans to retire from management in three years' time. A daughter from his first marriage and a son from his second marriage are interested in taking on a management role in the company. The company is just big enough for two managing directors and owners. The daughter, aged 35, has already made a career outside of the family enterprise and would like to start in a year's time as managing director. The son, 23, has just completed a university degree. The father considers the following governance questions:

- Shall the shares be handed over to both children; and at what time?
- How can he compensate the children who do not get shares in the company, if he has no personal assets?
- What if conflicts occur between the half-siblings?
- Should a board of directors with external members be created? What succession plans do we have?

A third family runs a mechanical engineering firm. It has developed a technology with great potential. The entrepreneur has ambitious plans: sales are expected to rise over the next five years from €150 million to €500 million. For expansion in France and the establishment of subsidiaries in the USA, India, and China, an external minority investor has joined forces with the company. The relevant governance questions for this family enterprise are:

- What changes in the management and control structures need to be anticipated?
- What role should the new investor play on the board of directors?
- How can appropriate control systems prevent wrong decisions?
- How can we ensure that employees in all subsidiaries comply with the legal rules and compliance standards?

These **three enterprises have the common features** that they are under the dominant ownership of one or more families, with a dynastic intention or generational approach.[2] However, the three family enterprises differ in ownership and management structure, whether they have a focused or a diversified business, and in size, culture, and whether or not they have nonfamily owners.[3]

*dominant ownership of one or more families, with a dynastic intention*

Family enterprises differ not only among themselves, but also from other types of businesses. For instance, publicly-listed companies have dispersed ownership of unknown shareholders that can buy and sell their shares at any time. Family enterprises also differ from state-run organizations, those held by private equity firms, or cooperatives.

Family enterprises constitute a unique and special category of businesses, with features that include: long-term strategic orientation, low disclosure obligations, and the increased continuity in management positions. Some of these characteristics give them competitive advantages; on the other hand, family enterprises face enormous risks, such as internal family conflicts destroying the business. In this book we seek to create a practical resource for approaching governance in family firms to help equip companies to face these issues. Below we highlight some of the **principal opportunities** that family firms enjoy, linked to the related risk factor:

- Family values can create competitive advantages, *but* continuous conflicts among family members undermine this.
- Family managers are more engaged with the company, and do not need so much control, *but* family managers may be less qualified and competent, act in their own interests, and require more control.
- Family members are oriented towards the long term, *but* some family members often want to maximize short-term dividends.

- Family enterprises focus on a sustainable business model, *but* family enterprises have risks associated with the business life-cycle.

Some family enterprises are highly successful and able to increase their value over generations, while others fall prey to internal disputes and crisis. The difference is that those that fail do not react properly to the challenges, do not have common vision and mission, a sound strategy or appropriate governance structures, and the roles of family members are not clearly defined and incorporated by each family member. The following chapters set out approaches for different aspects of governance, both for the family and the business, addressing not just the structures, but matters such as values, conduct, and principles.

*Employees who can identify with a corporate culture demonstrate an increased motivation for their job*

## Sound family business governance

Empirical analyses show that family enterprises are more successful when they have established optimally designed management, control, and family structures.[4] Despite this, many family enterprises neglect governance. A report published in 2010 indicated an alarming number of insufficiently governed family enterprises.[5] This neglect exposes them to considerable risks. **Indicators of inadequate governance** are:

- No obligation for family members to prove their competence when working in the business.
- No clear definition of the board of directors' competences for exercising control.
- No management of opportunities and risks in the company.
- No rule regarding an exit mechanism.
- No rule regarding interactions with nonfamily shareholders.
- Limited family cohesion.
- No arrangements for managing conflict in the family and the company.

It is surprising that family enterprises pay insufficient attention to governance, because this began to be discussed many years ago. In 1996, Craig Aronoff and John Ward published *Family Business Governance.*[6]

This laid the foundation for a structured discussion about the professionalization of governance in family enterprises. Between 1996 and 2003, only about 10% of published work about family businesses in academic journals was about governance in family enterprises, whereas today that has risen to about 20%.[7] A governance model for a family enterprise was comprehensively presented for the first time in *Family Business Governance – Successful Management of Family Enterprises*.[8]

Nonetheless, family firms are now paying more attention to governance, partly reflecting the fact that there are, internationally, 12 governance codes for family enterprises. The world's first formal code for family enterprises only was published in Germany in 2004.[9] As a result, around 60% of owners' families in Germany know the code, and 90% think that good governance influences the performance of the family business.[10]

The **aim of good family business governance** is to set the basis for a sustainable increase in economic value and emotional well-being.[11] Family owners want "deep pockets and warm hearts." A study published by Ernst & Young established that the value of a family enterprise consists of around 70% economic value and 30% emotional value.[12] It is disquieting to note, however, that the emotional value can become negative when conflicts erupt, which in turn can reduce the economic value. However, with the help of sound family business governance, both economic and emotional value can be maintained.

## Economic and emotional value

A higher **economic value** is demonstrated by higher sales, better results, a higher company value, and increased dividend payouts. **Emotional value** has been called the "family Pattex" (Pattex being the brand of a glue produced by the German family business Henkel). Some family business owners say that it is not the dividends but the emotions that create an attachment to the company; the individual family members are proud to belong to a business-owning family that has no conflicts. Further indications of a high emotional value are:[13]

- The family owners have common values and goals, which followed and passed on from generation to generation.

- Specific family traditions and rituals are performed by all family owners.
- The family owners have a strong willingness to learn.
- Participation in joint family activities is a pleasure for all family owners.
- The family owners support each other.
- There are clearly defined boundaries between the rights and duties of the owners in relation to the family enterprise.

## A family business governance system[14]

Effective governance helps a family business to achieve both economic and emotional value. Because family enterprises are different, each enterprise has to establish its own governance, which is optimally summarized in a family constitution. A structure for doing so is the family business governance model (Figure 1.1). Governance in family enterprises consists of two overlapping components:

*each enterprise has to establish its own governance, which is optimally summarized in a family constitution*

**business governance**, which deals with establishing appropriate structures of management and control within the company; and
**family governance**, which deals with managing the family and establishing cohesion among family members.

Better business governance increases economic value by **transparency and accountability** with regards to management and control of the enterprise.

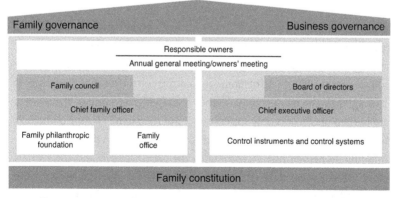

FIG 1.1 / The family business governance model (adaption of the model by Alexander Koeberle-Schmid, Peter Witt, Hans-Jürgen Fahrion, and Bernd Grottel)

This fosters long-term success through the professional conduct of owners, the board of directors, and managers. In addition, a management system covering risk, control, and compliance allows managers to ensure that monitoring can be carried out throughout the whole company. Additional supporting roles are played by the auditor and the internal audit function. Ethical codes, regulations about liability, and an appropriate remuneration system are also important governance instruments.

Good and adequately formulated family governance can increase the emotional value owners associate with their company by strengthening the cohesion of the business-owning family, by **increasing the engagement** with the company on the part of the family, and by **reducing the likelihood that emotional conflicts** will arise. To do so, a family council and family manager (also known as a chief family officer) play an important role by organizing family activities, by implementing a family intranet, or by being the first point of contact if conflicts arise. In addition, a family philanthropic foundation and a family office play important parts in increasing emotional value and in organizing the business-owning family. One could also think about a family bank, a family assembly, a family residence, a family history book, a conflict-management procedure, rules about dealing with each other and with the public, and family development programs, where the next generation is prepared for becoming future CEOs or board members. Not all family enterprises, however, will need all family governance instruments.

How the individual aspects of family business governance are configured depend on the individual circumstances of the family enterprise and their challenges (see Chapter 2). It depends on whether the business is owned by a sole owner, a sibling partnership, or a cousin consortium, and whether it is managed by the owners only (owner-managed), by some of the owners (family-managed), or is only supervised – not managed – by the owners. It also depends on the size of the business, its culture, and whether there are nonfamily owners or not. According to the classifications and the various factors listed above, different aspects of family business governance are necessary. Figure 1.2 shows how these different aspects of family business governance may become relevant. It is important to note that family

| Ownership structure | Management structure |
|---|---|
| Sole owner<br>• Ownership succession plan<br>• Board of directors | Owner-managed<br>• Management succession<br>• Board of directors<br>• Risk control compliance management system |
| Sibling partnership<br>• Annual general meeting<br>• Ownership succession plan<br>• Conflict management | Family-managed<br>• Management succession<br>• Board of directors<br>• Risk control compliance management system |
| Cousin consortium<br>• Annual general meeting<br>• Conflict management<br>• Chief family officer<br>• Family meeting/assembly<br>• Family educational programme<br>• Family philanthropic foundation<br>• Family office | Family-monitored<br>• Management succession<br>• Board of directors<br>• Family council<br>• Risk control compliance management system |

FIG 1.2 Definitions of the different stages in family business governance solutions for various types of family enterprise

business governance needs to be individually formulated by each family enterprise in order to fit the situation of each family and business.

Sound family business governance depends upon **strong decision-making by the owners** about the values and goals of the family, and about family ownership and the enterprise. Important family values include tolerance, respect, honesty, and mutual responsibility. Business-owning families should also set values for the business. It also helps to establish strategic principles, such as being an innovative market leader, maintaining an equity ratio of more than 40%, or prioritizing organic growth. Families should decide what they want to give the company (such as responsible ownership, and reinvestment of profits) and what they expect from the enterprise (fair processes, interesting business model, dividends).

## Responsible ownership and fair process

The principles of family business governance are **"responsible ownership"**[15] and **"fair process."**[16] **"Responsible ownership"** consists of four fundamental roots: family values, stewardship, emotional ownership, and patient capital (see Chapter 4 for full definitions). In practice, a **responsible owner** has the following traits:[17]

- He/she acts like a long-term affiliated owner.
- He/she wants the family enterprise to survive long term, preferably in family hands.
- He/she identifies him/herself with his/her own company.
- He/she maintains a relationship between family and business.
- He/she is fully informed about the current situation of the company.
- He/she wants to transfer his/her knowledge to the next generation.
- He/she wants both the family and the company to be successful.

**"Fair process"**[18] consists of three aspects. First, there should be individual arrangements or rules. These are set within the governance system and documented in the family constitution and articles of incorporation. These cover rules for succession, for distribution, or for exit. The rules must be clearly formulated, changeable, and consistent with the goals and values of the family business. They must be communicated to all owners and they need to be accepted. The second aspect of fair process is that compliance with the rules is to be ensured by a defined institution, such as the board of directors. The nonexecutive and nonfamily board members can, for example, objectively decide whether the agreed requirements for the new CEO are met by the candidate from the family. Third, transparency about all rules needs to be assured for all involved family members such that that they accept the decisions taken. "Fair process" means that decisions do not lead to emotional conflicts, because they follow clear and formally accepted rules.

*"Fair process" means that decisions do not lead to emotional conflicts*

## Business first or family first?

The culture and the country of origin have significant influences on family business governance.[19] Western cultures are more business-oriented, and Eastern cultures more family-oriented. In Western countries, few family members may work in the company. In Eastern countries more family members do so – sometimes they all do. Word pairs can illustrate whether a culture is more **"business first"** or **"family first."** Examples are:

- meritocracy versus representation
- most competent leadership versus personal growth
- ownership rights versus family membership equality
- efficient versus effective
- individual responsibility versus collective responsibility
- accountability versus protection
- results versus process
- formal versus informal
- legal contract versus moral commitment
- controlled versus open
- decisive leadership versus participatory
- profit versus fun
- high trust in outsiders versus low trust in outsiders
- independence versus security.

Families have to decide whether governance – both of the family and of the business – is oriented more towards the family's or the business's interests. In a **"family-first"** business, the CEO is usually a family member; family members can work in the business, sometimes without limit as to their number; remuneration and dividends depend on family needs. If the approach is **"business first,"** the position of the CEO is held by the most competent person, and often only one family member can work in the company and only as CEO; remuneration is market-based, and dividends are only paid out if the company is profitable.

Irrespective of the company's orientation, families should always consider the two principles of "responsible ownership" and "fair process." This is especially important when the culture is more family-oriented, because otherwise conflicts can easily arise and the family might end up destroying the business.

*families should always consider the two principles of "responsible ownership"*

**B E S T - P R A C T I C E**
**R E C O M M E N D A T I O N S**

**1** Business-owning families should implement a strong and healthy governance system.

**2** When developing appropriate family business governance, owner families should consider their individual challenges (Chapter 2).

**3** Owner families will find that strong governance can help build emotional value as well as economic value.

**4** Business-owning families should consider that the business needs appropriate strategies, structures, and rules, both for the business and for the family.

**5** Owner families should develop their family business governance individually according to the ownership, family, and management structure as well as the size of the company, and if there are owners other than the family.

**6** When designing family business governance, business-owning families will find it helpful to be guided by the principles of "fair process" and "responsible ownership."

**7** While every firm will have a tendency towards being oriented more towards the business or the family in its overriding culture, governance should encourage the business towards an orientation of "business first", *and* the family to the principle of "family first."

**8** Business-owning families are advised to document their family business governance in a family constitution.

**9** Business-owning families should regularly review their family business governance, and further refine it if there are changes to the family or business.

## IMPORTANT DEFINITIONS

**Annual general meeting (AGM):**   The meeting of the owners once a year where important decisions are made, such as the election of the board of directors, the approval of the annual accounts, or a decision about profit distribution. In some countries, it is also called an owners' meeting or shareholders' meeting.

**Board of directors:**   A governing body of a company that consists of executive and nonexecutive members. The latter provide advice and/or monitor the executive members. In some countries, the board may consist only of nonexecutive members with clear monitoring tasks; it is then called a supervisory board. When the board has no or little formal decision power, it is often called an advisory board.

**Business governance:**   Structural organization of management and control in a family enterprise aiming to ensure the long-term success and term continuity of ownership in family hands.

**Chief executive officer (CEO):**   Person who manages the enterprise. As well as developing and implementing corporate strategy, s/he is also responsible for the implementation of business governance and the family business culture, a lean organization, and ensuring that company policy aligns with the family's goals and values.

**Chief family officer** (or *family manager*): The person who is mainly responsible for family governance issues. The chief family officer manager performs the function of chairperson or president of the family council and helps to keep family members united. S/he often acts as a mediator, facilitator, and communication conduit for a family. S/he is responsible for ensuring family cohesion, and organizing family activities.

**Chief investment officer (CIO):**   Person in charge of all investments in a family office. The CIO heads the family office when its sole purpose is to manage the financial investments of a family. However, when the role of the family office is larger, it is usually headed by a chief executive officer (CEO).

**Conflict management:** Procedures that are used to resolve problems when conflicts arise.

**Family activity:** Joint activities of the owners' family to increase cohesion and commitment, such as family weekends, youngster days, and family meetings.

**Family bank:** A way to provide family members with financial support under specific conditions. It can help individuals create their own entrepreneurial endeavors.

**Family constitution:** A document that clarifies the relationship between a family and its business, and defines the strategy and structure of the enterprise. Mission, vision, important issues about the owner business model, governance, as well as rules that apply to family members, are normally documented. Other terms often used for a family constitution are family protocol, family code, family charter, generation contract, etc.

**Family council:** A governance body that focuses on family and ownership matters. The family council represents an institutionalized form of periodically holding family meetings. The primary advantage of this formal format is the disciplined approach to holding these meetings, even when they appear not to be needed. Family councils primarily promote communication, provide a safe harbor for the resolution of family conflicts, and support the education of next-generation family members in responsible ownership, family dynamics, financial issues, and philanthropic issues.

**Family residence:** Historic place where the family gathers for special occasions.

**Family education:** Activities to educate business-owners in a sense of responsible ownership, such as education days, development programs, or seminars.

**Family enterprise:** An enterprise that is predominantly owned by a family with the aim of handing it over to the next generation.

**Family governance:** Organization of the family owners aimed at strengthening cohesion within the family as well as their identification with the business, and therefore family solidarity

**Family history book:**   A comprehensive book about the history of a family, preferably with many pictures and written in a journalistic way.

**Family meeting or family day:**   Meeting of owners and other family members where issues about the family and the business are discussed. It is often combined with an AGM as well as fun activities.

**Family office:**   The family office is the person, desk or legal entity that manages the wealth of a family. It usually also provides legal and fiscal advice to family members related to their wealth.

**Family owners:**   The owners of a company, originating from the owner family.

**Family philanthropic foundation:**   A family philanthropic foundation, or family charitable trust, is an institution that organizes and funds the charitable activities of a given family. It can be set for the lifetime of a person or a specific generation, or may be an enduring entity.

**Management board:**   The group of executives who manage a company. Those are the executive directors.

**Owner family:**   The family who owns an enterprise. The boundaries of the owner family need to be defined. Normally it consists of the owners, their partners, and their children.

**Owners:**   The shareholders, partners, or limited partners of a company.

**Risk, control, and compliance management:**   Instruments that allow for control of the processes in the company. They help monitor risks and to ensure that employees comply with laws, rules, and regulations.

# 2

# Challenges to the Governance of the Family Enteprise

> "Our culture highlights the value of (1) being honest, (2) working hard, (3) having fun, and (4) being grateful, and, finallcy, (5) paying it forward to others."

Interview with Bruce T. Halle, chairman, Discount Tire, Scottsdale, Arizona, USA

Bruce Halle is chairman of Discount Tire, a US tire retailer that has an annual revenue of $4 billion, with 856 stores and over 15,000 employees in the United States. He founded the company in 1960 in Ann Arbor, Michigan, moving the headquarters to Scottsdale, Arizona after realizing that there were tremendous growth opportunities in the western states of the United States during the 1970s. Mr. Halle is an active philanthropist and the architect of a unique company culture where thousands of employees get to live the American dream of opportunity and personal and financial growth.

*Ernesto J. Poza:* **Discount Tire has been tremendously successful, and still growing at 9.9% a year, with a philosophy of responsible growth. What do you mean by "responsible growth"?**

*Bruce Halle:* Well, we own all of our stores; we do not franchise them, and we prefer to own, not rent, the real estate in our 856 locations. The capital requirements to fund this business model are daunting. At about $3 million to build, equip, stock, and open one of these company-owned stores, opening 100 new stores a year (something that our management capabilities and employee bench strength could easily accommodate) would require an annual investment of $300 million. But because we prefer to keep our debt-to-capital ratio low enough to protect our independence, we only build 40 to 50 stores a year, reinvesting only $120 million or so a year. We are not interested in chasing growth, we "grow responsibly."

**What else is responsible for your company's extraordinary success?**
Our unique culture is a big part of it. It is based on a value system, which, by the time I was 12 years old, had already been instilled in me. But a lot of it is so intangible. Our culture highlights the value of (1) being honest, (2) working hard, (3) having fun, (4) being grateful, and, finally, (5) paying it forward to others. Now it is easy to talk about this value system, but a lot harder to implement in 856 stores all over the country. In the first few stores,

I did it by example. Later on, I did it by picking and training people who exhibited those qualities and/or were looking for this view of the world as a better way. In the last 20 years, I still travel to all the stores and meet all our employees and their families, but it is the store managers who lead by their example and make it possible to have thousands of loyal followers of these principles. Store managers share 10% of store profits up to $200,000, and 20% of all store profits once they exceed the $200,000 profit level ($210,000 profit means a bonus of $42,000 on top of their base pay of $60,000, to $70,000). Store employees are paid more than industry standards. And, since we promote from within, store employees aspire to the opportunities that they have seen so many of their team members reach as we keep building new stores; they could become a store manager with a significant bonus and a small business owner-like financial profile.

We also started the company with new policies that differentiated us from other tire companies. Our competition was mainly the tire manufacturers. They owned or franchised retail stores, but were much more focused on manufacturing than selling and servicing the tires through retail. So, their stores were only open Monday through Friday. We opened our stores on Saturday and that proved to be our biggest retail sales day of the week...By the time we were established, we already represented a very different and much better tire-purchasing experience for our customers. We do remain closed on Sundays, so our team members can spend the day with their families.

**Now that the second generation is active in management and serving on the board, and the third generation is already beginning to attend college, what do you see as the main challenges to family business governance at Discount Tire?**

I would like to focus on two challenges that have been particularly difficult for me: letting go and *succession*. It is not uncommon for entrepreneurs to find these difficult to achieve but, for me, the need to keep control was more about continuing to do what I love to do, am good at, and have been doing for the past 50 years. I did not want to be put out to pasture at age 65 or 70.

What would I do if I quit? I play tennis – and by the way, I can no longer play like I used to, I no longer jump over the net after winning a game – but I cannot do that all day every day. So what was hard for me to give up was not the power, or the glory, but the work itself.

*So what was hard for me to give up was not the power, or the glory, but the work itself*

For a long time, this unwillingness to let go also got in the way of me planning my succession. After all, I started my business with six tires and no plan at all, other than providing for my family. But over the past 15 years I started to let other people do more things. Then I got lucky, and just like I had found great store employees with the right values, I began to find great executives and planners, next-generation members with great potential, and outside help. The current president, a son from my second marriage (my first wife died of cancer), has finesse and ability with people, coupled with an analytical and strategic capability that inspires confidence. The current chief executive officer (CEO), a nonfamily key executive who started as a team member in one of the Ann Arbor stores; the chief financial officer (CFO); my former banker, and others in the top team, have all inspired me to come to grips with the need to relinquish control in order to make my dream of continuity in the Halle family a reality.

**You have sophisticated trusts as part of your estate plan, and in them you set rules that would help govern the family business and family wealth relationship in your absence. Why, then, have you recently invested so much time and effort in other governance system initiatives?**
Well, yes, the trusts provide *family trustees* and *beneficiaries* with distributions so that they can do whatever they want to do with their lives. But I want them to participate in the continuity of the family business as responsible adults, responsible trustees, and truly responsible owners. So, besides the money and the rules, we formed a family council to initiate all the activity of educating second- and third-generation family members on family enterprises; on what has made Discount Tire successful thus far; on the legacy and the family

values and on the role of trustees and of family members serving on the board of directors. The family council also began to write a *family constitution* a couple of years ago, and has already approved a *family employment policy* and a set of other policies that we fully expect will guide the family in its relationship with Discount Tire for generations to come.

**What other initiatives are helping you with the governance of the family business relationship?**
Several years ago we began to engage both second- and third-generation members in our philanthropic initiatives. Right now, individual second- and third-generation members have their own funds to support the causes that they most care about. But they are also involved in discussions about the larger *philanthropic initiatives* of the Halle Family Foundation.

Family members have been participating in the company's quarterly review meetings with our top management. These have included a fair amount of operating details. So we are just now beginning to have separate "family board" meetings to review quarterly financial results. Our aim is to someday restructure the board to include independents to serve along with family members on the board. We will be discussing this subject in our family council meeting in June. We are also beginning to explore having our own family office and will be talking specifically about what services and functions we want from our family office in that meeting.

As you can see, much of the governance system is being developed in the family council. With owner education, financial transparency, our religious faith, and these governance mechanisms – board, family council, family constitution, and family office – we hope that the second and third generations will develop into responsible owners and responsible stewards of the legacy. You cannot expect a trust to do that for you.

## Family business governance is critically important

Chapter 1 helped us understand what family business governance is and why it is such a complex subject. Let us now address why it is fundamentally important to family enterprises, and discuss the search for continuity by considering some of the most common challenges. As you will soon discover, any one of a very large number of issues may present a formidable challenge to a family business. In each case, the challenge reflects weakness in, or absence of, structures and measures to regulate the family–ownership–management relationship in the family firm. The challenges are predictable and widespread, but the solutions need to be tailored to each individual firm. These challenges and dilemmas often require proactive leadership from the incumbent CEO. We will recommend several initiatives and steps that CEOs and others in the family and the business can take to address them successfully.

The desired outcome of effective governance is rational economic and socio-emotional decision-making by the owners and managers that is not overwhelmed by traditional family dynamics. Achieving effective governance is difficult, but is still a priority for family firms seeking continuity. It unquestionably constitutes the final test of greatness for leaders of family enterprises.

*Achieving effective governance is difficult, but is still a priority for family firms seeking continuity.*

## Challenges to family business governance[1]

### Nepotism

A family-first attitude in selecting managers and employees for the family enterprise is a significant barrier to governing the family – business or family – wealth relationships. When surname, not merit, is at the heart of the selection process in the firm or family office, a clear message is sent: family preference is in command, not economic, business logic.

This prioritization of the family agenda typically precludes the more balanced (or family + ownership + management) governance required by family companies intent on continuing across generations of owners or owner-managers. Unchecked, it leads to declining financial performance and, over the longer term, value destruction in the enterprise or the family's wealth.

## Insufficient *professionalization*

Even without nepotism, family firms can suffer from the inability to change, delegate, and institutionalize a successful business model beyond the founding generation.

Professionals bring different competencies and skill sets, as well as different perspectives on the strategy and managerial approaches to be used. Professionalization is a fine complement to the family's role in the enterprise. Notice that we are not arguing in favor of replacing family employees with nonfamily "professional" employees, but rather for increasing the professionalism of family employees and complementing this by the professional knowledge and skill sets of nonfamily employees.

Professionals also redefine management and expectations of management and act as a conscience for the appropriate role of family and the appropriate role of management in the successful leadership of the enterprise.

## Succession

For a parent, the need to pick one, and perhaps only one, descendant to lead the family company is not an easy task, precisely because the parent is also the owner and perhaps the CEO and/or chairman. Many CEO-parents who doubt the viability of a sibling partnership avoid this extremely difficult decision by turning the succession matter over to the board, or by ruling out next-generation family members from coming into the business. Regardless of how compelling the argument may be in favor of a particular successor, choosing one offspring over another for the top job can be extremely difficult and emotionally distressing for a CEO/chairman/parent.

A board is in the unique position of being able to enhance the perception of the quality, independence, and fairness of the succession decision by shifting responsibility away from family members. This third-party stamp of approval significantly increases receptivity to the new company leader on the part of both key nonfamily management and family members.

## Loss of family identity and values

**Family legacy**, coupled with a renewed sense of purpose brought on by a multigenerational family vision, help to create and sustain an enterprising family's **continuity plan**. But these often erode as families grow in generations, numbers, and wealth.

While some members of the family may be managing the family business or serving on its **board of directors**, others can serve the family well by nurturing its continued engagement with the original values of the founder and the founding family. The family members not actively managing the day-to-day activities in the business or the family office can play a significant role in engaging the next generation in rediscovering the nonfinancial legacy of the owning family.

## Entitlement culture

Another significant challenge for successful multigenerational families is the entitlement culture: an attitude towards high levels of acquisition and consumption assumed as a birthright. Warren Buffett is credited with a wise principle: "Give each child enough money so that they can do anything, but not so much that they can afford to do nothing." Families who develop a list of principles that guide their relationship to wealth and enterprise and capture them in a family constitution are also proactively governing the family and leading it towards responsible **stewardship** of its business.

## Family conflicts

Speed is one of the competitive advantages found in many entrepreneurial firms, resulting from quick strategic decision-making by owner-managers. But, in later generations, a family that is paralyzed because of conflicting visions for the enterprise across generations or across branches of the extended family can become inward-looking and turf wars can ensue. In the process, a family business can forget a unique advantage in relation to often larger, more international and bureaucratic corporations – its nimbleness.

Sir Adrian Cadbury, former chairman of Cadbury Schweppes, the large British chocolate and beverage maker, observed that:

> Paradoxically, the less important some established family benefits are, the more trouble they can cause. I was once involved in a dispute in a family firm over the produce from a vegetable garden. The family home, factory and garden were all on the same site and the garden was cultivated for the benefit of those members of the family who lived on the spot. When this apparently modest benefit came to be costed out, it was clear that it was a totally uneconomic way of keeping some members of the family in fresh fruit and vegetables. Any change in the traditional arrangement was, however, seen by those who benefited from it as an attack on the established order and the beginning of the end of the family firm.[2]

## The belief that fair means equal

The founder of another family firm, this one a Latin American industrial conglomerate, transferred all his shares to five next-generation members equally upon his death. The founder, and father, clearly loved all his children equally. But because in that loving family fair meant equal, the founder transferred a successful business to siblings who were totally unprepared to be a sibling team or to govern the relationship between family and business effectively.

Not all of the children wanted the same thing for their individual futures. So, equal was not fair. One of the sons wanted to launch a new venture. The inherited family business had a couple of years of reduced profits and dividends, which put this son's plans at risk. In the absence of different **classes of stock**, different **voting rights,** or even a **buy–sell agreement,** he ultimately forced a **liquidation** of his equity stake. While he was successful in redeeming his shares and obtaining the seed capital for his new venture, he ultimately felt so disloyal to his own loving family that he cut himself off from his widowed mother and four siblings. He never again attended family gatherings or remained close to the family, as if his dissolution of his ownership stake in the family company also required his exile from the family.

## The current leader's unwillingness to transfer power

The critical and urgent need to build institutions of family governance is often not obvious to the entrepreneur or family CEO. In a study conducted by one of the authors, the most statistically significant finding was that CEOs of family businesses perceive both the business and the family much more favorably than do the rest of the family and nonfamily managers, especially on matters such as business planning, succession planning, communication, growth orientation, career opportunities, and the effectiveness of their boards. In the absence of expressed dissatisfaction with the status quo, the CEO-parent may be the last to recognize the need to change and create the institutions that will effectively govern the family business and family wealth relationship post-succession.[3]

In the interview above with Bruce Halle, chairman of Discount Tire, the major factor was not a desire for control and power, so much as his sheer love of the work and disinclination to retire. By nurturing his ability to identify talented executives to whom he was comfortable delegating, he was able to resolve this issue.

## Dilution of wealth

Besides the erosion of wealth that may result from unnecessary expenses, taxes, and a culture of entitlement, high dividends and the break-up of the business can negatively affect the family's access to new investments. Diluted wealth can also take the family out of the running on a wide range of business opportunities because of a shrinking pool of family capital. Distributions motivated by needs for current consumption and the break-up of business interests fueled by family conflict prevent wealthy families from reaping the benefits of patient family capital; that is, capital that remains pooled together over generations.

## The erosion of the entrepreneurial culture

The entrepreneurial stage is recognized as one that endows the business with the capacity to be nimble and opportunistic. But it does not take long for successful family businesses to be expected to comply with standard accounting principles that promote greater transparency – and the accompanying paperwork – and to have to comply with a growing number of industry standards and government regulations. Increased regulation and a greater need for coordination create the impetus for more meetings, more memos, and more email that make the business of the family naturally more bureaucratic and risk-averse. IKEA's CEO, Mikael Ohlsson, recently attributed a slowdown in global store openings to this phenomenon. And while he assigns part of the responsibility to governments and regulatory bodies, he takes full responsibility for the growing number of barriers to speed and agility within a maturing IKEA.[4] Collectively, these multiplying new requirements may contribute to the family enterprise or family office experiencing time delays that the business did not experience during its entrepreneurial phase.

More importantly, there is the distinct possibility that family members themselves may have begun **wasting company time and resources** (for example, arguing over who gets to use the company plane or the country home for a holiday; typically, both are administered by a nonfamily staff member). In this case, the family begins to represent an agency cost to the enterprise rather than the resource that it represented during earlier generations.[5] And, more importantly, by focusing inward, it can lose its ability to keep an eye on new competitive dynamics, the ever-changing marketplace, and the financial landscape.

## Lack of transparency and oversight

Neither boards of directors nor professional managers can make their value-adding contributions to family business without good metrics and clear scorecards. Shareholders themselves can seldom act as responsible shareholders and hold management accountable in the absence of financial knowledge and financial controls. A business with an entrepreneurial culture often resists the call for greater transparency – after all, the founding entrepreneur stayed on top of everything. Next-generation leaders, however, are well served by investing in metrics that can take the pulse of the enterprise in real time. Lack of transparency can also give rise to an absence of caring for the business by later generations of the family. Without caring, continuity is threatened.

*Without caring, continuity is threatened.*

Lack of oversight (by, for example, an independent board of directors) often breeds complacency and resistance to change. It may also lead to self-dealing and giving some shareholders' interests priority over those of all shareholders; which can create significant family conflict and legal fights between members of the family, and (in the case of family-controlled but publicly traded family companies) between family members and other shareholders.

## Altruism

Research has found that altruism, or attending to the welfare of a relative, is a prominent feature of many family enterprises. Some scholars have argued that altruism represents a form of agency problem that often leads family firms to make decisions that are economically irrational. And while it may be true that what is irrational to some is perfectly rational to an owner-family aiming for maximum utility from its relationship with an enterprise (which includes socio-emotional benefits such as a good reputation, family benefits, family emotional well-being, and other nonfinancial objectives), altruism presents the **risk of an increasing cost structure** that may be unsustainable in the long term by the family enterprise.

## Keeping control in the family

Publicly traded firms, through their capacity to create a market for corporate control, hold management accountable. The market for corporate control makes top management accountable to all shareholders. The absence of the equity markets' influence prevents this disciplining function in privately held family firms. Even family businesses that are publicly traded, by definition, have an overriding measure of family control.

In the absence of market-induced accountability, owning families have to step up and, in collaboration with their family council and board of directors, hold top management – both family and nonfamily executives – accountable to all stakeholders' interests.

**Family governance**, then, is an essential discipline for the long-term well-being of the family business and the family's wealth. It defines a family's **ability to discipline and control the nature of the relationship** between family members, shareholders, and professional managers in such a way that the business prospers and the family promotes and protects its unity and its financial, human, and social capital – as much for the family's sake as for the company's. After all, a family's unity and its human and social capital are the source of long-term comparative advantages of the family business firm. Patient family capital, reputation, and influential knowledge and networks represent unique resources that a family business can translate into competitive advantage.

## Which hat to wear: parent, owner, or CEO?

Because of the complexity implicit in a system that is composed of three subsystems (family, ownership, and management), each potentially with different goals and operating principles, family businesses are vulnerable to the consequences of blurred boundaries and overrun frontiers. Nepotism is perhaps the most obvious of boundary infractions. Research in the social sciences – both psychology and economics – suggests that emotion can lead to behaviors and actions that rational thought would seldom support. As a result, family patterns or dynamics, replete with emotional content, can easily override the logic of business management or ownership returns on invested capital.

There is often a lack of awareness on the part of company employees and family members that decision-making may be shaped by a family, ownership, or management consideration, and that the one chosen may be inappropriate. This often leads to **incongruent policies** and **bad decisions.** In the most extreme, but still quite common, example, family rules may overtake the business. For instance, a younger son may insist on starting work after 10 a.m. every day, despite the requirement that, as a customer service manager in an insurance company, he should report to work by 7 a.m. His father, to whom he reports, may choose to avoid the conflict and anxiety his tardiness provokes by ignoring it and allowing it to continue. Avoiding resolution of this disagreement out of fear or altruism only diminishes problem-solving ability. If such selective inattention is unchecked, it may grow over the years. Succession hurls many of these unsettled issues to the forefront of family business management, often at a very vulnerable time in the life of a family business.

In the case of the Latin American industrial conglomerate discussed earlier in this chapter, such blurred boundaries between ownership, management, and family, and not just the mistaken belief that "fair is equal," most likely led the founder to transfer shares to all five next-generation members equally upon his untimely death. The siblings were totally unprepared to effectively differentiate between family and ownership of the business, and were therefore unable to keep the business profitable and the family united.

## Simultaneous optimization of family-ownership and business

Effective governance empowers leaders of families in business to make the most of the unique strength of a family enterprise: the synergy between a strong, unified owning family and a well-run family enterprise or family office. Many families fail to govern the family – business relationship, to the detriment of their business and their wealth.

*Many families fail to govern the family – business relationship.*

**Solutions** to the governance challenge have to be **comprehensive, holistic,** and **systemic,** not based on advice from a single discipline, like the law. Yet family business owners often use an individual accountant, family psychologist, or trusted lawyer for particular tasks or projects that relate to building a governance structure. Implicit in systems theory is the capacity jointly to optimize interrelated subsystems in such a way that the larger system, in this case the family business, can be most effective and successful in the pursuit of its goals. Intuitively, reaching this state would seem akin to reaching nirvana, and it is just as difficult. Yet thousands of family businesses, many of them featured throughout the book, have achieved precisely that. They have balanced the goals and needs of families, individual family members, shareholders, and the business itself in what appears to be a masterful walk across a tightrope. They have done so by implementing the structures, systems, and cultures listed in the best-practice recommendations section.

Family enterprises can indeed inspire a commitment to the greater good across generations. But this takes leadership by the incumbent CEO and/ or chairman on the seven recommendations listed; these are the action levers of family business governance.

The current CEO, chairman, or president of a family enterprise or family office can hardly leave a finer legacy and contribution to family business continuity and continued family wealth across generations than the creation of an effective governance structure. The next several chapters of *Governance in Family Enterprises* make specific and relevant recommendations on how you too can build effective governance in your family enterprise.

| **B E S T – P R A C T I C E** |
| **R E C O M M E N D A T I O N S** |

**1** Family forums or councils that promote transparency, responsible ownership, and continued family unity.

**2** Boards of directors that promote accountability, conflict resolution, and strategic growth.

**3** Realigned ownership structures that prune the family tree, ensure corporate control, and promote agility.

**4** Strong organizational cultures that preserve customer orientation, quality, productivity, and innovation.

**5** Family offices that capably manage the pooled financial resources of the family.

**6** Fair policies in a comprehensive family constitution or charter.

**7** Solid managerial practices – such as strategic planning for growth and the employment and retention of key nonfamily management.

# 3

# Evolution of Governance Structures and Systems

"Partnerships only work when the partners want to remain partners and continue to see the benefits of keeping the family's capital together and of continued family unity."

Interview with Julio Cazorla, managing director, family office, Grupo Landon, Barcelona, Spain

Julio Cazorla is the nonfamily managing director of Grupo Landon, the family office for the Gallardo Family in Barcelona, Spain. The Gallardo family founded Grupo Almirall, a publicly-traded but *family-controlled* pharmaceutical company that has recently diversified into the larger healthcare industry. Almirall has 2,700 employees and €873 million in annual revenues. The Gallardo family remains active in the management of Almirall and several other companies and investments.

*Ernesto J. Poza:* **Could you walk me through the evolution of the governance of the family – business relationship at Grupo Landon?**

*Julio J. Cazorla:* Well, in our case, it all started with two second-generation brothers with a deep curiosity and profound sense of mission regarding family business continuity. One brother, then CEO of Almirall, the other the chairman of the board, shared a deep preoccupation with the continuity challenge and sought knowledge and advice from IMD, the international school of management in Lausanne, Switzerland, and a globally recognized family business consultant they met there, Ivan Lansberg. During a day-long seminar with him just outside of Barcelona, family members decided to launch a *mentor committee*. The committee would be composed of six third-generation members, all cousins. This committee would be the vehicle for the academic and professional development of the third generation of the Gallardo family.

The two second-generation brothers were very busy running and overseeing the business and suggested to the third generation that they continue working with the family business consultant to help map out a multiyear succession process. All six third-generation members began developing the vision for the next generation, clarifying their roles and expectations and working on their own relationships with each other.

**Did the second-generation brothers have any concerns of their own?**

The two brothers had some additional concerns. As 50:50 partners, they had learned to work with and accommodate each other, but what would happen once one of them was absent? Would strategic decisions or business operations be blocked or encumbered? Would the suddenly restructured ownership pre-empt a stable and successful succession? Then, in 1997, the acquisition and consolidation of Prodesfarma, another pharmaceutical [company], provided the catalyst for the separation of some assets from the combined company. What was now more a conglomerate or group, than a single business entity, created the need to find a way to manage nonoperating business assets separately. Jorge and Antonio Gallardo asked themselves a fundamental question: "Should we continue as partners in the operating company as well as other investments, *Should we continue as partners* or begin to separate assets outside the business and begin to manage them individually?" They asked Ivan Lansberg for advice on this issue. The family business consultant suggested that they ask their children instead. The cousins, who had been learning and working with the consultant in the mentor committee, issued a resounding yes as an answer to the question of whether to continue the *family wealth partnership.*

The brothers then made succession and continuity planning a priority task, notwithstanding all their other duties. Soon they realized that their direct involvement approach was not sustainable and proceeded to seek help on several interrelated fronts: the launching of a *family council,* the writing of a family constitution, and the creation of a modern-day *family office.* That is precisely when I joined the Grupo Landon, almost 12 years ago, and launched the family office. The young family office began then to assist in the projects just mentioned and to provide help in the establishment of *ownership councils,* boards of directors for each of the enterprises, and a *holding company* consolidating the various businesses. The governance system evolved over the span of these 12–15 years, from aspirational words to concrete actions guided primarily by the *family*

*constitution.* This document was the first joint project by the second and third generation working on behalf of continuity. As the various drafts were completed, many and profound deliberations between the two generations took place, leading to the eventual approval of a final draft in 2009.

**Please tell me a little more about the family constitution. It is not the standard "protocol," as it is referred to in Spain, is it?**

No, our family constitution is not meant to be a legal document developed by company lawyers, as is so often the case in Spain. The family constitution was developed by family members and has been the blueprint for the development of ownership and family structures like the family council and the ownership councils, policies regarding the employment of family members in the business, decision-making via super-majorities (two-thirds vote) on the ownership councils and the board, and the selection of family members to serve on the boards of directors. The constitution also highlighted important family values that needed to be preserved, and advocated the creation of *conflict-resolution mechanisms* and the use of third parties to prevent paralysis and inaction in the face of problems or opportunities.

These were particularly important because the family was committed to systematically seek consensus, but was equally committed to not imperil the business through blocked decision-making. Since the independent outsiders on the board constitute one-third of the vote, the family could make those decisions by itself (family consensus), or with the assistance of the independent outsiders. The family constitution spelled out the need for win–win behaviors in the extended multibranch family, and specified the functions, membership, and authority of the family council, the ownership councils, and the boards of directors. It also addressed policies guiding the development of *shareholder agreements* on *shareholder liquidity*, dividends or distributions, and buy-sells.

**Grupo Landon has ownership councils as well as a family council?**

Yes, the ownership councils promote and oversee the various shareholder agreements and supersede rights of association that in corporate law in Spain allow individual shareholders to appoint their pro-rata number of directors (based on percentage of stock ownership). So in the interests of keeping the partnership working, ownership councils were created for each of the enterprises in the Group. The councils operate per the shareholder agreements to consolidate the extended family votes via renouncing to the *individual's right to representation* in the interest of continuing to pool the financial and managerial resources of the multibranch partnership. The ownership councils became the conscience for the principle of continued *patient [long-term] family capital* that the second generation considered important to preserve. And mechanisms for establishing *fair market value* for the shares and for facilitating *buy-sells* between shareholders are also in place, all in the interest of keeping the partnership healthy and conflict-free.

The two brothers remain active in the management and the

governance of the Group, hold regular "Seniors' Meetings," where they continue to provide much oversight and family business leadership, and meet with me to discuss any important subject affecting family unity. There is a shared belief that partnerships only work when the partners want to remain partners and continue to see the benefits of keeping the family's capital together and of continued family unity. The brothers expect that the next generation will similarly use this litmus test in their governance of the family-business relationship going forward.

**Let us discuss the family council further. It has been in operation the longest now; 15 years or so, right? How has the family council evolved over time?**
The family council was and remains the fundamental venue for the deliberations and work by family and business leaders. The family council wrote the family constitution and developed the ownership councils. The family council was one of the earliest structures implemented in the furtherance of effective governance. It has significantly

evolved over time. Beginning as a third-generation committee, it grew to include both generations. After drafting and approving the family constitution, it began to meet regularly to educate family members who were not active in the business, to discuss family matters and promote family bonding and family unity and to be a catalyst for developing the structural infrastructure (boards and ownership councils) with my assistance as managing director of the family office. In the past two years, or eight years into the governance-building process, the family council invited three independent directors (the chairman of a large insurance corporation, the dean of a prominent business school, and myself) to meet with the council in executive session. While in *executive session*, the family council has evolved into the *family board* of the overall holding company. Standard practice today, per your recommendation to our board as our family business consultant [referring here to Ernesto J. Poza], is for family members to meet alone as family and owners for the first half of the scheduled meeting, and discuss family subjects and develop consensus on topics to be discussed in the second half of the meeting as an executive committee. In this way, the family does its work and prepares itself to influence the work of the holding company board, the family council/family board. The individual businesses that make up the Group have their own boards with independent directors... and a couple of family members serve on each of those boards too.

## Any concluding comments, Mr Cazorla?

Ours is a very comprehensive approach to family business governance that over a ten-year period has evolved to create strategic deliberation and decision-making bodies and the policies that allow the bodies or structures to function (akin to hardware and software in computers) without undue interference by the family in business matters or inappropriate influence by the business on family matters. Family, shareholders, and the operating businesses all have their platforms for continued success, and yet they all work to optimize the best interests of the partners, the owning family, as it successfully transitions to a third generation. It is a never-ending, continuous process that aims to keep family capital patient for the family's *socio-emotional well-being* and for the preservation of the family's pooled patient capital or *long-term orientation advantage*.

*It is a never-ending, continuous process that aims to keep family capital*

## Evolution and sustainability

The lifespan of the average US corporation has shrunk to about ten years.[1] This means that the family firm intent upon **continuity** has to attend to planning and **systemic thinking** and acting. Business leaders throughout Europe and Latin America, in conversations with the authors, agree that in their respective countries, too, turbulence has increased significantly and the long-term sustainability of companies is under attack.

Shortening product life-cycles, global hyper-competition, drastically changed supply chains, volatile capital markets, disruptive new technologies, and short-term thinking in top managements of businesses everywhere are making the goal of long-term continuity a quickly vanishing dream. And while the goal of successful succession and continuity is not universal, it still represents a worthy ambition for many families in business, and to a large extent defines the essence of family enterprise.

An evolutionary perspective would seem very timely, if the goal of so many family enterprises of continuing and even thriving from generation to generation is going to be achieved. Creating **governance architecture** is an essential leadership response to this challenge; a challenge that only becomes more difficult over time. Sustainability across an extended period of time is predominantly achieved today by family-owned and family-controlled enterprises. Zildjian Cymbals, from Norwell, Massachusetts, USA, for example, is almost 400 years old. Founded in 1623 in Istanbul, it is now the world's largest manufacturer of cymbals. The Timken Company, a specialty steel and bearings company based in Canton, Ohio, USA, was founded by a German immigrant to America, and remains a global powerhouse in its industry, more than 110 years after its founding in 1899. Tim Timken, its current chairman, argues that product innovation, and consistent values going back to his great-great-grandfather, drive the Timken Company's longevity. What is most important for families in business to address in order for the evolution of the family enterprise to continue for generations? Based on the last 20 years of research into family enterprises and more than 25 years of consulting to family companies, the authors have discovered three factors that significantly contribute to effective governance of a family business. These will be discussed next.

## Effective governance is more than just structures

Effective governance (EG) = Transparency (T) × Governance structures (GS) × Principles and policies (P)

Or EG = T × GS × P ›› 0

Governance is generally thought of as being provided by a board and perhaps a few other structures such as the **ownership structure** – and, in the case of a family business, the family council. But governance, as discussed in Chapter 1, is much more than a structure: it is a system; a holistic approach. This governance formula states that, for governance to be effective and contribute to business continuity over time, three fundamental and interrelated elements are necessary. **Transparency** and communication (strategic and financial); **governance structures** (such as boards, ownership structures/trusts, and family councils); and principles and policies (often contained in a family constitution and in shareholder agreements or company by-laws) are all required. In order for governance to be effective, these three building blocks have to be present in sufficient quantity to ensure that the effective governance factor (EG) will be significantly larger than zero.

The governance formula is a multiplicative function – that is to say, if any of the individual building blocks or independent variables is absent, or largely absent, effective governance will tend towards zero. At zero, or a similarly low value, effective governance will make no meaningful contribution to the sustainability and continuity of the family firm over the generations. It is therefore imperative that leadership initiatives by the CEO/chairman and others ensure that all three building blocks are in place. Taking the three dimensions in turn:

**Transparency** requires clearly communicating strategic plans, financial statements, financial analysis, and overall wealth/estate information to shareholders in a timely, clear, and actionable way. This is especially important the older the company and the greater the number of owners. This transparency is created via communication and the education of shareholders in ownership forums (such as **shareholder meetings** and family councils; see Chapter 8) to enable engaged and responsible ownership by shareholders.

**Governance structure:** these are the institutions and governing bodies that serve leading families globally in their efforts to build resilience to the challenges of wealth. They include: family councils, shareholder meetings, boards of directors (at the business unit and the holding company level), and, in later generations, family offices that help manage everything from investments to **concierge services** offered to family members.

**Principles and policies** that are often contained in family constitutions and shareholder agreements developed by leading enterprising families in later generations include:

1. **Employment and participation policies**. These spell out the requirements for being an employee. These policies then further define the criteria that family members need to meet in order to be deemed capable of carrying out a managerial role. They also often address the requirements that family members need to meet in order to serve on the board of directors or chair committees of the board or the family council.

2. **Dividend, distribution, and reinvestment policies.** Family constitutions sometimes define shareholder expectations with regard to shareholder returns from their investment in the company. These represent a proactive approach to managing shareholder expectations of management, whether as part of the family constitution or as a separate agreement. Some families set percentage guidelines (for example, 20% of annual profits will be distributed in the form of dividends or bonuses), while allowing for flexibility in the face of extraordinary circumstances, such as a new product launch or a company acquisition.

3. The mission, duties and coordination of each of the various governing bodies.
4. Shareholder and trust agreements that address buy-sell, rights of first refusal, voting rights, and control structures.

All these practical vehicles to create an architecture for effective governance are addressed in detail in subsequent chapters. But, to re-state, finding solutions to the fundamental challenges in the evolution of the family enterprise requires a systemic approach. It needs to include initiatives in all three areas: transparency, governance structures, and principles and policies.

## The long term

First-generation entrepreneurial family businesses typically comprise a single operating entity with all the financial resources contained within it. Tracking the financial resources is clearly the responsibility of the controller, chief financial officer, or founding owner. It is often only in later generations, when wealth is present in other ventures or asset classes, that the family firm features **wealth management**, and the information systems needed to support it, as a separate entity.

In order to keep shareholders in a family firm committed over the long term, share owners must be treated even more transparently and professionally than shareholders in a management-controlled S&P 500, FTSE100/250, Nikkei, or DAX-listed company. The advantage of patient family capital and caring oversight by responsible shareholders can then be tapped and can offer truly distinctive competitive strategies. It allows the family business to deploy distinctive competitive strategies.

Families have to reinvest continually in the development of a **culture of trust**. It can be difficult, for example, for an individual family member to trust a relative's assessment of the business and its performance, owing to family dynamics; and solutions to disagreements via the sale of stock are often out of the question, as shares in a privately held family company are illiquid and unmarketable. A culture of trust is important in the continued effective leadership of a family firm over the long term. Even in publicly traded but family-controlled firms, family dynamics can significantly affect strategic behavior. Consider the Ford family's commitment to the long-term success and sustainability of the Ford Motor Company in 2008, at a time when the auto industry as a whole was in a precarious condition and, at least in the United States, was requesting government bail-outs. The Ford family instead insisted on retaining their valued principle of independence and requested that top management find private sources of funding. Top management successfully negotiated multimillion dollar lines of credit with banking institutions before the need was apparent and before the full impact of the 2008 financial crisis had been felt.

*A culture of trust is important*

In terms of wealth management, the entrepreneur and family business owner will tend to focus and keep many eggs in one basket – the enterprise. This is in sharp contrast with risk-reduction approaches suggested by **modern portfolio theory**, an investment theory that has had widespread influence in the management of wealth over the past 50 years. Family shareholders thus often depend significantly on their equity in the firm, much more so than shareholders, who own widely traded shares of management-controlled companies. And if they are not "in the know," because they are not involved in management, this dependence turns to a heightened sense of risk. Adults tend to resist blind dependence on people or things they do not understand and trust. But what can family business shareholders do about their dependence on a significantly valuable and undiversified asset?

Family shareholders expecting to fulfill their responsibility must be able to make sense of what the numbers say about the firm and its competitiveness. Financial literacy is essential for every shareholder, not just those active in company management. Without it, family business shareholders can easily become just as indifferent or impatient, fickle and greedy as hedge fund managers and investors in public equity markets.

*Financial literacy is essential for every shareholder*

The time dimension or investment horizon of individual family members is also critical. Family shareholders inactive in the business, with little understanding of management and the time cycles involved in new strategies or new investments, can hamper the company's effective operation. They can bring about erosion of the founding entrepreneurial culture, which valued the role of hard work and patient capital and tacitly understood the benefits of **owner–manager alignment**.

*The time dimension or investment horizon of individual family members is also critical*

If family unity suffers as a result of this pressure by some family members for high financial returns and/or short time frames, this may result in a loss of will and vision. Family owners have to understand and ultimately agree what their returns will be in both economic (dividends, capital gains, and career opportunities, for example) and noneconomic (purpose, reputation, family unity, and philanthropic opportunities) terms. Without this understanding, a family business may lose a powerful source of competitive advantage: its patient pool of family capital. In the longer term, some family members may abandon business continuity in favor of immediately recapturing, via sale of the company stock, the value created by previous generations. Such a family business will be incapable, in the future, of adopting a strategic profile that is different to that exhibited by hedge funds and institutional investors on Wall Street, the French Bourse, or the Bolsa de Santiago (Chile).

There is no way of avoiding the evolutionary changes that we discussed in Chapter 1. A first-generation entrepreneurial firm with a sole owner, the founding entrepreneur, that survives under family control will inevitably move – over time – to perhaps a **sibling partnership**, then perhaps a **cousin consortium**, and eventually to a **family dynasty**, even if the progression is neither as linear nor as predictable as described here. Some family firms, for example, go from a sibling partnership in the second generation to a sole owner in the third, after one of the family branches buys out the other's interests in the company.

Similarly, the management structure will migrate from a founder-dominated entrepreneurial structure to a focused structure containing departments and/or divisions, which evolves to a more diversified family business structure with multiple business units, and eventually perhaps a family office with oversight and investment responsibility for a dozen companies, ventures, and other asset classes. And the ownership structure will likely evolve from a sole owner, to a multiple-owner managed firm, and to a firm managed by owners plus nonfamily managers, to a family-monitored enterprise comprising operating companies and a variety of other assets.

## Evolution by design[1]

When the evolutionary process is led by the CEO, chairman of the board, or family council chair, and not left to chance, then the three dimensions of transparency, governance structures, and principles and policies are the leader's tools. There are four distinct stages in the evolution of a family – enterprise and a family's wealth. Each stage has its challenges, and deploys these tools differently in the service of effective governance of the family business relationship.

In stage one, virtually all of the family's invested capital is committed to a highly entrepreneurial business. In this stage, there is no need for complicated financial systems or a family office; the owner/entrepreneur already knows all there is to know about his company's finances. Distributions and dividends to family members are small to nonexistent (since the capital is all being reinvested to grow the business) and the entrepreneur-owner and the business are often one and the same.

In stage two, the family often begins to professionalize the business. Professional family and nonfamily managers can make a substantial contribution to more effectively governing the family – business relationship. Professional best practices both raise the standards of performance for owners and build a useful moat between a family's behaviors and dynamics and the preservation of the positive organizational culture. Nonbusiness assets are often added to the family's investment portfolio at this stage too. Typically, the management of nonbusiness assets still falls to the individual owner, with perhaps some assistance from the CFO, the accountant, or financial advisers. A board of directors that is primarily family, possibly complemented by a couple of dependent outsiders, such as the company lawyer and accountant, may meet four to six times a year. Some families launch family councils at this stage, usually in preparation for an approaching succession. Some have also begun to write a family constitution, or at the very least a family employment policy to prevent the negative consequences of excessive nepotism or **altruism**.

During stage three, the family often begins to professionalize the management of its nonbusiness investments, which now constitute a substantial portion of the family's wealth. Depending on the size and nature of nonbusiness assets, some functions are performed by family – offices, either by service providers or a **multifamily office**. The multifamily office (a family office established to serve the needs of families other than the founding family, such as the Rockefeller family office) could assist the family with its wealth, and help govern the relationship between the family, the business, and its non-business investments. Transparency is expected in the investment manager's and/or family office's management of the non-business assets. Greater transparency in the business is also expected by family members, especially those not employed in the family business. By stage three, some business and non-business assets have already been transferred to the next generation and are no longer a part of the family's patient capital pool. Family council meetings are held to assist in educating heirs on wealth management and their responsibilities as shareholders or **trustees**; a board of directors most likely now includes independent outsiders and limits the number of family members who sit on the board; a family office may help the owning family develop the agenda and logistics of family council meetings, as well as providing investment and wealth management assistance. Also at this stage, the family may have established a **foundation** to carry out its philanthropic goals. Liquidity and access to capital for growth purposes can be central concerns, so the business family sometimes executes an **initial public offering** (IPO) and takes the company public at this stage. Proceeds from the IPO may be used to diversify the estate or create a family bank or family venture capital company that funds new ventures by next-generation members. Family policies to promote and regulate this trans-generational entrepreneurship process via the use of business plans and **venture review boards** that include independent outsiders are often implemented.

In stage four, the family may no longer own the operating business that was the original source of its wealth. As an enterprising family, it has likely professionalized the management of its investments too. For these families, asset management, wealth preservation, and wise wealth utilization become the new family business.

In stage four, the family office indeed is the family business. It may be involved in ensuring that shareholder returns from a portfolio of businesses, real estate, private equity, venture capital, or angel investments are appropriate and that investment risk is being managed proactively. Transparency is significant and absolutely necessary; multiple business boards and holding company boards meet quarterly; family councils and family assemblies (see below for a discussion on family assemblies) meet to *Transparency is significant and absolutely necessary* handle the family's business; a variety of **shareholder agreements** regulate buy-sells and other owner transfers, and ownership councils for the various businesses (as described by Mr. Julio J. Cazorla in the opening interview for this chapter) meet on an as-needed basis.

## The founder exits; a family office is started

Today, a growing number of second- (and later) generation family firms are creating family offices to assist shareholders in their owner duties and responsibilities. The services offered vary depending on the company, but typically family offices shoulder primary responsibility for joint family investments, **family philanthropy**, family private equity and venture capital investments, tax and legal advice to shareholders, tax-return preparation, the filing of required legal documents on behalf of the shareholder, shareholder education, the planning and execution of family council meetings, shareholder meetings and **family assemblies**, and administration of shared assets or properties.

Examples of the family office include Rockefeller's Room 56 (so named because the family office operated out of Rockefeller Plaza's Suite 56), and the family office at Cargill, the largest private corporation in the world. In a similar way, many much smaller family firms rely on their own family office or a shared-service family office, a multifamily office. The latter, usually housed in the family office of a larger family enterprise, represents a way to outsource the administration of a family office, with corresponding cost savings. The services they provide to the large business-owning family can be retained by the smaller business-owning family for a fee; usually 1–2% of assets under management.

Family offices assist shareholders with the responsibilities born out of their ownership relation to the company. In so doing, they often help make the owner – company relationship a more positive and disciplined one. Family offices can also support a business model that puts the enterprising family at the heart of family business strategy and family wealth decision-making. This means that trans-generational strategies (which include entrepreneurship, family business, real estate and private equity investments, and even alternative investment classes) can all be part of the family's enterprise from generation to generation. Like family councils, family offices enhance a family's ability to govern the relationship between the family and the company, enabling more professional management of the firm, and fairer and more timely handling of shareholder and family issues and requests. (For a more comprehensive discussion of the family office and its services, see Chapter 10.)

If a multigenerational family business does not have a family office, it typically will have a staff person at the operating company who coordinates all shareholder communications and stock transfers, and acts as the liaison between the family shareholders and the shareholders' financial and tax advisers.

## The family assembly

Not all members of a large multigenerational family may be able to work together as members of a family council. The extended family may be too large for this. As a result, larger families sometimes create an annual family assembly to operate in conjunction with the family council. Family assemblies are another vehicle for education, communication, and the renewal of family bonds. They create opportunities for participation for all family members at least once a year. The family council can work on behalf of the assembly during its two or three meetings per year and then report on its progress during the larger annual family assembly. If the family in business has created a family office, then the staff at this office are typically in charge of organizing and managing the annual family assembly.

## The annual general meeting

The annual general meeting (AGM) presents an opportunity for review of management and company financial performance. During this meeting, family members exercise their responsibilities as shareholders and are informed of the company's performance, the **returns on shareholders' equity**, strategic initiatives, and the **dividends** to be distributed. The board of directors is elected at this meeting. Shareholders may vote on other matters on the agenda, including the selection of auditors, changes to the articles of incorporation, and dividend policy. Only shareholders may attend, not extended family members or spouses who are not legal holders of stock. The AGM usually takes place annually. However, special meetings may be called to address important and time-sensitive issues.

If the stock is held in trust for the benefit of family members, this meeting is often referred to as the **trustees'/beneficiaries' meeting**. Depending on the provisions of the trust, some or many of the functions performed in an AGM, as discussed earlier, are carried out in the trustees'/beneficiaries' meeting.

## BEST-PRACTICE RECOMMENDATIONS

**1** In order to make family businesses that are seeking continuity less fragile over time, the incumbent generation needs to build redundancies in governance structures and systems (for example, by not relying exclusively on a board of directors, but also launching a family council and writing a family constitution) while continuing to nurture the unique resource that is patient family capital.

**2** Transparency and ample communication with the owners and future owners regarding company strategy, company finances, competitive challenges, and shareholder returns on the family's invested capital are essential. Education of shareholders on these subjects (something akin to a mini-MBA) may need to precede the information-sharing, so that understanding, not loyal compliance, is the outcome.

**3** Governance structures are very important even if they do not constitute the whole governance system. Create boards with independent directors, restructure boards that are all family; use family councils, family assemblies, and family offices. Leading enterprising families around the world consider family offices to be the most effective at addressing the challenges posed by wealth and growing families.

**4** Develop principles and policies that both preserve the legacy and regulate the relationship between the family and its enterprise. As Sir Adrian Cadbury, former chairman of Cadbury Schweppes, the large British chocolate and beverage maker, eloquently put it, "The sooner a family firm regularizes the relationships between the family and the firm, the less time will have to be spent on matters of allocation between them, which can create trouble out of all proportion to their economic significance."

**5** Professional management of the family enterprise is another essential building block in the governance architecture of the family business. Hire the best nonfamily managers, reward their independence (not just their loyalty), and listen to their suggestions for keeping the business growing profitably. When businesses grow profitably as fast as the family is growing, zero-sum dynamics are arrested and their attack on family business governance is neutralized.

## chapter 4

# Responsible Ownership in Family Enterprises

"It is important to integrate family shareholders into the company and into the entire entrepreneurial family. This can only be achieved by organizing common activities. It will not just magically happen."

Interview with Franz M. Haniel, chairman of the board of directors, Haniel, Duisburg-Ruhrort, Germany

Franz M. Haniel, chairman of the board of directors at Haniel, talks here about his aim of forging a family identity and training family members to become professional owners. Haniel is an internationally successful, family-owned diversified group of companies. In 2012, it employed around 56,000 employees, generating sales of €26.3 billion in more than 30 countries. Haniel has been a family-owned business for over 250 years, with its headquarters in Duisburg-Ruhrort, Germany, throughout this time. *

*This interview is translated into English and has already been published in *Führung von Familienunternehmen* (*Leading the Family Enterprise*) by Alexander Koeberle-Schmid and Bernd Grottel.

*Alexander Koeberle-Schmid:* **More than 255 years after it was founded, Franz Haniel & Cie. is today owned by about 650 owners. How would you characterize this group?**
*Franz M. Haniel:* It is a large group of people each of whom is proud to be a part of one of the longest-established and most successful entrepreneurial families, and thus feels strongly attached to it. We are a family whose members are scattered all over the world. Yet, no matter where the individual owner lives, all of them feel that, emotionally, Ruhrort, the cradle of our family business, is an important home base.

**Your range of owners appears to be very heterogeneous. Is it a great challenge to forge an identity within the Haniel family? How do you proceed?**
We have established a wide range of occasions where family members can meet each other. These include the shareholders' meeting, of course, as well as board of directors meetings and advisory board meetings. But there are also opportunities for further training – a factor we value very highly. For example, we organize a meeting for junior owners, which lasts one and a half days. Participants are given an introduction into the basics of the company's business management as well as the roles of boards and committees in the company and the family. Additionally, there is a financial reporting seminar. All of those seminars serve the same purposes for participants: to understand what the company does, to understand why the family is special, to establish affection towards the company and the family, and also to provide training on particular specialist subjects. The objective is to become a well-trained, responsible owner.

**What characterizes a professional and responsible owner of Haniel?**
They have a vested interest in the company and in the family. Secondly, they are someone who epitomizes the Haniel virtues such as decency, honesty, reliability, and responsibility. Thirdly, they are someone who can demonstrate in their private life

*They have a vested interest in the company and in the family* as well as in their professional environment that they are successful and that they are visionary in terms of business and steadfast in the principles by which they are guided. Fourthly, they have an integrative personality, which is what a large family needs to stick together, after all.

**A lot of working hours are needed for the organization of common activities. Do you have staff who are expressly in charge of that?**

No, we have no designated organizing staff. Owners' events are organized by company employees who do this in addition to their usual tasks. They do an amazing job and are highly professional.

**I am under the impression that your owners are proud to be members of the Haniel family. In what way does this high emotional value become manifest?**

Our emotional value does not result from our products, but rather from the fact that there is a strong sense of community. The additional emotional value that welds us together lies in the awareness of belonging to a successful, long-

established entrepreneurial family. In addition, everyone knows that they are integrated in a family whose members support each other.

**How do you establish contact among family members?**

In addition to the numerous ways of getting together in person, owners are also given the opportunity to contact each other online. We have something called Haniel Family Net. First of all, this is a means of sharing information. It provides owners with information concerning the company, but it also allows owners to submit information or queries to the company. Its second purpose is to facilitate organizational processes within the family and to cultivate the family network by providing communication platforms.

**To sum up, what are the success factors for ensuring that family enterprises will survive even if their number of shareholders increases?**

It is important to integrate family shareholders into the company and into the entire entrepreneurial family. This can only be achieved by organizing common activities. It will not just magically happen. Furthermore, what is needed is a clear common understanding of values and roles. Every family member has to continue to realize: what does the company stand for, what does the family stand for, and what is my role in our family and in our company? Knowing what I may and what I can expect from the company as well as what the company can and must expect from me is essential. The third factor is training family members to become responsible shareholders.

# "Firm, family, fortune."

Interview with Karl-Erivan Haub (CEO) and Christian Haub (CFO), Tengelmann, Mülheim an der Ruhr, Germany

In this interview, Karl-Erivan W. Haub (chief executive officer at Tengelmann; pictured right) and his brother, Christian Haub (chief family officer at Tengelmann; pictured left) talk about

family and company objectives and values as well as shareholders' rights and duties. The Tengelmann Group is a multisector European retailer. With a network of 4,346 stores and 83,826 employees, the group generated sales of €11.08 billion in 2012. The holding company is located in Mülheim an der Ruhr, Germany, where the family business was founded in 1867.*

*Alexander Koeberle-Schmid*: **Family enterprises are especially successful if they are built on a clear foundation of objectives and values. What are the objectives and values that you have defined for your company?**

*Karl-Erivan W. Haub*: It is our foremost objective to hand over to the next generation a successful company. Even if no family members were in charge of the management of the company by then, we always want to have control over third-party management. In addition, as a diversified family enterprise, we want our family holding to remain 100% in family ownership. Among our important values are continuous innovation, maintaining an entrepreneurial approach, and dealing with our employees in a respectful way, while putting a strong emphasis on their performance.

**What are the objectives and values you have defined for your family?**

*Christian Haub*: We are a German-American family. Our motto is: "Firm, family, fortune." Our firm

---

* This interview is translated into English and has already been published in the book *Führung von Familienunternehmen* (*Leading the Family Enterprise*) by Alexander Koeberle-Schmid and Bernd Grottel.

is given priority over family and fortune. Inter-generational cohesion within our family is what we think is especially important. We want to deal with one another in a trusting, fair, and appreciative way.

**What do you, as manager of the company, expect from your other owners?**

*Karl-Erivan W. Haub*: First of all, I expect that they identify to a considerable extent with the family enterprise and with the family. This includes the expectation that owners are loyal towards the family enterprise, especially in public. Furthermore, I expect them to behave in a way that is worthy of a professional owner, and for everyone to contribute to the best of their abilities.

*We want to deal with one another in a trusting, fair, and appreciative way*

**What can owners expect from their management?**

*Christian Haub*: First and foremost, some basic financial security. In addition, they receive a regular dividend payment, although we do not believe that this is something owners should rely on, because each owner is supposed to make their own living and not live at the expense of the company. Also, they have the opportunity to develop their abilities within the family, be it as the person in charge of our foundation, as family manager, as a nonexecutive member of the board of directors, or as managing director. All this is subject to rules that we have established in order to avoid conflicts.

**What rights and duties do your shareholders have?**

*Karl-Erivan W. Haub*: The most important rights are the dividend right and the right to be eligible for the board of directors. This board is of utmost importance to the company and the family. It provides advice to, and control of, management, and is empowered to appoint or recall members of the management team. It is the duty of every owner to enter into a marital agreement that excludes any gain or statutory share related to business assets. In addition, they are obliged to observe absolute confidentiality towards the public: conflicts must not be aired in the media.

**What happens if owners violate their duties?**

*Christian Haub*: This falls within my range of duties as family manager. I consider it to be my responsibility to point out to each owner and to all family members what their rights and duties are – that is, to warn them, if necessary. Should another warning be necessary, this may – if the worst comes to the worst – result in expulsion. In order for this to become effective, a qualified majority of owners' votes is required, obviously without the vote of the owner or family member who is to be expelled.

**You are required to hold an AGM at least once a year. What do you discuss in those meetings?**

*Karl-Erivan W. Haub*: Due to the fact that our number of owners is still rather low, only formal decisions are made in our owners' meeting. This usually takes about two hours. During the meeting, for example, the annual accounts are approved, the management board responsibilities are discharged, new members of the board of directors are elected, and any changes to the shareholder agreement are put to a vote. Future developments and strategy, however, are deliberately not part of the agenda. These are topics we deal with during our board of directors' meetings or during our family day.

**In your opinion, what are the factors that determine the lasting success of family enterprises?**

*Karl-Erivan W. Haub*: As a family enterprise, what is needed in order not to fail, because of the life-cycle risk, is continuous innovation, true to Schumpeter's principle of "creative destruction." Each generation must strike gold once or twice, for no business model can be perpetuated endlessly.

*Christian Haub*: I wholeheartedly agree with the last point my brother made. I would like to add that a wisely developed management and control structure, in line with the principles of good governance, is an important success factor. If there is no fair and professional system of rules, you are effectively opening the floodgates to conflict. Furthermore, and this is what I consider to be my responsibility as family manager, it is essential to the success of a family enterprise that cohesion within the family is safeguarded. Against this background, my brother and I regard ourselves as team players with complementary roles and clearly defined responsibilities. He represents the company and its assets; I represent the family and its assets.

## Being a responsible owner of a family enterprise

The American motivational speaker and writer Denis Waitley observed: "A sign of wisdom and maturity is when you come to terms with the realization that your decisions cause your rewards and consequences. You are responsible for your life, and your ultimate success depends on the choices you make."[1] Such an approach can be found in many successful entrepreneurial families. They care deeply about their business and their family; they consult one another before making important decisions, to lower the risk of mistakes; they take responsibility for their decisions; their vision of and commitment to the business are strong. They take pride in steering the enterprise and the family through the storms that will inevitably occur, and guiding them to harbor.

People tend to think that it is easy to be an owner. But being a responsible family business owner can be difficult and challenging. Some decisions are tough: having to sell part of the business, stopping the heritage product line, forgoing dividends because the business needs liquidity, making employees redundant for the sake of survival – there are many examples of tough decisions. Yet the amazing strengths of family businesses come from the very fact they are privately owned. Their resistance, resilience, long-term vision, the passion and efforts made to preserve and maintain the business over time are some of the underlying reasons that explain the higher economic performance of these businesses.

*Yet the amazing strengths of family businesses come from the very fact they are privately owned*

## What does responsible ownership mean?

What does "responsible ownership" mean? Is it in the family's DNA, or does it need to be acquired? Responsible ownership begins with "ownership," which brings with it the ultimate power of decision-making in a business. The role and the importance of ownership have long been overlooked. Historically, management has received much attention – from owner families, the media, and business schools. Later, much weight has been placed on governance with the business board and its functioning – or lack of it. It is only relatively recently that attention has been turned to ownership[2] to understand better the role it plays in a company's performance, longevity, and commitment. A quite different type of ownership distinguishes family-owned and private businesses from other businesses. Ownership is concentrated in the hands of a few people, which gives them considerable power but also makes them visible and identifiable, thus more accountable for their decisions. In addition, as detailed in Chapter 1, the family-business ownership structure evolves over time and goes from one owner-manager, to a partnership of siblings in a second stage, and later to a cousin consortium in a third stage, growing in numbers each time.

The second part of responsible ownership is **"responsibility,"** which means the capacity to act in the best interest of the business, the employees, and the community, as well as the family and the other owners. Responsible ownership has four fundamental roots:

*the capacity to act in the best interest of the business, the employees, and the community*

1. *Family values*: integrity, respect, commitment, and many other values typical of successful families. They can be instilled from a very young age, generation after generation.
2. *Stewardship*: ensuring protection of the best interests of the business in the long term. Owning a family business is not about "me" – how much power, prestige or money I can get from it – but about my commitment to it and what can I do to serve and protect it.
3. *Emotional ownership*:[3] a sense of ownership that is far more than material ownership or an investment. Children have a natural sense of "owning" their family and its tangible possessions, such as houses, but this does not automatically extend to their appreciation of the family business. The emotional sense of ownership of a business has to be nurtured

*Owning a family business is not about "me"*

in children and young adults. When this occurs, it leads to higher commitment and participation of family members in the business, and strengthens corporate culture and performance.

4. *Patient capital:*[4] this refers to the willingness of family business owners to provide equity, and to be willing to balance the prospect of a short-term return on their investment with the merits of a well crafted, long-term strategy that safeguards the family heritage. Such owners are prepared to receive less today to reinvest more in the business and increase its perennity and future value.

## Education

One could argue that there is no need to acquire specific skills to be an owner. It is true that shares through inheritance or purchase on the stock exchange may come about easily; "responsible ownership," on the other hand, typically requires awareness, and then understanding and knowledge. Values and an emotional sense of ownership can be instilled from a young age, through both the family and the business. The closer young adults get to the business, the family council, or the family foundation, the more likely it is that they will develop a strong **emotional attachment** to it. An environment that welcomes the next generation into the business and its governance is particularly helpful.

Once values and emotional ownership are acquired, responsibility and stewardship can be developed. All four dimensions of responsible ownership will help ensure resilience and continuity, and that capital is available when the business needs resources, or that a sacrifice will be made when necessary to help the business survive.

Educational initiatives can also include an early donation of shares, perhaps in small quantities. This can be combined with more formal education on finance, the business, and on economics generally, to create some valuable learning about ownership and why it is important to protect it. In addition to the case studies in this chapter, the Bekaert

Academy discussed in Chapter 13 is an excellent example of an education program to create responsible owners. In particular, owners (through the family council or the owners' board) will be keen to set appropriate education programs to raise the level of financial literacy. It is important that all owners understand how to read **financial statements**,[5] such as a balance sheet, a profit and loss (P&L), or a cash-flow statement, and that they are aware of key financial ratios (such as the debt–equity ratio, return on assets (ROA), and the earnings per share (EPS) ratio). Being familiar with these financial concepts enables owners to understand what is happening in the business, to realize its current and future value, and to feel knowledgeable enough to ask relevant questions. Such education helps family owners to gain the skill set necessary for exercising their duties as responsible owners.

## Benefits

As well as helping the business and the community, responsible ownership reinforces family cohesion, enabling family shareholders to speak with one voice and give a strong sense of direction and leadership to the business, usually resulting in higher performance.

*responsible ownership reinforces family cohesion*

## Owners' rights and duties

Owners have **legal rights**. It seems obvious, but many family owners are unaware of these, in particular if they are not directly involved in the management of the business. Legal rights and duties vary according to jurisdiction and to the legal form of the company. Experts or specific legislation should be consulted to see what is applicable in each country, but some of the most common legal rights include the following:

- *Attend*: a right to attend all shareholders' meetings, or to be represented at those meetings.

- *Voice*: a right to vote and express opinion at shareholders' meetings. The vote may be in accordance with the rights attaching to different classes of shares. Same shares have preferred voting rights and thus more weight in the decisions (these may be known as preferred shares, A shares, or voting shares).
- *Information*: the right to receive financial information as well as information on development, strategy, or control mechanisms, and on the organizational structure of the company. This is similar to the information published by listed companies in their annual reports, without having to be as costly and sophisticated.
- *Remuneration*: a contingent right to receive a share of the profits of the business, as well as a right to receive a share of the property of the business upon dissolution.
- *Elect and dismiss directors*: the right to select who sits on the business's board.
- *By-laws* (articles of association): the right to approve and amend the by-laws of the company. The by-laws may contain additional rights or duties for shareholders; in family businesses they often limit the transferability of shares to other family members by giving them a pre-emption right.
- *Auditors*: the right to approve the external auditors.

The **legal liability** of shareholders in a corporation is limited to the nominal value of their respective shares, but other forms of businesses can involve a higher degree of liability, going all the way to being personally responsible for all the debts of the company. In a shareholders' agreement, shareholders can also restrict their own rights, such as setting a limit on when and to whom shares can be transferred or sold. In an agreement they can also add duties, such as the duty to elect a certain number of family members as directors. The rights and duties defined in a shareholders' agreement are contractually binding.

In addition to legal and contractual rights and duties, responsible owners also have **moral duties**, as stewards

*responsible owners also have moral duties*

of the business and of the family legacy. Examples include a moral duty to ensure the well-being of the business, to protect employment and employees, to grow the business whenever possible, to consider environmental impact, and to protect the community. Exercising moral duties distinguishes responsible ownership from mere ownership. Moral duties stem from family values, cultural influences, and emotional ownership. If I love my business, I will protect it. If respect is a family value, I will treat employees and clients with respect and consider their interests.

It is important to note here that some rights can also be perceived to include an aspect of duty, in particular when shareholders have enough consolidated voting power in their hands, which is most often the case in a family business – listed or not. For instance, a shareholder who has US$20,000 invested in General Electric (GE) shares will have a technical right to vote in the election of the board, but in reality no influence at all because of the small percentage of capital the shares represent. In a family business, though, individuals, branches of the family, or the family itself hold significant portions of the capital and can have an influence. Therefore, for instance, to be true to their duty of protecting the business, it is not only their right to elect board members, it is also their duty to dismiss them (family or not) if they do not act in the best long-term interests of the business.

## Tasks of responsible owners

There are many ways in which responsible owners can seek to enhance and protect the business, and protect their employees and the community. These include:

- Providing a clear long-term vision. When asked about the difference between a family and a nonfamily business, a Japanese family business owner said, "It is very simple: for us a "quarter" is 25 years."
- Clarifying, communicating, and inculcating values and ethical standards for the business.

- Setting overall objectives for performance and risk levels that enable the business's long-term development, well-being, and legal compliance.
- Overseeing and monitoring the performance of the business to assess that its management is in alignment with their long-term objectives and the values they set.
- Delegating responsibilities to the board and management, and, once done, not interfering with their action and decisions, unless major problems or fraud are detected.
- Seeking family harmony and unity – in particular, but not exclusively, between owners who work in the business or have a role in the governance structures and those who do not.
- Enabling a climate of transparency, respect, and trust.
- Enabling and growing emotional capital.
- Setting in place measures for welcoming the next generation.
- Setting and attending relevant education programs, including those aimed at financial literacy.
- Maintaining ownership in adverse economic conditions being committed.

Family owners usually set and review objectives, and perform the above tasks either through an owners' board, or a shareholders' committee, or directly through the family council. Elements of their functions and ownership policies are set in the family constitution.

The strength of family businesses comes from responsible ownership. It provides the capacity to foster resilience and long-term vision: a treasure to keep, protect, and grow.

## Types of ownership

While all owners may become responsible owners, not all of them are equal in the way they can or want to be involved. Aronoff and Ward[6] established a classification of owners that has become standard, and in which many families can recognize themselves. It consists of the six following categories (Figure 4.1):

1. *Operating owners* are actively involved in management of the business, the family office, or the family foundation, on a day-to-day basis.
2. *Governing owners* oversee the function of, and hold positions on, the business board or some of its committees, the family council, the family office board, or the family foundation board. Governing owners may also be involved in management, not as operating owners, but more as ombudsmen, for instance.
3. *Involved owners* are more remote from business and governance than the previous two categories, but are attentive to issues facing the operations, understand the business's strategy, and promote the corporate culture.
4. *Proud owners* are not involved, and may not understand strategy or governance, but have strong emotional ownership levels.
5. *Passive owners* are happy to share the benefits of the business and to receive dividends, but have low or neutral emotional ownership levels and take no responsibility for the business.
6. *Investor owners* are invested in the business for its financial performance, keeping or selling their shares based on performance, and having no emotional ownership of the business.

| OPERATING OWNER | GOVERNING OWNER | INVOLVED OWNER | PROUD OWNER | PASSIVE OWNER | INVESTOR OWNER |
|---|---|---|---|---|---|
| Actively involved | Position on | Remote | Not involved | Not involved | Not involved |
| Management | Board | Attentive to issues | Strong emotional ownership | No responsibility | Keeps or sells shares based on performance |
| F. Business F. Office F. Foundation | F. Business F. Office F. Foundation F. Trust F. Council | Understands strategy | | Dividends | No emotional ownership |

FIG 4.1 **Typology of family business owners**

*Source*: Aronoff, C.E. and Ward, J.L., "6 Kinds of Owners," in *Family Business Ownership: How to be an Effective Shareholder* (Palgrave Macmillan, 2002, pp. 7–9. Adapted with kind permission.

Out of these six categories, the first four are or can become responsible owners, perhaps with the help of training programs. The last two are merely owners. They delegate responsibility to others. It may take considerable effort to turn them into responsible owners.

It can be helpful for family members to review periodically where they fit in these categories. Such reviews can indicate, for instance, that no one in the next generation is interested, at that point of time, in becoming an operating owner, or that more and more family owners are clustered in the "passive" and "investor" categories, indicating a drop in emotional ownership and a higher likelihood of the business being sold.

## Indirect ownership

A business is not always held directly by family members. Often shares are held in a trust or a foundation (such as Stiftung in Germany or Stichting in the Netherlands). This is mostly done to protect the business and ensure that individual family members cannot decide to sell it against the wishes of a larger group of owners, or against the interests of the business itself. At times it can also optimize tax efficiency. These entities are governed by a **board of trustees** or a foundation board. By-laws (articles of association), the vehicle itself, or the law may exclude owners from participation in these boards, or limit their number.

*Often shares are held in a trust or a foundation*

This indirect ownership model can be tricky if it becomes intangible and abstract for family members: they may manage the business but not own it; they may govern it but not be able to decide on some important issues related to the business. It may even result in a low sense of emotional ownership or in a lack of drive and motivation because it is one step removed. These potential negative outcomes are important to monitor in order to put in place balancing measures whenever needed.

In order to counter some of the negative aspects of the trust/foundation model, some families have devised hybrid solutions, where voting shares are held by the trust or the foundation, and nonvoting shares by family members. Or, for publicly listed companies, a block of shares is held in a foundation to ensure majority of voice and unity of ownership among family members, while the rest are held directly and can be bought or sold on the stock exchange. These solutions allow a sense of direct ownership and commitment, as well as the ability to sell if in need of liquidity – while protecting the business, since individual owners cannot make major decisions against the best interests of the business.

## Shared ownership

A business may need fresh capital to grow on a scale that is beyond the means of the family. For example, one branch may wish to leave, and its contribution to the capital of the business may need to be compensated for in order not to prejudice the long-term survival of the business. The family usually has two broad options to seek fresh capital, if selling the business or borrowing capital is not an option. The first is to find a **private investor,** or a small group of private investors, to co-invest with them, in which case it remains a private business. The second, if the business is large enough, is to go public and prepare for an initial public offering (**IPO**) (Figure 4.2).

*Often shares are held in a trust or a foundation*

Both options can be positive and constructive for the business, provided families are aware, well in advance, of the positive and the negative impacts of the decision to open up the capital and share ownership,[7] and they make plans to mitigate the downside. Some of the negative impacts can include (a) a loss of control, which families may struggle to accept, even if only a fraction of the capital is traded, and (b) a possible shift in strategy and vision if the market or the private investor wants to prioritize short-term revenues ahead of long-term stability. Some of the positive impacts can include (a) increased liquidity for the owners and the business, (b) a consequent potential to improve business performance, at least in the short term, and (c) an opportunity to prune the family tree and concentrate family ownership in the hands of the more committed family owners, leading to reinforced family unity.

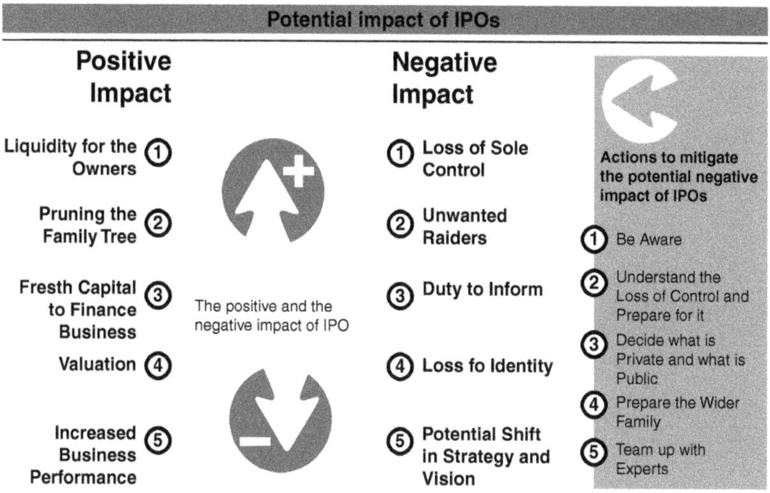

| Potential impact of IPOs | | |
|---|---|---|
| **Positive Impact** | **Negative Impact** | |
| Liquidity for the Owners ① | ① Loss of Sole Control | **Actions to mitigate the potential negative impact of IPOs** |
| Pruning the Family Tree ② | ② Unwanted Raiders | ① Be Aware |
| Fresh Capital to Finance Business ③ | ③ Duty to Inform | ② Understand the Loss of Control and Prepare for it |
| Valuation ④ | ④ Loss fo Identity | ③ Decide what is Private and what is Public |
| Increased Business Performance ⑤ | ⑤ Potential Shift in Strategy and Vision | ④ Prepare the Wider Family |
| | | ⑤ Team up with Experts |

The positive and the negative impact of IPO

FIG 4.2 / The potential impact of IPOs

*Source*: Kenyon-Rouvinez, D., "The Aftermath of an IPO – What Families in Business Ought to Know Before They Go Public," *Tharawat Magazine*, vol. 9, January 2011, p. 62. Reproduced with kind permission of Tharawat.

**B E S T - P R A C T I C E**
**R E C O M M E N D A T I O N S**

**1** Being a responsible owner is not easy. It comes with rewards, but it also requires couragsse to make difficult decisions and sacrifices at times. Ownership is central to the performance of family businesses.

**2** Responsible ownership has four roots:

   a. Family values.

   b. Stewardship.

   c. Emotional ownership.

   d. Patient capital.

**3** Few people are born "responsible owners," but anyone can become one provided the right values, attitudes, structures, and education systems are made available.

**4** The benefits of responsible ownership are increased family cohesion, a stronger sense of direction and leadership, and higher business performance.

**5** All owners have legal rights. Responsible owners also recognize their moral duties – such as protecting the business and the family legacy, or respecting the interests of employees, employment, and the environment.

**6** Responsible owners set a clear vision and objectives for the business; they enable a climate of transparency and trust, and they welcome and educate the next generation of owners.

**7** Responsible owners are more likely to maintain ownership in adverse economic conditions and are committed to being an entrepreneurial family.

**8** Owners can be classified into six categories, graded according to level of involvement. The evolution of the family within these categories is a powerful indicator of measures to implement and education programs to initiate.

**9** Ownership may be transferred to a trust or a foundation to protect the business, or offer tax efficiencies. This may cause a drop in emotional ownership, and so corrective measures and education programs may have to be put in place to avoid this.

**10** Opening up the capital to a private investor or to the public can prove to be a positive tool both for the business and for the family, provided family members are well aware of the less positive implications, and anticipate the impact of the change.

# Structures for the Business: Business Governance

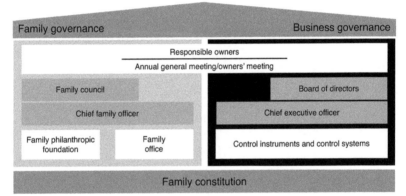

This figure highlights the business governance covered in Part II and acts as a navigational tool for the reader.

## chapter 5

# Professional Board of Directors*

/ **"If the board is appropriately staffed, it can be of valuable assistance in setting strategies and developing the business model further."**

Interview with Bettina Würth, Chairwoman of the Advisory Board, Würth Group, Künzelsau, Germany

The Würth Group has an advisory board which holds competences similar to that of a board of directors. Bettina Würth, chairwoman of the advisory board, here gives an account of the role of the board within the Würth Group. Würth is a family business that was founded by Adolf Würth in 1945. The Group is a world market-leader in its core business, the trade in assembly and fastening materials. It currently consists of over 400 companies in more than 80 countries and has more than 65,000 employees on its payroll. The Würth

* Alexander Koeberle-Schmid kindly thanks Joachim Groß, Arno Lehmann-Tolkmitt, and Rainer Lorz, as well as his colleague board members, for their support in the development of the knowledge about professional boards and their support in the development of the four steps board model for family enterprises.

Group generated total sales of €9.98 billion in 2012.**

*Alexander Koeberle-Schmid*: **Ms. Würth, in the governance report of your annual report, you describe the enormous importance that is attached to governance in your family business. Why is governance so important?**

*Bettina Würth*: Firstly, business governance and transparent decision-making have always been integral parts of our corporate philosophy, a fact that we also like to demonstrate beyond our corporate borders. Secondly, the Würth Group has reached an overall size exceeding that of a traditional family enterprise. This means that within the Würth Group we now have a system of executive bodies and dual decision-making which is similar to that of typical publicly-listed companies.

**The board of directors or advisory board holds a central position in governance. Why do family businesses need this type of body?**

Depending on the size of the company and the business sector in which the family enterprise operates, I think it is a good idea to have an advisory board. If the board is appropriately staffed, it can be of valuable assistance in setting strategies and developing the business model further. It is important to ensure that the advisory board comprises professionals with different types of expertise, who will be able to assist family members in making operational decisions, as they are likely not to be trained auditors, tax consultants, or lawyers.

*I think it is a good idea to have an advisory board.*

**Which specific tasks is your advisory board responsible for?**
Based on what is stipulated in our "compendium" – that is, our company constitution – the board members of the Würth Group have responsibilities that are comparable to those in a publicly-listed company: these are monitoring and advice. That said, the advisory board members should of course use their authority

** This interview is translated into English and has already been published in *Führung von Familienunternehmen* (Leading the Family Enterprise) by Alexander Koeberle-Schmid and Bernd Grottel, published by Erich Schmid, Germany.

to support the Würth Group and its operating management.

**How would you characterize the way Group executives and you as chairwoman of the advisory board work together?**
Due to our history, it is natural that the family, especially my father and I, work closely together with management. In a company such as the Würth Group, it is not practical to confine oneself to being a member of an advisory board that is involved in company issues only three times a year.

**Does the advisory board offer any particular mechanisms intended to maintain or limit the influence that family members have over the Würth Group?**
The constitution of the Würth Group includes election regulations for the advisory board as well as the supervisory board of the Würth Group's family trusts, according to which a certain number of board members are appointed by the family. The purpose of this mechanism is to create a balance between family interests and the interests of the Würth Group management. Moreover, there is a family council where management provides family members with accounts of the current state of the company and recent developments.

**You have an audit committee. Which members of the advisory board are part of this committee and what specific tasks are the members of the audit committee responsible for?**
The audit committee has three members: an auditor, a lawyer with experience in finance, and me. We are responsible for monitoring compliance as well as financial statements.

**You assess your advisory board's efficiency. How do you do this?**
Assessment of the board's efficiency takes place every other year. It is carried out by means of a questionnaire and a comprehensive evaluation session. A neutral third person, who is not a member of the board, is in charge of assessment, evaluation, and moderation of the evaluation session. The assessment aims to improve the board's work.

**What were the results of your efficiency assessment, and how have they been tackled?**
We have gained some insights concerning the editing of reports

and the composition of committees. Also it made us realize that board members wish to be included in strategic issues to a greater extent, and to receive more information on certain monitoring areas such as risk management. In my capacity as chairwoman of the advisory board, I take these topics into consideration and try to come up with appropriate solutions, together with my team.

*board members wish to be included in strategic issues*

**What role does your advisory board play in a crisis situation?**

If there is such a situation, the advisory board would try, to the best of its knowledge and belief, to be of service to the family and the business. There is no patented remedy for that. However, all members of the board use their comprehensive experience and knowledge to help make the company as crisis-proof as possible.

## Different boards for different family enterprises

### Example 1

In Company A, a family enterprise, the founder was the sole owner.[1] One day, he was killed in an airplane accident. His two sons were not in the business. Fortunately, there was a board of directors, which was to prove to be crucial in ensuring the survival of the company. Nonexecutive board members helped manage the difficult succession. External help was necessary, because each son received 50% of the shares and both had ambitions to become the next CEO and different interests at the beginning. The external board members helped to establish an executive team comprising the two brothers. The **nonexecutive board members are of considerable assistance** in this company, especially in the case of conflicts, for example, when the two brothers cannot agree on a decision. The main roles of the nonexecutive board members are to listen, mediate, and advise the two brothers. Monitoring them is a minor role, since the two managing directors are also the owners, who have the ultimate decision-making authority and could even fire the nonexecutive board members if they both agree.

### Example 2

A large diversified family enterprise, Company B, with 50 family members, decided that family members should not be allowed to work in the company. The business has a board of directors with nonexecutive family members only. The CEO is a nonfamily member, and the chairman is a family member. This **board exercises considerable powers** over strategic business decisions to ensure that executives act in line with the interests of the owners. The nonexecutives make decisions on all top management positions, about large investments and divestments, about mergers and acquisitions, about taking loans, and about the budget.

## Example 3

In Company C, one family member, who has nine cousins, is the CEO and is also responsible for sales and marketing. There is a nonfamily chief financial officer (CFO) and a nonfamily chief operating officer (COO). On the board, there are five nonexecutive members, two of whom have a family background. The chairman is a nonfamily member who is CEO in another company. The reason why the board is composed this way is that the company is run by a family CEO with a view to ensuring alignment of interests with the other family owners. However, the **risk of conflict** owing to family tension, which may have arisen if the chairman were also a family member, is reduced. The task of the nonexecutives is to ensure the quality of leadership and take personnel decisions at the executive level. In this respect, the board also monitors the decisions and the performance of the family CEO, to prevent misuse of his power.

These three examples show that **family enterprises are diverse.**[2] A focused family enterprise with one owner needs a different type of board than a family enterprise that owns different companies and where the management team consists only of nonfamily. Another major influencing factor on the type of board needed is the way in which a company is constituted; for example, whether it is listed or not, and in which jurisdiction.

## Why establish a board of directors?

Not all family enterprises have, or even need, a board of directors. Where a business-owning family has the choice, it has to decide whether a board will help to deal with their challenges and professionalize the business. We list some of the **common objections** below, followed by some reasons that counter these points.

*it has to decide whether a board will help to deal with their challenges and professionalize the business*

- *"I see no benefit in a board of directors for the enterprise."* A board can be particularly helpful in the succession process, because nonfamily nonexecutives are often better able to approach the decision about the next CEO in a professional and objective manner (see Chapter 6). A board can motivate and inspire the executives, and can create space for deeper discussion and reflection. It increases the accountability among customers, suppliers, and banks.
- *"I do not want external people to know about our problems."* Nonfamily members as nonexecutives can act as mediators in conflict situations. Those board members who are not employed in the business, independent of whether they are family members or not, may identify problems that managers have missed.
- *"A board slows down our decision-making process."* If a CEO has to present a proposal in front of nonexecutive board members, he or she is forced to think clearly about the consequences of the decision. This slows down the decision-making process but can also allow for deeper reflection, better identification of risk, and prevent a poor decision.
- *"My fear is that I cannot get rid of the board of directors anymore."* The contractual term that a board member serves can be as low as three years. And, if all owners agree, they can be voted out any time. Setting up a board is a reversible process: the owners collectively could choose to abolish the board.
- *"I don't want to lose control."* A board functions primarily as an advisory body and a forum for discussion, testing and challenging ideas, including those put forward by executives. It can also assist in an emergency when the next CEO or managing director needs to be selected.

Despite these objections and fears, most family enterprises have a board of directors.[3] These owners have transferred some of their rights, very often the right to monitor the executives, to their board of directors. This is a step that many business-owning families take when the size of the company and its complexity increases; when the number of family owners goes up; when there is a succession in leadership due within five to ten years, or when there are nonfamily owners, or when there are owners who work in the company and others who are only shareholders. Once the board is established, most **owners are satisfied** with its operations. This is because the board, provided it is well structured, assists the professional management of a company.[4]

## A four-step model for a professional board of directors

For boards to be able to operate professionally, their tasks and composition have to be adapted to the context. Due to the diversity of family enterprises, there are no recommendations that apply to all equally. There, however, is one recommendation that applies as a general principle: the need for appropriate checks and balances, with the **CEO position and the chairman position separate**.

Figure 5.1 shows a helpful **four-step model** for establishing a board.[5] It encourages owners to start thinking about the benefits, tasks, duties, and qualifications of the board, before thinking of particular personnel to be recruited.

The first step in the model is to define the **benefits** of the board. The second step is to define the **tasks** and duties needed to create the aspired benefits. These may include monitoring, advice, personnel selection, networking, and family communication. The next step is to regulate the **contingent factors** in relation to the individual situation. Regarding the structure, it is necessary to stipulate the size of the board, the term of office of each member, the number of meetings and the composition – family, nonfamily members, chairman. In addition, the competences of the board as a body and of the different members needs to be determined. Arrangements for liability, reporting, selection process, and committees need to be established, and the remuneration of the board members needs to be defined. The fourth step is the **evaluation process**. In summary, the four steps are:

- What benefits should a board generate?
- What are the specific duties of the board?
- How should the contingent factors be set?
- How could the effectiveness and efficiency of the board be increased?

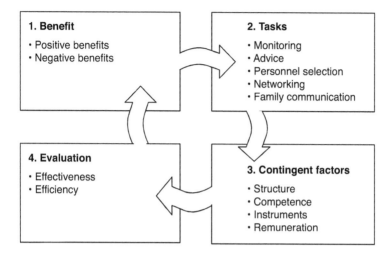

**1. Benefit**
- Positive benefits
- Negative benefits

**2. Tasks**
- Monitoring
- Advice
- Personnel selection
- Networking
- Family communication

**4. Evaluation**
- Effectiveness
- Efficiency

**3. Contingent factors**
- Structure
- Competence
- Instruments
- Remuneration

FIG 5.1 / Four-step model for a professional board of directors in family businesses, especially the nonexecutive side (adaptation of the model by Alexander Koeberle-Schmid, Joachim Groß, and Arno Lehmann-Tolkmitt)

Business-owning families who already have a board can also use this model to **improve its performance**. This can mean adjusting the composition or remit of the board as the context changes. Examples of a significant change include new markets, new products, increased size of the business, a rise in the number of family members, or a change in the composition of the management – for instance, moving to a nonfamily CEO. If there are changes in the family or the business, the duties and composition of the board of directors need to change, too.

## Step 1: The benefits of a professional board

Before a board of directors is implemented, the owners need to consider the benefits that the board should generate for the firm and the family.[6] The answers differ tremendously, depending on the type of family enterprise. Some of the **potential benefits** are summarized in Figure 5.2.

| Our board should ... | Our board should not ... |
| --- | --- |
| • Support the management with comprehensive expertise<br>• Increase the quality of decisions<br>• Intensify the self-discipline, accountability and responsibility of managing directors<br>• Assure the realization of goals and compliances with rules and values<br>• Ensure communication to owners<br>• Mediate in conflict situations<br>• Assist in the succession process | • Intervene in daily business<br>• Intensify groupthink dominated by one person<br>• Produce extensive reports<br>• Generate complex structures<br>• Avoid a critical and controversial debate<br>• Speak out for the interests of individual owners |

FIG 5.2 / The pros and cons of having a board in a family business (adaptation of the overview by Alexander Koeberle-Schmid, Joachim Groß, and Arno Lehmann-Tolkmitt)

In addition, it helps if the business-owning family defines those aspects that the board should *not* do. This will depend on legal considerations. It is important that the **limits** of the board's remit are clearly communicated by the owners' family to the nonexecutive members, the managing directors (and, in the case of family, external shareholders to them). The limits also differ according to the type of family enterprise, but some examples of what the board should not do are mentioned in Figure 5.2.

## Step 2: Tasks of a professional board

It is helpful to define the overriding tasks or duties in five categories: monitoring, advice, personnel selection, networking, and family communication (see Figure 5.3).[7] The next step is for owner-families to elaborate in more detail the specific requirements and tasks of each duty. They also need to ensure that they are compliant with company law.

### Monitoring

Monitoring the managing directors ensure that managers **act in line with the interests of owners**. A common problem in family enterprises is that an owner who is also the managing director retains his/her management

|  | Firm | Society/Family |
|---|---|---|
| • Operational<br>• Strategic | Monitoring | Networking |
| • Strategic<br>• Operational | Advice | Family<br>communication |
| • Selection<br>• Remuneration<br>• Dismissal | Personnel selection | |

• Considering family
opinion
• Communicating with
the family
• Assuring cohesion
within the family

**FIG 5.3** Possible tasks carried out by boards, particularly performed by nonexecutive board members, in family enterprises

position longer than is beneficial for the company.[8] In addition, family owners who work in the business often use company resources like the company gardener or the company's aircraft for personal reasons.[9] Often, they have more information than the other owners; they have a deeper insight into the company and know the operating figures earlier.

**Operational and strategic monitoring** can reduce those problems.[10] **Operational monitoring** means controlling *ex post* the financial and risk situation of the business. This also includes getting critical information from the external and internal auditors. A family enterprise should implement a risk management and internal control system, and processes for compliance management (see Chapter 7). Such instruments should be capable of delivering information on whether, for example, risk thresholds are violated or a fraud has occurred. The board can then respond immediately.

Strategic monitoring helps guard against managing directors making unwise decisions. Before a strategic decision is taken, an in-depth and wide-ranging discussion should be held. It helps to prepare a detailed overview listing major transactions requiring approval by the board. On the board itself, nonexecutives should be in the majority. This list of pending transactions often

*Strategic monitoring helps guard against directors making unwise decisions*

consists of the approval of strategic planning, goals, budget, investments and divestments, mergers and acquisitions, and of all financial contracts with banks and other financial institutions. The board should approve all major contracts, especially in cases where family members are working in the firm or have business relationships.

## Advice

The existence of a board enables executive directors to discuss their doubts, fears, and challenges with the nonexecutive board members on a strategic level. This can be a particularly valuable opportunity if there is only one executive on the board, as in the case of a sole owner. Such discussions create the space for managers to reflect on their decisions, leading to more informed strategic decisions and an improved positioning of the business.[11] Such a forum can **generate new ideas**, and lead to deep conversations about business strategy.[12] However, the board members always ought to operate within the defined values and goals of the owners' family. In addition to strategic advice, the nonexecutive board members may offer support in a technical and operational specialism that the business may lack, such as accounting, legal expertise, or new markets.

## Personnel selection

One of the most important duties of a board concerns the **search for, appointment, remuneration, and dismissal of company executives**.[13] Monitoring is illusory if the board does not have the power to dismiss managing directors in cases of misconduct or poor performance. The selection of executives should normally be carried out in close coordination with the owners.[14] Family members who work in the business typically have the same interests as other family owners, therefore they should be preferred, especially if they have the same ability as nonfamily executives. However, the nonexecutive board members (or in some cases only the nonfamily nonexecutives) should be involved in the **selection process**, especially if a family member is being considered for appointment. The following aspects are relevant in the selection process:[15]

- The nonexecutive board members should develop a **profile** for a vacant post. In addition, the board should define whether the candidate should have working experience outside the business. This is especially relevant for family members, because it indicates to them whether they should have worked in another firm and for how long.
- The nonexecutive board members should define the **remuneration** and **reasons for termination** of contract. Such reasons may be if goals are not achieved, or if the company has underperformed in relation to competitors.
- If a family member applies for a position and receives **approval by the board**, a development plan for him/her should be drawn up (see Chapter 6).
- During this development phase the nonexecutive board members should give regular **feedback**. A board member could function as mentor or coach.
- If the candidate is successful at the end of the development phase, which will be decided by the board, he/she will win a **long-term contract** or may possibly be promoted to become the next CEO. If targets are not achieved, the candidate cannot become CEO and thus should leave the company or could continue to work in the same position.

A board's most difficult task is to **dismiss a manager**. If the board recognizes that a managing director has not achieved the set goals, then consequences should quickly follow. This is particularly difficult when the individual is a family member. The decision becomes even more difficult if, for example, the father is the chairman and his son is the CEO. In such a case, the nonfamily nonexecutive board members could form a committee that is empowered to dismiss the family CEO. In order to enforce these personal decisions, regardless of family affiliation, the board, and in particular the chairman, needs to have the necessary authority.

## Networking

Nonexecutive board members can create opportunities for the business through their **network** of relationships.[16] The company may gain access to information, wider networks, and possibly government departments. Access to resources and risk reduction are the two business advantages from such networking. However, not all networking will have positive effects. For example, if the board's network includes banks, while this can lead to improved credit conditions, it can also increase dependence on the bank, because if the company goes through an economic slump, the bank will become nervous and may recall its loans earlier. It is advised that there is no member of the company's bank on the board.

## Family communication

The board of directors often has the task of **maintaining communication** between the business-owning family and the company.[17] This is an especially important role if there are many owners. The board informs the owners about decisions taken, gives the owners qualitative information about the decisions, and information about the financial and strategic position of the firm. The duty of the board is to ensure an orderly and adequate flow of information to the family owners.

The board also needs to take into account the **owner's opinions** when making a decision. Board members should convey the owners' thoughts to management. So, for example, the owners should formulate their expectations of the company with regard to matters such as financial stability, profitability, growth, risk appetite, and diversification. The board then transmits this to the management and bears it in mind when making a decision.

One or more members of the board can assume specific duties in relation to the family. For instance, they could organize family activities such as a family social weekend, a family assembly, or family seminars, where owners learn about being professional owners. These joint activities could contribute to the cohesion of the family and strengthen the engagement with the business on the part of the family. Such a role is increasingly popular in family enterprises.

## Step 3: Contingent factors

When discussing the benefits of a board and its proposed tasks, the owners' family should define the contingent factors of the board of directors, especially the nonexecutive part.[18] This also depends on the type of the family business. This section defines four contingent factors for a professional board of directors: **structure, qualification, instruments, and remuneration** (see Figure 5.4).

### Structure

The **size of the board** depends on the legal constitution, the duties, the complexity of the business, the representation of the family, and the potential for conflict within the family. The bigger the team, the more complex the discussions, so the size of the board has to accommodate

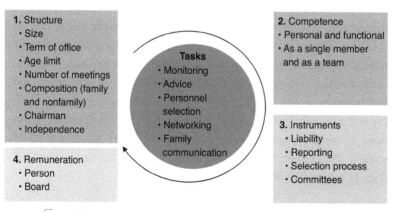

**FIG 5.4** Contingent factors in boards of directors in family enterprises, especially for nonexecutive directors

these. Three board members is a recommended minimum: one executive, two nonexecutives. A maximum should be seven to nine. However, the nonexecutives should always be in majority.

The **term of office** of the nonexecutive members should be established, bearing in mind the likely need for continuous adjustment of the composition of the board in relation to company needs. A period of three years offers the possibility to react to changes in the business environment. In addition, it is recommended that the term is designed to be rolling, so that each year a board member is elected, there is no loss of expertise. Furthermore, one could make sure that the accumulated tenure of the nonexecutives is not too long. A **maximum term**, for example of 12 years, can be established. An **age limit** can also be used to ensure that board members do not stay in post for too long. Experience has shown that 70 to 75 years is a good limit for nonexecutives. This should apply to both family and nonfamily board members.

The purpose of the **board meeting** is to discuss relevant company issues, make decisions, and resolve conflicts. Typically there are two to six meetings per year, with more meetings needed in crisis situations. At least four meetings per year should be held covering the following main issues: outlook, financial statements, strategy, and budgets. In addition, executives hold their own meetings.

When making appointments to the board, and especially in the case of nonexecutive members, the owners should make sure that there is sufficient **external representation**.[19] There is a risk that where personal, financial, and commercial relations are significant, the independence of nonexecutive board members is reduced, and the whole body could degenerate into a body without sufficient authority to influence and make decisions. Some groups of people should therefore be excluded from becoming board members; for example, the company accountant, tax adviser, banker, and lawyer, as well as friends and business partners.

There should, however, be **family members on the nonexecutive side** of the board. They act generally in the sense of all the family owners, and can represent the values and goals of the family.[20] Family owners have a strong incentive to monitor the actions of the nonfamily management, because it is their money. If there are only nonfamily managing directors, then the nonexecutive side should consist of mainly family members. If there is a family managing director, there should be more nonfamily nonexecutives, to reduce potential sources of conflicts between family members. Family members on the board can be responsible for the task of communicating with the family. However, there should not be too many family members on the board, because that could lead to a small AGM.

The **chairman** plays a key role. He/she directs the board's work and is the first person to be addressed by management and owners. For the purposes of good governance, to ensure sufficient checks and balances, the position should be held by someone other than the CEO. In the collaboration between those two, the chairman is in close contact with the CEO. In line with principles governing the composition of the board as a whole, if the CEO is a family member, the chairman should be a nonfamily member, and vice versa. The chairman should not be so dominant that the problem of "groupthink" occurs and the other nonexecutive board members do not speak up. He/she should create an atmosphere that encourages open discussion.

## Competence

The second contingent factor is the competence of the nonexecutive board members. It helps if individual members have **specific qualifications** to offer to the company.[21] What specific skills are needed depends on the situation of the family and the business, as well as on the duties of the nonexecutive board members. Board members ought to have knowledge of the company's products, markets, customers, and competitors. Awareness of the firm's strategy and issues concerning innovation and finance is particularly important. Knowledge of investing, accountancy, risk management, internal control systems, and compliance management is also indispensable.

Nonexecutive board members also ought to have relevant **personal qualifications**. They should also have a deep understanding of the dynamics of families and family enterprises, and should have management experience. This should be complemented by qualities such as the ability to work as part of a team, clarity of communication, integrity, and reliability as well as sufficient availability such that board members have the time to prepare for meetings as well as attend. The board should also reflect diversity in terms of age, gender, and cultural background. Finally, each board member should be highly motivated. Individuals can be best inspired by offering them the exciting opportunity to shape the future of the business and to learn something in the process.

## Instruments

Strong boards need the help of appropriate instruments to work effectively and efficiently. National law will cover important areas such as a **director's liability**, and of course these must be understood in detail. Risk can be reduced by an appropriate directors' and officers' insurance.

Furthermore, there are three important instruments that the family owners need to define: reporting mechanisms, the selection process of board members, and the creation of special committees, where appropriate. It also helps if the necessary defined processes of the four-step model are included in the articles of association or other by-laws.

An appropriate **reporting system** is necessary to inform board members so that they can perform their duties. In preparation for a board meeting, managers should provide the relevant information in a structured manner, at least two weeks before the meeting. A board booklet that follows the structure of the agenda should include all the information in one document. In addition, it is extremely useful if board members receive a succinct monthly update. The use of eye-catching visuals such as graphs, green and red light images, and so on can help members gain a quick overview of the current situation. On a quarterly basis, the board should receive the balance sheet, the profit and loss (P&L) statement, the cash-flow calculations, and a risk management report. In addition, the board may request special investigations and

*receive a succinct monthly update*

reports if they perceive a need to investigate irregular practices. It is also a duty of executives to report any irregular practices to the nonexecutives immediately, especially if certain events occur, such as fraud or cancellations of important orders, that have a negative effect on the company and can destabilize it.

The **selection process** to the board is crucial. There are three ways to appoint a nonexecutive board member: (1) admission rights to certain owners, (2) posting rights for certain owners (that is, entitlement on the part of some owners to become board members without election), and (3) election at an AGM. Admission and posting rights mainly apply when a family is organized in branches, or the former CEO and family owner wants the right to sit on the board while his/her child becomes the next CEO. The election process, mainly by qualified majority, should be based on a pre-selection, where the chairman or CEO or other family owner prepares a shortlist of candidates. Preparation should include analysis of the current composition of the board and the competences required by the company, resulting in a search profile. In addition, it should be determined whether the nonexecutive board member should come from outside the family, as well as the requirements for independence and diversity – which may be with respect to age, gender, cultural background, and/or representation of family branches. With this profile, designated board members or owners can start to screen possible candidates, who can then be presented to the owners, with election at a subsequent owners' meeting. Each owner should have the right to propose a candidate for election.

**Committees** play a special role, especially if there is a CEO who is also the chairman of the board.[22] They help to professionalize decisions. Examples are an audit committee, a nominations committee, and an advisory committee that is set up for special issues. Ad hoc committees, set up for a specific period, may be useful when, for example, large investment or acquisition projects are planned. Committees can also be implemented to mediate conflicts.

Audit and nominations committees ought to consist of nonexecutives only. In the other cases, one executive board member could sit alongside nonexecutive members to help inform management's decision-making process. All committees should maximize their use of the committee members' knowledge to help the company.

## Remuneration and other costs

The cost of maintaining a board of directors comes under five broad categories. These are: (1) the initial set-up, (2) remuneration and expenses of board members, (3) the cost of preparing reports to the board, (4) paying for the participation of the management and other employees at board meetings, and (5) the premium for the directors' and officers' insurance.

**Remuneration of nonexecutive board members** depends on the size of the company, the number of board meetings it holds, the complexity of the company, and the duties of the board. In Germany, for example, nonexecutive board members are paid on average approximately €17,000 a year.[23] Family enterprises with an annual revenue of less than €10 million pay about €4,000 a year; companies with revenues between €50 to €125 million roughly €11,500 per year, and firms with more than €500 million in sales pay about €40,000 per year. The chairman receives 50–100% more. The general principle of the compensation should be: pay the nonexecutive board members well, and expect a lot.

## Step 4: Evaluation

Each team needs to ask itself what has been performed well and what has been carried out less well through regular evaluation.[24] To design appropriate **board evaluation**, it is helpful to address five questions:

- Who will be evaluated?
- What will be the content of the evaluation?
- Who will be subject to evaluation?

'•Who will carry out the evaluation?
'•How can the evaluation be structured?

1. **Who?**
   - Whole board
   - Non-executive board members
   - Single board members
2. **What?**
   - Task performance
   - Structure and composition
   - Qualification
   - Reporting design
3. **For whom?**
   - Owners
   - Board

4. **By whom?**
   - Board
   - Extrenal evaluators
5. **How?**
   - Completion of questionnaire by board members
   - Analysis of questionnaie and discussion of results with external evaluators
   - Recommendations by external evaluators
   - Adjustments

FIG 5.5  Evaluating a board

The answers depend on the type of family enterprise. However, many family enterprises use a similar evaluation design as shown in Figure 5.5. The content of the evaluation can be based on the model presented here for professional boards: task performance, structural performance, competence performance, instrumental performance, and appropriateness of remuneration. Normally, the whole board is evaluated by answering a questionnaire, which is then analyzed by an external evaluator who will discuss the results with the board members as well as the owners.

The results of the board evaluation can also lead to a review of the intended benefits of the board (step 1 of the four-step model; Figure 5.1). This completes the circle of a professional board aiming at continual improvement in the way in which it assists management to make the best decisions in the interests of the company and its owners.

## BEST-PRACTICE RECOMMENDATIONS

**1** Owner families should consider setting up a professional board of directors to assist the success and sustainability of the family enterprise. Its composition will depend upon the ownership and management structure.

**2** Professional boards of directors should formulate goals for executives based on the goals and values of the owners.

**3** Board directors should perform their tasks effectively and efficiently: monitoring, advice, personnel selection, networking, and communication with the family.

**4** Professional boards should engage in deep discussion with management on strategy, the budget, and company performance, with the objective of preventing management from making unwise decisions.

**5** Professional boards of directors are advised to have between three and seven members, where the nonexecutives are in majority, the CEO is not the same person as the chairman, a term of three years is set, with an age limit of 75 years. They should meet at least four times a year.

**6** The entire board, but also the individual members, should have considerable experience and relevant specialist qualifications.

**7** The board of directors should receive comprehensive, structured reporting at least two weeks prior to the meetings. Board members should be well prepared for the meetings.

**8** If the CEO is a family member, the chairman should be a nonfamily member and vice versa.

**9** The board of directors should evaluate its performance annually.

**10** Board members should be adequately remunerated in line with high expectations of their performance.

# 6

# CEOs and CEO Succession*

"There is a special emotional link to something that has existed for 350 years. We have the fifteenth generation now running the company."

Interview  Henri van Eeghen, COO/director of Cordaid, the Hague, The Netherlands, and Tini Hooymans, former nonfamily director on the board of the Van Eeghen Group, Amsterdam, The Netherlands

In this interview, Henri van Eeghen shares his career progression and choices. He is joined by Tini Hooymans, former nonfamily director on the board of Van Eeghen.

Henri van Eeghen is a member of the fourteenth generation running the company (with the fifteenth generation now in charge). A former

chief operating officer (CEO) of the Van Eeghen Group, Henri is currently chief operating officer (COO)/director of Cordaid, a philanthropic organization. He holds numerous directorships and speaks six languages fluently.

*This chapter is based on a chapter written by D. Kenyon-Rouvinez in *Family Business Governance, Erfolgreiche Führung von Familienunternehmen* (Erich Schmidt Verlag, 2010). Permission to reproduce this here has been granted by Erich Schmidt Verlag.

We also speak to Tini Hooymans, former nonfamily director on the board of Van Eeghen. Tini Hooymans is a member of the board of management of TNO (a company based in Delft, The Netherlands) and served on the supervisory board of the Van Eeghen Group from 2004 to 2007.

The Van Eeghen Group is a 350-year-old family business based in The Netherlands. Founded in 1662, it is an international producer of quality health ingredients. The group has diversified into other sectors such as communications and precious metals.

*Denise Kenyon-Rouvinez*: **Henri, can you describe your career path?**

*Henri van Eeghen*: In the middle of my MBA in Canada I went to work for a Finnish company, a multinational in the paper industry. I spent the summer there. A few months later, a member of the board offered me a position I could not refuse. I started with some training in northwestern Canada, then took up a position in Osaka. At the age of 27 they sent me to South Korea to set up a new company. We worked hard, employed local companies, supplied high-quality

materials, and within two years beat our target. At 31, I was offered work in Finland as the company's first foreign employee in a director's position. I had two factories under me and some 4,000 employees, learned Finnish, and was also given the opportunity to oversee mergers and acquisitions (M&A). We made a lot of investments, in Asia, in Africa, and Europe. The company had a subsidiary in the Netherlands. I had never really thought of coming back, but the group asked me to go there and see. I was running the subsidiary, the M&A initiatives and managing a division. That year I spent 160 nights in hotels; my family life was pretty poor. I knew I had to make a change, sent in my resignation, and left. For a short period I did an interim job. Then I was asked to run a family company in The Netherlands.

**What made you decide to join the family business?**

*Henri van Eeghen*: During the time that I was in Finland I was asked to join the supervisory board of our family business. About four years after that, my father asked me whether I would consider joining the family company [full time] as the CEO. I said not under the current circumstances, with my father still very involved. The risk of conflict was too high, considering my father's character and my own.

In the meantime, I had joined a family company that was in the process of being sold to a venture capital company. It was a considerable and very profitable company. I helped them through the process and stayed for four years.

The pull from my own family company became more and more pressing. I did not want to feel that I was married to the business and had to run it for the next 20 years; in the end I agreed to consider joining provided that if, after five years, I wanted to do something else, I should feel no pressure to stay. I eventually stayed for five years. I did some internal restructuring of the company and started up a new business.

**Did the business have any conditions for you when you joined?**

*Henri van Eeghen*: For my hiring there were no conditions set, apart from the fact that the CEO had to be a bearer of the name van Eeghen. It is in the by-laws of the company.

**Tini, were you on the supervisory board when Henri joined the business?**

*Tini Hooymans*: I served on the board of the Van Eeghen Group from 2004 to 2007. When I started, Willem, Henri's brother, was the CEO. Willem himself felt that he could concentrate more on the vitamin business if someone else was taking care of all the other activities.

**Tini, did you have a formal process in place to recruit Henri and did you have a possibility of a veto?**

*Tini Hooymans*: Yes and no. We certainly received Henri's CV. I was on the board together with the chair who was also nonfamily, and Maarten, another of Henri's brothers. The three of us discussed whether Henri was a good candidate and we decided in all objectivity that, yes, he was. But, on the other hand, there were no other candidates and in that respect recruiting for a family business is different. We were happy, though, because Henri had all the qualifications needed and more.

## Henri, has the family business changed conditions to entry?

*Henri van Eeghen*: Yes, when I was running the company we also initiated changes to the governance system. With the supervisory board, we were very much in favor of having more competition among family members who had an interest in joining. We decided on a few ground rules, one of them being that people should have a minimum of five years' outside work experience for a position that became vacant in the business; more for the CEO position. The second was that if a position became vacant there should be a competition among family members interested in joining. Another new rule of engagement that applied to me, as well as the others [CEOs] to come, is that after five or ten years' time you are free to move on if you want to. The only constraint is to give sufficient time for the group to find a successor.

## Henri, when and why did you decide to leave the family business?

*Henri van Eeghen*: After four and a half years, I was approached by a search firm to see if I would be interested in running Cordaid, which I was. Then the process of recruiting a new family member started. We set out a description of the function and the responsibilities, very much as we would if searching for an external candidate, and sent it out broadly within the family. There were a number of applicants. The supervisory board did all the interviewing. One candidate was proposed to the shareholders at the shareholders' meeting, he was considered to be the right person for the job and was accepted unanimously.

## What are the advantages and disadvantages of being an heir to a business and its CEO?

*Henri van Eeghen*: There are two sides to it. I underestimated the way family members look at their company. I thought I was just going to run another business. Even though we had 30 shareholders, which is a relatively large group, they had an emotional influence on how we were running the business. In the beginning I did not accept the emotional ties of the family members, and the fact they wanted/needed to come to the business. Then I realized it was important, accepted it, and spent more time with the family members, especially with the older generation.

On the other hand, if you wanted to start new ventures and new ideas you had a lot of latitude to do so. And as you were a family member too, there wasn't a whole lot of scrutiny in terms of quarterly results, half-year results. Yearly results were the most that people were interested in. There was never any pressure. So, in terms of administrative burden, the family company was fantastic.

Luckily too, none of the 30 shareholders had financial needs that would require for them to exit the business. It is not unusual at a shareholders' meeting for shareholders to say: "We like the plan you have for the coming year, we don't need the dividends, why don't you reinvest them in the business?" It happened at least twice during my mandate, which is really great because the money went back into the company, and we did not have to borrow.

**Tini, as a nonfamily observer, what struck you about the van Eeghen family?**

*Tini Hooymans*: Everyone was quite competitive and professional, also the shareholders. The supervisory board had six meetings a year, one of which was with all the shareholders. We had very strong discussions, tough discussions about where we were heading with the company. They were very involved. Dividends were not a question or an interest – the future of the company was. I think that is the big difference between family and nonfamily businesses. The van Eeghens are deeply involved in the company and very proud of it.

**You have a vibrant pool of talent in the next generation, 40–50 of them. There must be something very special about the family that it still breeds motivation and competence. What is it?**

*Henri van Eeghen*: I think there is a special emotional link to something that has existed for 350 years. We have the fifteenth generation now running the company. We are proud of it and of the fact that it is a company that has renewed itself many times over.

We have a few ground rules, nonwritten rules, that have probably helped: our business is not about size but about profitability; it is not about size in terms of turnover, but in terms of employees. Another ground rule is: know all the employees who work for you. So that limits you to 400–500 people, because otherwise you just won't remember everybody. That was one philosophy; another is that if profitability is a driver, as a medium-sized company, you always need to find niche markets. And

*Our business is not about size but about profitability;*

a third one is that, in our family business, we always leave room for a newcomer to remain entrepreneurial and add to the business; we accept failure and learn from it.

Our family values also have a deep influence on our longevity. The way we were brought up was, "Do what you are good at and then excel at it by putting in a lot of effort." The second value is "live frugally," which may come from our religious background; we don't want to identify with material things. The third is that we must give back to society, it is a major part of who we are.

## Identifying the right CEO and grooming his/her successor

"If I were born again, I would still be an industrialist. I complain because it's very hard work with no weekends, but I would still do it," said Sakip Sabanci who, along with his brothers, took over the family business and with energy and initiative led the Turkish Group (a diversified group with 57,000 employees worldwide and revenues of US$14.6 billion in 2012) to become one of the world's largest companies.

With the role of CEO comes **power and prestige**, which many people like, and they may want nothing other than to have that role. The role also comes with many **responsibilities**, and requires great dedication, talent, and leadership: a rare combination of skills that can be found in some families, but which sometimes needs to be sought outside the family circle.

The mere fact that the business is a family business adds several layers of complexity to the task, and makes the role of the CEO (and other senior managers) fundamentally different to that of other businesses – even if the business is listed on the stock exchange or otherwise not fully owned by the family. Here are a few reasons why:

- *The power of family ownership*: in a family business, ownership is clearly identified and usually in the hands of relatively few individuals who will impose a strict framework in which the board and the CEO can operate.
- *The power of the board*: often comprising family and nonfamily members, it can exercise a great deal of control and authority over the CEO.
- *Increased responsibility*: of the CEO towards the company, the employees, the profitability, and the longevity of the business.
- Deep emotional ties to the business, the family, and its history.

This means that CEOs of family businesses can leave their egos at the door. Their own wealth, the wealth of their parents, siblings, and cousins, as well as the wealth and future of their own children, the economic stability of their employees, and of their region: all are in their hands. They have to roll up their sleeves and work hard to grow the business for the next generation.

From a family business governance point of view, three things matter in terms of management: (1) understanding in what ways managing a family business is different from managing any other business, (2) deciding whether competence can be found in the family or if there is a need to hire a nonfamily CEO, and (3) grooming the next generation of CEOs and key executives.

## Managing the family business: why is it different?

The general framework in which the CEO of a family business operates is defined by the family owners and the board. This might not be obvious to a nonfamily CEO, who may be used to far more freedom. Owners, through the board, let the CEO know about the vision they have for the business, their strategic objectives, their tolerance to risk, and their guiding principles, which translate into what is allowed and what is not allowed in the business. The CEO operates within those guidelines in the day-to-day management of the business,

*The CEO operates within those guidelines in the day-to-day management of the business*

Essential management functions – marketing, production, finance, legal, human resources, etc. – are broadly the same in family enterprises as in nonfamily businesses, but there are three distinctive management tasks of a family business that relate primarily to the way in which business is conducted. These are:

• The corporate culture.
• The alignment of business policies with the family's values.
• The structure of the organization.

## Corporate culture

From the **values and guidelines** received from the family owners, the CEO can transform, preserve, and transmit the essence of what makes the family business unique. This creates a true competitive advantage: the corporate culture.[2]

Why is corporate culture so important? Simply because it has a significant direct impact on performance. Employees who can identify with a corporate culture demonstrate an increased motivation for their job, their work, the family they serve, the people they meet. They feel strongly committed to their company and are more likely to apply themselves beyond their contractual job description, which can play in favor of the business, especially in difficult economic times. Suppliers and clients also prefer to do business with a company that has a defined and long-lasting identity.

*Employees who can identify with a corporate culture demonstrate an increased motivation for their job*

They may do business with the firm's competitors as well, but the day the firm needs a shorter delivery time or some other extra favor, it has a higher chance of receiving it, in the cases where a strong culture and identity has created a close bond between the company and its clients and suppliers.

Nonfamily businesses often struggle to create and maintain a corporate culture. Contributory factors are more frequent changes of CEOs and board members, and the large number of shareholders who have no impact on the management of the business. Very few nonfamily businesses have been able to create a corporate culture in such an environment. Jack Welch at General Electric and Warren Buffett at Berkshire Hathaway are two exceptions. It is notable that they both stayed with their companies for very long periods of time.

In family businesses, the corporate culture is derived from the family's values. Family values tend to be long-lasting. When the families are clear about their core values, they are able to transmit them from one generation to the next, thus enabling the corporate culture to gain influence over time.

## Aligning business policies with the values of the family

Family values are not only the source of corporate culture; they also shape some of the most important policies of a family business. The CEO makes sure that these policies are applied. Examples of business policies that are directly influenced by family values include **employment and compensation policies** and the **debt/equity ratio** – many families have a strict principle not to borrow money. Such has been the case at Miele in Germany (see Chapter 11). Studies of long-lasting dynasties have shown that most have a no-debt principle.[3]

It is the responsibility of the CEO to clarify, bring to life, and communicate the corporate culture and business policies. Families often have strong core values, but they are not always able to describe them succinctly or point to their specific impact on the business. Clarity helps to build a stronger, more coherent structure from the shop floor all the way up to the owners. This can lead to noticeable gains in efficiency and effectiveness.

## Leaner organizational structures

**Clarity** and alignment between values, corporate culture, and business policies, **generates trust**. If done well, everyone has a clearer notion of how to operate and within which guidelines. Employees have a strong and deep identification with the business, and higher motivation and autonomy. Because the framework is clear, empowerment becomes more of a rule, and **fewer levels of hierarchy and control** are needed, which in turn leads to leaner organizations, reductions in costs, and increased profit margins.

Leaner organizational structures are one of the characteristics of highly performing family businesses. Reaching higher performance through an optimized organizational structure is one of the goals of the overall governance system, and of the CEO in particular.

*Reaching higher performance through an optimized organizational structure*

## A family CEO versus a nonfamily CEO: opting for competence

Families often deliberate over whether the next CEO should be a family member. The answer is complex, and strongly influenced by the vision the family has for the business and for the future generations of the family. Three elements need special attention when selecting a CEO: competence, values, and drive.

Equally important is the capacity of the future CEO – whether or not a family member – to understand the way in which the role of CEO in a family business differs from that in a nonfamily business. In a nonfamily business, the CEO function is often the strongest and most powerful function. In a family business, CEOs often need to tone down their egos, since the ultimate power in the firm resides with the family owners, who may or may not be involved in the business, may or may not be on the board, may or may not have significant knowledge of the business world, and may be very young. A CEO of a family business, with the exception of the founding generation, serves the business and the ownership vision and values. **The family and its legacy** are at all times "bigger" than the CEO.

> "If you are not the founder, you are not the original entrepreneur. Even though I'm the CEO, my father's imprint is indelibly on the business."
> Marcy Syms[4]

CEOs of family businesses can be viewed more as **stewards of the business** than change leaders. Change, though, remains important. To survive over a very long period of time, family businesses need to adapt, but change most often affects strategy and goals – not mission and the corporate culture. Making this distinction requires tremendous skills on the part of CEOs.

**A family CEO** is more likely to be in strong alignment with the family values and the corporate culture, even compared with a nonfamily CEO who has spent many years in the business. If the family CEO candidate also has the competence and skills needed, and the requisite drive, he/she is likely to be a very good choice.

A nonfamily CEO is likely to present a very different mix of attributes. Competence and drive would probably rank highest, in addition to readiness to bring about change, and a higher appetite for risk. He/she is probably highly motivated by the function. But the core values of the nonfamily CEO may not be aligned with the family values, in which case the CEO will have a tough time, and the corporate culture is at risk. A business can even be destroyed in this way.

This cultural fit or "nonfit" is not restricted to nonfamily executives; some family members may also have values or attitudes that are not aligned with those of the family. Such was the case with one fourth-generation family business who had a very promising 30-year-old family member in its executive committee. He had drive and obvious entrepreneurial skills. He made two highly risky acquisitions, one of which failed miserably. The other acquisition, though, was an excellent choice for the business and was a great success. In a family context, where the owners were highly risk-averse, this young family member quickly destroyed the faith the owners had in management. He was asked to leave the business. He started his own venture, and is now a happy and successful entrepreneur. Inside the family business, it took several years and many discussions to re-establish trust between the owners and management.

## The transition from a family to a nonfamily CEO

The debate over family versus nonfamily CEOs is tough, especially for families considering the question for the first time. Appointing the first nonfamily CEO is a move into the unknown and a big emotional step:

*Appointing the first nonfamily CEO is a move into the unknown and a big emotional step*

- What will he/she do with the business?
- Will I still know what is happening in the business?
- Will he/she know how to get a good deal?
- Will he/she take care of our employees?

The prospective of the first nonfamily CEO can be so daunting to some that they never move on from discussing it. Those who do go ahead, however, are often engaging in a massive act of faith: they take a deep breath and put their fears to one side until the new CEO proves that he/she is the person they needed.

## Some arguments in favor of nonfamily CEOs

An obvious reason for selecting a nonfamily CEO is that there is no successor within the family. There are, however, other reasons why families should consider switching to a nonfamily CEO.

Family reasons:

- *A lack of a competent successor* is one. Most family members love their business, but not all have the skills and the strengths needed to become CEO.
- *Lack of motivation* on the part of the family candidate. CEOs of family businesses tend to be in the position for a significant period of time – on average 15–20 years. During that time they will be questioned, challenged, criticized, and, sometimes, perhaps, praised. They need to stay strongly motivated. Demotivation at the highest levels trickles down through an organization. Similarly, attitudes of entitlement or arrogance can be corrosive. As William Dean Singleton said, "Show me a generation that's not interested in the business – and I'll show you a business that's going to be sold."
- *Family rivalry* is a third reason why families consider switching to a nonfamily CEO. Some families are so entrenched in their conflicts that no matter what the family CEO proposes it will be rejected by the board or the family owners. Or a conflict arises because some feel very strongly that the next CEO should be chosen from their branch. In such

situations, the family CEO is caught in a deadlock, and the business is unable to move ahead.

Positive reasons:

- The person appointed can add vibrant new energy to the business.
- The nonfamily CEO can bring in new or missing abilities. Family businesses attract numerous highly competent people who share the values and the vision of the family and are devoted to the business. Giving them the opportunity to make it up to the top of the organization may well help the business improve its performance.
- Switching to a nonfamily CEO creates **healthy competition and stimulation** for family candidates themselves. Human nature is such that, when people know far ahead that they will be the next leader, they may not give their all. If family candidates know that there will be real competition to become the next CEO, the board and the family can create a fertile environment for people to give their best and bring renewed energy and drive to the business.

Other considerations also have an impact on the choice of CEO:

- *Are you "family first" or "business first"?*[5] The former see the business as a means to keep the family together and provide employment for family members; such businesses are nearly always led by a family CEO. "Business first" families see the business as the center of their attention; whether there is a family CEO or nonfamily CEO is irrelevant.
- *Leadership skills for the twenty-first century.* During the twentieth century, firms focused heavily on technical skills – engineering, finance, marketing – when choosing the next CEOs, whereas today the most sought-after skills relate to people; **the capacity to connect to the outside world and motivate employees**.
- *Impact on the governance system.* The switch to a nonfamily CEO has a deep impact: employees are no longer reporting to a family member, which may be unsettling, so the switch ought to be accompanied by a review of the overall governance system, to ensure that family owners, the board, and managers are aligned on the company's vision, mission, values, and key objectives.

## The succession process

Choosing the right successor is so essential to the long-term success of a family business that all three layers of governance should be involved: family, board, and CEO. The owners let the board know if they wish the next CEO to be a family member; they also make sure that the family values are transmitted to the next generation. The board will review competence, screen CVs, interview the candidates, and at times act as mentors. The current CEO and the executive committee will groom the potential successors.

*all three layers of governance should be involved: family, board, and CEO*

## Grooming the next CEO

This is an important task of the CEO and the executive committee, not only because of its impact, but also because of the length of the process – another way in which family businesses differ from nonfamily businesses. In family businesses, it is frequent to see potential successors being groomed for a period of time, in excess of ten or even 15 years. In large nonfamily businesses talented managers are groomed for a long period of time, but not necessarily to become the next CEO; that choice often occurs only months before the current CEO departs. In family businesses, because the number of potential candidates is much lower, the process is more obvious to the entire organization and the heirs apparent are more visible earlier in the process.

> "To some people, ownership equals leadership. I'm not part of that group. Leadership is something you have to earn." Howdy Holmes[6]

Having **a clear established process** during that long grooming time helps. Here are a few points to consider:

- •There are a number of prerequisites for a family or nonfamily manager to be identified by the CEO and the board as potential candidates to be CEO. They must have been in the business for a number of years, demonstrated good management skills, have established good relationships with employees throughout the organization, and **have earned their respect.**

• To avoid lengthy processes and **false illusions,** identified candidates need to know what is expected of them and have **a clear competence development plan,** which highlights the different stages they need to go through to prove themselves. Three things in particular need to be articulated clearly in the plan: (1) the duration of each stage, (2) the conditions for moving to the next stage, and (3) who will assess performance. In family businesses, the CEO and the candidates often elaborate the plan together – this is true at least for potential family candidates.

• The duration of each stage may vary depending on the importance of the job and its **scope of responsibility.** A period of two to five years is generally long enough to gauge the candidate's competence for the challenges in that stage.

• Each stage needs to consist of a project involving **direct responsibility** of the candidates, and the scope of responsibility is increased from one stage to the next. The process may start with the leadership of a significant project – being in charge of an acquisition, for example. This may be followed by market responsibility with direct profit and loss (P&L) responsibility, followed by business unit responsibility, before moving to senior management and executive committee positions. (Figure 6.1).

• Not having a plan can have devastating consequences. Young family members are often at a loss when they enter their family business. There is no plan, no job description for them. Candidates are either positioned too high too quickly, or kept at middle management levels for too long. Both situations have negative impacts for the company and the individuals. Reaching too high too quickly puts successors in positions they cannot manage successfully, **losing them credibility and damaging their self-esteem.** When successors are kept at a low level in the company for too

*Not having a plan can have devastating consequences*

long, they become bored and frustrated. In either situation, individuals are likely to leave the family business.[7]

- Each stage of the competence development process needs to be planned with care. It must present a true challenge and set realistic objectives. Each stage must be aimed at helping the candidate earn respect and build credibility.
- The conditions for moving from one stage to the next should be known from the outset. **Clear qualitative and quantitative objectives** must be set and reached: relating to financial results, relationships with superiors, leadership skills, knowledge of products and competition, creativity and so on; intermediary objectives should also be set.
- The evaluation of how well and how quickly these objectives are achieved is the basis of the **evaluation process and** of the **performance assessment**.[8] A 360-degree evaluation can also be included once or twice in the process. In addition, all potential candidates to the CEO position need feedback, family candidates even more so as it is probably the only time they will get the chance of **objective and honest feedback**.
- Deciding on **who will perform the evaluation** and give feedback is crucial. It needs to be someone in a senior position, with relevant expertise, who can objectively assess candidates, is neutral to family conflicts and emotions, has the courage to say if a candidate has reached his/her maximum competence level, and is trusted and respected by the owners and the board. It is difficult to find all these qualities in one person, so appointing a small team is probably better. This could consist of, for example, a board member, the head of human resources, and an external adviser. The team should include at least one family representative if the candidate is nonfamily, but preferably no family members if the candidate is a family member.
- While honest feedback is usually given very effectively to nonfamily candidates, it is much rarer to see it given to family members. The reasons are multiple: respect for the family, presuming that the candidate

will always be fully committed and so does not need feedback; not wanting to hurt feelings; not wanting to make enemies of the wrong people. These are all the wrong reasons. Honest feedback, positive or negative, can only help candidates to improve their performance. Highlighting the areas where people need further development can only help them become better leaders.

*While honest feedback is usually given very effectively to nonfamily candidates, it is much rarer to see it given to family members*

• The higher the candidates rise in the hierarchy, the more the board, the CEO, and the executive committee need to pay attention: first, to the quality of their relationships with other family members and their ability to build consensus,[9] and, second, to the alignment of their values with the family values and corporate culture. Assessing these dimensions is just as important as assessing skills and competence.

At the end of the competence development process, when the choice of the next CEO has been finalized, the CEO, the business board, and the family owners announce who the next CEO of the business will be.

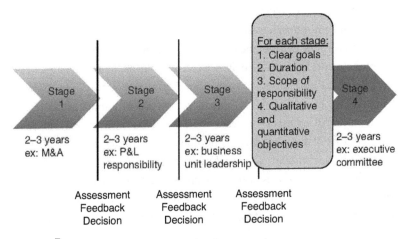

FIG 6.1  **Example of a competence development plan**

## Thinking outside the box: considering alternative leadership patterns

Some families feel strongly that the business should always be run by a family member, while others put the emphasis on competence. Either approach can be effective, provided that the business puts checks and balances in place to ensure good governance, and selects and develops their leaders thoroughly.

Interestingly, there are also ways to have the best of both worlds. Here are a few insights into the **leadership systems** of some highly performing families.

1. The first system consists of alternating family and nonfamily CEOs. As previously discussed, this provides a healthy challenge for family members and retains talent within the business.
2. The second system consists of a family CEO coupled with a nonfamily chairman and a strong nonfamily presence at the business board level. This system enforces natural discipline and drive into the CEO and all family members working in the business.
3. The third system consists of a nonfamily CEO and nonfamily management, coupled with a family chairman and a strong family presence at the board level or a stronger influence of the family council. This system offers a counterbalance to a trend observed in many families who switch to nonfamily CEOs and then become distanced from the business. They move out of management first, then a few years later have reduced their presence on the board, and ultimately end up losing interest in the business altogether. By reinforcing the family presence in the upper levels of governance simultaneously with the switch to a nonfamily CEO, these families strongly indicate to the owners, to the employees, and to all stakeholders that they remain deeply committed to the business.

The essence of good business governance in a family business context is to maximize its unique competitive advantages: a strong corporate culture, a leaner organization, and a clear alignment of business policies with the owners' values. When the CEO and the executive committee manage to reach a perfect alignment throughout the governance system – from the bottom of the firm to the owners – then the firm is clearly positioned for higher performance.

## BEST-PRACTICE RECOMMENDATIONS

**1** Managing a family business is fundamentally different to managing a nonfamily business, in terms of culture, business policies, and organizational structure.

**2** One of the key competitive advantages of family businesses is their corporate culture.

**3** A family's unique values and guiding philosophies are at the core of the business's corporate culture.

**4** **Different business sizes,** life-cycles, industry circumstances, and generations call for different leadership styles.

**5** Succession planning takes a long time and is complex.

**6** Clear competence development plans, performance appraisals, and honest feedback help CEO candidates build credibility throughout the organization.

**7** While it is often difficult for families to move from a family to a nonfamily CEO, the switch can prove beneficial.

**8** Technical skills are not enough: the personality of the CEO, and his/her capacity to motivate both employees and shareholders, are key to ensuring the long-term viability of the business.

**9** There are many leadership patterns and systems available: thinking out of the box may help families to implement one that best fits their purposes.

## chapter 7

# The Benefits of Control Instruments and Control Systems

**"We celebrate instances where people have demonstrated integrity or passion or respect."**

Interview with A. Vellayan, executive chairman, Murugappa Group, Chennai, India

A. Vellayan, executive chairman of the corporate board of the Murugappa Group, explains here how control, compliance, and risk management shape the governance system at the heart of the Group.

A. Vellayan is a member of the fourth generation descending from the company's founder, A.M. Murugappa Chettiar. He is also the chairman of EID Parry (India) Ltd and Coromandel International Ltd, and on the board of Kanoria Chemicals Ltd. He holds a diploma in Industrial Administration from Aston University in the UK and a Master's degree in Business Studies from the Warwick Business School in the UK.

The Murugappa Group, headquartered in Chennai, is one of India's leading business conglomerates. It is market leader in diverse areas over 28 businesses from engineering and finance to sugar and bio-products, and has a workforce of over 32,000 employees. Today the Murugappa Group is firmly rooted in its homeland; it has sound traditional values and high ethical standards. The Group's business philosophy is summarized in a quote from the ancient Indian treatise on wealth creation and governance, the *Arthashastra*: "The fundamental principle of economic activity is that no man you transact with will lose, then you shall not."

*Denise Rouvinez-Kenyon*: **Your corporate governance policy includes "good audit process and reporting." Could you explain how auditing is organized?**

A. *Vellayan*: We have a group corporate board, and we have individual boards for each of the listed underlying businesses. Each of these boards has an internal audit committee chaired by an independent nonfamily director. The chairman of each of these internal audit committees has fairly independent freedom over the managing director, or the chairman of the specific board, to question operations, policies, and functions. In addition, all the Ombudsman's complaints come to the chairman of the internal audit committee.

In each of the listed businesses, the internal audit team comprises six employees plus six or seven people to whom we outsource. There is always a total of 12–14 people in the team. The internal auditors report directly to the managing director, and then to the chairman of the audit committee to ensure independence. They meet quarterly. Internal audit is supported by internal technical audit (production efficiencies, plant maintenance, health, safety) and also financial audit (external audit). Technical audit is important as it reports potential problems, and helps us address them while we still can.

The external audit is run by large established firms (Deloitte, KPMG, etc.) but is organized in such a way that we rotate the firm in charge every five years, to lessen the risk of familiarity. And if we can't rotate them, we at least rotate the partner in charge. Also, we have no auditors on our business boards.

**How do you ensure integrity and transparency in reporting?**
We have what we call the "five lights" program. It is based on our principles, which are: (1) integrity, (2) passion, (3) quality, (4) respect, and (5) responsibility.

Although these are just words, what happens is that I go out across the group and across companies, hearing and collecting examples of what has happened over the year. We celebrate instances where people have demonstrated integrity or passion or respect. But we also point out areas where people haven't conformed to the company's values.

We have open communication with employees and all businesses. This is very important because you cannot control physically what happens. You can only control and anticipate the way people think, the way they comply to the rules, values, and principles.

These five lights stem from our family values. We have modified them to suit business purposes and they are now applied throughout the business. We are expecting people to comply with these principles and to have respect for people we are dealing with. We are also requiring people to come to work, not just from 9.00 to 5.00, but to have a passion and take responsibility for what they have taken on.

And we expect the same from our family members. Family values shape our governance system and risk management, in particular operational risk. Take prudence, for example: we are moderate in our lifestyle, we don't overspend on ourselves, we don't buy very expensive cars, as we don't want to draw attention to ourselves. In a country like India, the family would be quickly viewed as exploiters rather than partners. Similarly, in the business we don't own a private aircraft, and instead we reinvest more in the business, which enables us to ensure stability. Our debt/equity ratio is pretty conservative and we can create value in the stock exchange by distributing 25% of profit after tax in dividends. The large reinvestment portion helps us create employment and keep capital costs low.

*Family values shape our governance system and risk management, in particular operational risk*

**Families may have a position of prestige in a region, and as a result reports may be biased as employees may want to please the family. How do you deal with that?**

On the corporate board, family members are in a minority. We have two family members, three independent external directors, and three nonfamily executives. They have the responsibilities as lead directors for the businesses. The three external directors sit in on my appraisal and the appraisal of my cousin who is the other family member on the board. [So] if they don't like what I am doing or what my cousin is doing, or if we are not performing or pulling our weight, these people have decision-making powers on our remuneration. That counters the weight of the family. As a family we want value creation and meritocracy over ownership and control.

*As a family we want value creation and meritocracy over ownership and control.*

### Where is the framework of risk management set?

This is a new area for us. We started a formal risk assessment process three years ago, based on recommendations from independent directors of the corporate board. We also felt it was becoming a pressing need as we were growing fast. We use external firms to help us evaluate strategic risk and financial risk. The other risks – operational, geographic, and internal – are handled directly by management.

We have four directors in each risk management committee. Every business board has one because each business is different. They each comprise four directors – largely nonfamily. They are market- and product-oriented, they look at our relative competitiveness, our relative risk profile, year-on-year, and how it is moving and where it should be two years from now.

At the group level we only do portfolio assessment of risk profile as an overarching objective for the group – are we too involved in agriculture, or in financial services, or too light in certain geographies?

**You have a fair number of family owners. Do they have a voice in how risk objectives are set, or do they delegate that to the board?**

The elders of the family have an interface with the external directors of the corporate board twice a year. At that time they are free to question, express advice on risk, growth or performance. [This] gives them comfort that there is an external group overseeing the family members at the top of the organization. All our independent directors have wide experience and credibility; our corporate board is not like a company board who spends a few hours on the board and goes. They spend 12 days a year, and it is quite intense because we have a corporate planning group and support staff. We meet every two months, so when they get feedback from the elders, they are able to integrate that in their review process.

We have three elders at the moment. They have all been involved in the business and have retired. They have the knowledge, they are also investors, and they have the freedom to interact with the independent directors of the corporate board.

**Do the elders in turn inform other family shareholders?**
Yes, the elders meet with the family council regularly. They communicate with the rest of the family.

**A number of families complain that setting control systems in place is too costly and end up not implementing them, or only partly. What would you say to them?**
We decided long ago that we needed value creation. When you say that you don't want control, what you are really saying is, "Leave me alone, I can operate on my whims and fancies, my gut feel." But you need to decide for the organization; the system has to run on its own, whether you are there or not. We feel that control systems are a safeguard from ourselves.

**Does human resources (HR) play a role in your risk management?**
HR plays a big role in hiring the people: they do the first screening and check for integrity. Then they help us identify key executives, most of whom are grown from the inside. Identifying the right people certainly lowers our risk profile.

People stay with our group because we treat them well and we empower them, and in turn they help us build stability.

## Control instruments and systems

Family enterprises have the ambition to thrive over many generations. To do this, they need strong values and high levels of trust. Values and trust are not enough, however, in a context where a single employee making the wrong decisions can threaten the viability of the company, especially as family businesses cannot easily rely on fresh capital. A formal system of control mechanisms is one of the best protections for shareholders' interests, and can assist the board and the management of the company. When set appropriately, **control mechanisms** protect the business assets by optimizing the balance between operational and strategic risks and opportunities. They can also help build trust among active and non-active family owners; if non-active owners are confident that effective controls are in place, there is less mistrust.

This chapter is an introduction to control systems for a family enterprise, and provides an overview for families operating medium-sized businesses if they wish to extend control beyond an external audit. Listed firms, and those in heavily regulated sectors such as financial services, will probably already have sophisticated control systems in place. Even those firms with compliance controls in place, however, may not be dealing with other issues, such as protection of shareholders.

## Control

Control is an essential part of well-functioning businesses, even if at times it can be perceived by some as intrusive. One of the classic frustrations of families who make the transition from a private ownership model to a publicly listed model can be the amount of resources involved in establishing control and **reporting systems**. Yet, once they are all in place, families are often pleased with the results, as the systems bring added protection to the members of the board, to the family members employed in the business, to shareholders, and to employees.

Control in any business is organized into three main dimensions:

1. Control performed by outside, independent people or organizations:
   - External audit.
2. Control performed within the company:
   - Internal audit.
   - Risk management.
   - Compliance management.
3. Reports:
   - Reports are distributed to shareholders, and highlight the way in which a company has been managed over the course of a specific period of time.
   - Intermediary reports can also be oral, and can for instance take the form of a brief presentation at a family meeting.

Controls do have their limits. No control system can be guaranteed to catch all risks, and determined fraudsters will often be well aware of control systems and find ways of avoiding them for long enough to cause some damage to the business. Controls are not a substitute for management or leadership; they are akin to the brake pedal in a car.

## External audit

The external audit is an **assessment** – made by an external accountant having attained an officially recognized level of qualification – that the accounting records are accurate, complete, and conform to the accounting standards of a specific country, for instance GAAP (generally accepted accounting principles) in the USA or IFRS/IAS (international financial reporting standards/international accounting standards) in Europe. It provides some assurance that the financial statements made by the company duly represent the economic reality. For diversified groups the assessment is made at the level of the individual companies, as well as at the group level (consolidated accounts).

Not all businesses are legally required to undergo an external audit – in many countries, small companies are exempted from a compulsory full audit. It is, however, often considered good practice for firms to undergo an external audit, especially if they have more than one owner. It tends to make for greater discipline and transparency, and reinforce trust among shareholders.

The two main areas that external audit covers are as follows:

1. **Statutory audit**

   A statutory audit checks that the company has respected all appropriate tax, legal, and accounting requirements. It ensures, within certain limitations, that the information included in the financial statements is correct. For instance, it will make sure that the debts reported have been assessed correctly, that accrued income has a realistic prospect of being received or that the buildings on the balance sheet have been evaluated at the proper value. However, a standard audit will not necessarily catch a well-hidden fraud or other operational issues and risks which are not in the mindset of either the auditors or those who drafted the laws or audit standards.

2. **Validation of reporting**

   External auditors can, within the limits of the **audit mandate** and the information made available to them, check that the reports issued by the company are complete and that they represent a fair assessment of the company in that all important elements, whether good or bad news, have been brought to the attention of the shareholders.

Many external auditing firms have moved into consulting services. It is a logical evolution given that, because of their yearly involvement with businesses and how deeply they get to know them, external auditors are well positioned to highlight areas that require attention. Examples include how a company can take

*external auditors are well positioned to highlight areas that require attention*

better advantage of tax laws, or how could it be organized in more efficient and less costly structures.

To provide transparency and mitigate any risk of conflict of interest collusion, external auditors usually report directly to the chairman, indirectly to the audit committee, and through the chairman to the owners of the company. The "audit report" is usually addressed directly to the shareholders. However, as a matter of necessity their usual operational contact is often the finance vice-president (VP) or director.

Auditors need to be careful of conflicts of interest. Examples might include the development of too close a relationship with the finance VP or director (or indeed the chairman), or the keenness of the audit firm to win or retain other work from the company, such as tax or management consultancy. Some audit firms ask clients to agree not to make offers of employment to the audit firm's employees, to avoid the risk that an employee might feel more likely to be made an attractive offer if he/she "cooperates" with management. Laws and **professional standards** in many countries limit the extent to which audit firms can provide other consultancy services to audit clients.

## Internal audit

Many businesses also have a system of internal audit, checking that activities are carried out in accordance with internal rules and policies, and that risk and other critical factors are being properly managed. Internal audit is usually organized as a task force team reporting to the board of directors, most often through the audit committee, and sometimes to both the board and the CEO.

According to the Institute of Internal Auditors (IAA), a body widely recognized in this sphere of activity, the purpose, authority, and responsibility of the function should be formally defined in a charter. This should include the following points and should be approved by the board:[1]

- definition of purpose
- definition of activity
- authority
- responsibility
- position in the organization
- relationship to the board
- authorization of access to records
- definition of the scope of internal audit activities
- ethics
- standards.

While internal audit is a standard function for listed family businesses, it is far less so for privately owned family enterprises. When faced with the request – by the board of directors, external auditors, or shareholders – families often find it an intrusion or unnecessary bureaucracy, and struggle to understand the benefits. However, the act of writing the charter often itself clarifies the value it can bring by showing family members how it can protect their interests and help avoid tensions arising between active and non-active family shareholders, with their very different levels of access to information.

Internal auditors must have the ability to be independent and objective. They cannot be bound to a specific family member or manager, or be asked to favor any individual person, group family branch, or business unit. This is an example of where the human resources department can play a strategic role, by hiring internal auditors not only for their skills but also for their integrity. Once established, their position and reporting lines in the organization are crucial for maintaining independence.

*Internal auditors must have the ability to be independent and objective*

In addition to the traditional role of internal audit, it is interesting to see in which direction the field is evolving. A recent survey by Forbes Insights[2] indicated that internal audit could go beyond simply control and risk management to play an active role in protecting and enabling business performance. Because of its unique position in the business, internal audit could play an active role in:

- identifying potential cost efficiencies
- offering strategic insights to improve business performance, and
- helping to identify risks that really matter.

This, however, can only be made possible when the internal audit team is not only asked to control and monitor risks, but is also aligned to the company's key strategic objectives.

## Risk management

### What is risk?

Everyone knows what an **opportunity** is. Businesses exist to exploit opportunities, such as a gap in the market for a given product. In order to do so the business needs to take **risks**. Risk is the flip side of opportunity. For example, to manufacture the product, the business must invest in a factory and thus spend money. The product may not sell well, or it may not be possible to sell enough of the product to cover the investments necessary. That is a risk. Another example could be that the products do not comply with a given set of applicable regulations.

Risk is a factor of two elements: probability and impact. In general terms, the greater the likely impact of a risk event occurring, the lower will be the acceptable probability of it occurring. Some risks are wholly or partly within the direct control of the business, such as the risk of fraud; others are less so or not at all, such as war breaking out or a key employee being killed in an accident.

*Risk is a factor of two elements: probability and impact*

A business can take steps to reduce the probability, or the impact (or both), by only committing a certain level of resources to a project at any time, and identifying milestones for the allocation of further resources. Every event, location, product, or individual may represent a risk or an opportunity – and usually both. Risk management consists of a number of processes to optimize the delicate balance between risk and opportunity. While some people view risk exclusively as negative, others define risk and opportunity as simply the positive or negative effect of uncertainty.[3]

Risk management involves a number of set tasks in a specific process that includes the identification of risks (or opportunities); **quantitative and qualitative analysis** of those risks; their assessment, management, and treatment, as well as careful follow-up of the process and its effectiveness (Figure 7.1).

Throughout these stages, it is important to remember that the overriding purpose of risk management is to optimize the performance of the business, by doing the following:

• Identify and quantify major risks, and manage them. For example, one family business sold its highly profitable explosives division because, while it only sold explosives to companies that built roads, dams, and

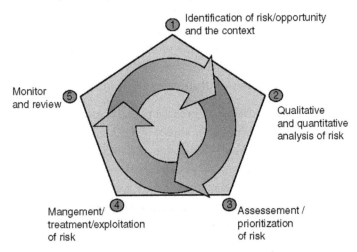

FIG 7.1 / **The risk/opportunity management process. Reproduced with the express authorization of Harvard-Smithsonian Center for Astrophysics**

other infrastructure projects, they could not guarantee that they would not be sold on, and end up being used in wars or other ways that would hurt people. While this was not a direct risk, it could be seen as an indirect reputational risk to the company and the family.

*Identify and quantify major risks, and manage them*

- Reroute, or reposition, when necessary by changing the course of an action. For example, when selling products in regions controlled by rebels or other unofficial armed groups, to do so under the supervision of the army.
- Add steps, checkpoints, and milestones in the process to be more cautious, and make sure the process exhibits agreed levels of safety before engaging further.
- Insure: insurance cover can be arranged to cover the financial consequences of many risks such as natural disasters, theft, or other special circumstances, but it is important to note that special insurance may be very costly, and that money cannot always completely compensate for the occurrence of a risk event.

*Hedge: when faced with currency risks*

- Hedge: when faced with currency risks, hedging will limit the downside (the impact) by also limiting the upside (the opportunity).

Businesses are faced with a number of different risks that can be usefully divided into four main categories: strategic, financial, operational, and geographic:

- *Strategic*: **exposure** to loss resulting from a strategy that turns out to be defective or inappropriate, or which simply fails.[4] An example could be choosing between rival technologies, not knowing if one will be the all-out winner and the other one a waste of investment as the market abandons it. For a family business-specific example, the decision to rely on family and retained profits for additional capital carries advantages in keeping the company in family hands, but may carry the risk that those financial resources are insufficient and the business fails due to lack of investment.

- *Financial*: this category relates to the risks that shareholders take by investing in a business, and also the risk a company may be faced with when deciding to allocate its capital between competing projects. Another dimension can be exchange-rate risk: for example, where a business has costs predominantly in, say, the US dollar; and its income predominantly in the euro. A significant strengthening of the dollar against the euro will reduce the dollar value of sales unless the euro price can be increased to compensate; this can even force companies to close their operations.

- *Operational*: operational risks can result from a wide variety of factors. Breakdown of manufacturing equipment; human error causing accidents or defective products or services; failure to comply with laws and regulations; industrial disputes; loss of a key employee; loss of a major customer or supplier; natural disasters such as floods and earthquakes; allowing the company's technology to become outdated; and so on. Operational risk factors are multiplied by lack of motivation, lack of skills, and poor planning. Ineffective or inexistent succession planning also falls into this category, and may put the business at considerable risk.

- *Geographic* (or political): risks linked to operating in a specific country or region, for example, because the country may be experiencing social or economic difficulties, or due to a lack of understanding of the local political and legal systems or the local culture. Local technical standards may differ from those the business is used to.

The particularity of family businesses is that they have – at least when privately owned – a great liberty to define the level of risks they are willing to take. However, this means that family shareholders need to be clear as to the level of financial, operational, and strategic risks they consider appropriate, so that management can operate within those limits, and the board can ensure that the strategies in place respect the owners' risk tolerance profile.

| Risk management model | | Probaility | | |
|---|---|---|---|---|
| | | Low | Medium | High |
| **Impact** | **Severe/Critical** | Substantial management required | Must monitor and manage risks | Extensive management crucial |
| | **Moderate** | May accept risks but monitor them | Management effort useful | Management effort required |
| | **Limited/Minor** | Accept risks | Accept risks but monitor them | Monitor and manage risks |

FIG 7.2  The risk management model

Risk management can also define risks in relation to their possible occurrence over different timelines: current risk (now), emerging risks (one to two years), and future risks (beyond three years). Such a classification helps to prioritize the resource allocation needed to address them.

Another way to assess management priorities is to classify risks according to both probability and impact, as shown in Figure 7.2. Such a classification can make risk management more systematic and can help management focus time and resources on the most urgent and most important risks.

## Compliance

In general, compliance means **operating in accordance with a rule**, usually imposed by a public authority, but it can also be a standard agreed by a family or an industry association and which is in principle voluntary, but which cannot in reality be ignored. An example may be a voluntary code not to have goods made in factories using child or slave labor. **Regulatory compliance** is often one of the critical factors defining whether a company can enter into and remain active in a given business; if a business does not comply with important regulations it may be shut down or subjected to heavy fines or other penalties.

Besides identifying the regulatory framework applying to a business, there are two fundamental aspects to compliance: operational and control. For operational compliance, the whole organization needs to adopt and "own" the need to work in a given way in order to ensure compliance. This makes compliance cheaper and easier to achieve, and can often result in the business becoming operationally stronger. The consequences of noncompliance for the business and for employees need to be clear.

Control systems are essential for coping with the increasing number and complexity of regulations. An organization cannot rely only on cultural efforts and operational integration of regulatory requirements alone; the board, which is ultimately responsible, needs to ensure that there are control systems in place to check at regular intervals that the business is not being put at risk through noncompliance. Organizations are increasingly adopting the use of consolidated and harmonized sets of compliance controls. This is often the role of the internal audit function.

## Reports

Publicly listed companies publish written annual reports, which give an overview of what the company has achieved over the year. Such reports usually include a message from the chairman, an overview of the key events of the financial year, financial reports, investors' information, people and remuneration report, and special employee events such as anniversaries of employment or special achievements. They usually also include an overview of strategy for the year to come, and information on the progress of key projects.

Similarly, a number of non-listed family companies decide to publish annual reports. They do so to share information with major stakeholders, in order to show their willingness to be transparent and increase their credibility. These companies often increase their perceived value of robustness and trustworthiness.

Diligent family businesses are particular in the way that they regularly share information with their shareholders and also more widely to family members even if they are not shareholders – such as spouses or young family members. Once or twice a year, when the family is gathered, the family CEO or the family chairman gives a brief presentation of the family business, explains its performance, and highlights the major events that have taken place during the period. This is a wonderful way to keep family members motivated. It usually reinforces shareholders' cohesion and the pride that family members have in their business.

*This is a wonderful way to keep family members motivated*

As well as formal reports to shareholders and other stakeholders, the internal reports required can be greatly influential on the effectiveness of control systems. Being clear as to what information is needed internally is key.

## Limits of control mechanisms: potential dangers in the family business context

It is important to emphasize that every system, no matter how solid, is likely to have points of weakness. The mere presence of systems of external and internal audits does not guarantee effective control.

*every system, no matter how solid, is likely to have points of weakness*

Here are some potential flaws:

- The CEO may be perceived as a person of absolute power who can dictate who will work or not for him. As a result, internal and external audit reports may be biased or incomplete as employees and external auditors may fear they could lose their job or their mandate if they were to unveil the whole truth. Such a position of power or influence may not necessarily be intentional; in practice, it is often a result of the economic impact of the family business in its region, or of the historical role the family has played in the region, or simply of the charisma of the CEO. It is important, though, that families are aware of it and set in place measures to balance that impact.

- Hiding of key facts or, in extreme situations, the keeping of two sets of books. If an individual or a group of individuals (for example, the executive committee, or the management of a division) wishes to hide or "massage" information, this can be difficult to detect. Two main defenses exist against this risk: first, the human resources systems which ensure that people with the right values and moral compass are hired in the first place and, of course, effective control and audit systems. No system can guarantee that it will catch the most determined fraudster, but maintaining world-class control systems, including a robust internal audit system, is the best defense. Reasons for hiding or misrepresenting information can be many and varied. A divisional manager may wish to hide losses or operational failures; he/she may even think it is in the company's best interests to present false figures to "save" tax or to ensure the bank does not stop the overdraft facility. If the problem is the active shareholders who wish to keep more profits for themselves and to deprive non-active shareholders, the best defense is a robust contingent of nonexecutive directors with an active audit committee, which directly oversees an independent and empowered internal audit function.

The best way to guarantee that a proper control system is in place is by submitting the company and everyone in management to proper controls (including an internal audit function), by working with highly skilled and ethical external auditors. Thus, the choice of people who operate both in external and internal control is of utmost importance and deserves the full attention of the board and of the family shareholders.

Underlying this is, of course, the need for clear "rules of the game." Whether called company policies, regulations, or guidelines, the issues that are important to the integrity of the company should be clearly expressed. They must be simple and workable, not create disproportionate bureaucracy, and must be readily understandable and usable by those who are expected to work by and comply with them. In time these rules will work their way into the company culture – if they have been sufficiently well thought through, expressed, and understood.

**B E S T - P R A C T I C E**
**R E C O M M E N D A T I O N S**

**1** Put in place clear, practical, comprehensible, and realistic rules of the game. Few things reduce morale more effectively than moral uncertainty in the workplace.

**2** Strong, clear, and transparent control systems are key to ensuring the business is run in a healthy manner and thus to protecting shareholders and maintaining the peace among family shareholders.

**3** It is important to make sure that sufficient thought is invested into the implementation and regular improvement of control mechanisms, including internal audit.

**4** External audit is often a legal requirement and is a very good discipline even when not compulsory. Families can maximize the efficiency and outcome of external audits by working with trusted firms and by making sure external auditors are granted access to all information they need.

**5** Ensure that links between auditors and business and its managers do not become too close. Occasional rotation of audit firms should be considered.

**6** Owners need to define the level of operational, financial, and strategic risks they are willing to take in order for management and the board to be able to operate within a clear framework.

**7** The board and management need to define and set in place appropriate risk management systems.

**8** Operational risk is one area where a family business is particularly vulnerable. Having the right leadership in place, having the right skills in family employees, and planning for succession are some of the most effective ways by which a family can minimize operational risk.

**9** Regular written and oral reports on business performance are a wonderful way to build family cohesion and pride, and demonstrate effectiveness to other stakeholders.

**10** Each and every system has its flaws; family shareholders need to be aware of this to ensure adequate supervision is in place.

# Structures for the Family: Family Governance

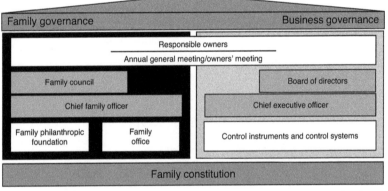

This figure highlights the family governance in Part III and acts as a navigational tool for the reader.

## chapter 8

# Family Councils and Chief Family Officers

"We use the family council as a safe harbor, a relaxed space where we update each other about our lives and aspirations."

Interview with Maria Luisa Ferré Rangel, chairperson, Grupo Ferré Rangel, Puerto Rico

The Grupo Ferré Rangel is a diversified group of enterprises in the media, real estate, and healthcare industries based in Puerto Rico in the Caribbean. The fourth generation of the Ferré family currently owns and operates its various media outlets. *El Nuevo Día* and *Primera Hora*, its banner dailies, together represent about 80% of the newspaper and advertising market in Puerto Rico. A variety of other media-related companies, along with a real-estate investment company operating both in Puerto Rico and the USA and a healthcare company operating in Chile, are also actively managed by Ferré family members.

The Ferré family name has a high recognition factor in Puerto Rico, and *El Nuevo Día's* daily circulation places it among the top ten dailies in Latin America and the top 45 dailies in the USA.

María Luisa Ferré Rangel, its fourth-generation chairperson and CEO, agreed to talk with us about her 20-year history with the family's family council. The council was founded by her parents when she was a young reporter at *El Nuevo Día*, where she was later editor. Her brother, Antonio Luis Ferré Rangel, serves as *chief family officer* (or president of the family council) and in that capacity helps María Luisa to ensure balance in the strategic deliberations and continuity efforts of this family-in-business.

*Ernesto Poza*: **María Luisa, please tell me about your family council meetings and their history.**
*María Luisa Ferré Rangel*: It all started in 1993, as my parents began to be concerned about a succession to the fourth generation, five siblings all working in the Grupo. [Note that while the Grupo Ferré is a fourth-generation enterprise, between the second and the third generation, a major restructuring of companies and assets led to the separation of branches of the family enterprise; the Grupo Ferré Rangel then is a fourth-generation family firm with a first-to-second generation composition. The fourth generation operates as a *sibling partnership*.]

My family began to meet monthly to discuss family and business issues.

Family council meetings were given top priority in the busy schedules of the owner-managers, all seven of us. The half-day meetings included discussions regarding the operating businesses, investments, sibling disagreements or conflicts between family and nonfamily managers, and the multiyear succession process itself. My father had estimated it would take ten years to complete all the work, so he created a deadline for the succession of December 31, 2004. All our initiatives seemed somehow guided by this goal or time-frame.

Family council meetings in the early days combined business subjects and the business of the family – or both. So in these meetings we developed our family constitution, with guidelines for the employment of family, a listing of family values, a declaration of the family's expectations of management and management's reasonable expectations of family owners, and a listing of our proposed governance bodies such as the family council and the board of directors.

Over time we realized that we were mixing the business with the family too much in these meetings, so we separated our meetings into an executive committee meeting to address business matters and a truer family council, to address family matters, and certainly a variety of investment and family wealth subjects that did not really belong on the agenda of the executive committee meeting.

## What is the family council's composition? And how does it interact with the board?

The family council is composed of the five siblings and the two parents. When the family council meets as the executive committee, it still deliberates and makes decisions related to the operating companies, the family office, group versus individual financial plans and investments, our ownership structure, and *by-laws*; all in preparation for a meeting with the larger board of directors, which includes key nonfamily management and independent directors. Hence, the executive committee of the family council acts as the board of directors for family wealth. In this function, it helps the family develop a single family voice or family consensus prior to the regular board deliberations; which

may very well challenge the family's position on the issue. We have had a few fundamental questions about our continued role in some of the companies, and after agreeing to remain [involved] in that particular enterprise, have been challenged by the board and reconsidered our strategy. But certainly, the family council operating as the executive committee helps us develop the family business/ family wealth strategy that we take to the board for review and approval.

*the family council operating as the executive committee helps us develop the family business/family wealth strategy*

## What has the family council helped you address and/or find solutions to?

When meeting on the business of the family, it has helped us educate the family about *estate-planning issues*, and make decisions regarding our investment strategies, the diversification of our family's wealth in geographic and industrial sector terms, and the management of risk in our overall portfolio of assets.

It has also significantly helped us develop family unity among very busy adults. We use the family council as a *safe harbor*, a relaxed space where we update each other about our lives and aspirations, our challenges and dilemmas, our spouses and kids, and their lives too. The fascinating thing about the family council is that it is such a disciplined approach to making space for just-family conversations that, whatever happens, whatever is bothering us, on or off the job, or is newsworthy in our individual or nuclear family lives, we know we will all be meeting again soon and will have an opportunity to discuss it with our loved ones. We know we will all be there for each other. We always close family council meetings with a luncheon, and the spouses are invited to attend. Now they don't all attend every month. But during the luncheon we do a brief state-of-the-business and state-of-the-family presentation so that family members not involved in the family business from day to day also update their information on the extended family and the Grupo.

**How has it helped you build bridges to the fourth-generation spouses and the fifth-generation children?**

It has helped us to make spouses part of the conversation, which is essential; particularly when it comes to the formation and education of the next generation. The spouses know what sacrifices are absolutely necessary to make and why; they are engaged in the legacy and are active team members in building future opportunities for that fifth generation.

And whether this has happened as a result of the family council meetings or is just another expression of family unity, the cousins in the fifth generation all like traveling together, and socializing together with their friends, all of which provides us with a much greater sense of security; they care for their cousins and very much watch out for each other.

**Are there any recommendations you would like to make to other families meeting in family councils or considering starting one?**

Select a president or chief family officer of the family council. He/she will stay on top of scheduling the meetings, getting the agendas together, and ensuring follow-up with other family members or the family office.

Meet regularly, even if you think there may not be enough to talk about in the next meeting. Being able to reliably count on the meeting happening makes a world of difference.

Be clear on the purpose of the meeting. Is it to talk about the family and the family's business, or is it to talk business? If it is a purely business subject, put it *Be clear on the purpose of the meeting* on the agenda for the top management, executive committee or board meeting instead. Prepare an agenda and take minutes so there is continuity between meetings. While the chief family officer remains the same, we take turns in serving as scribes of the minutes.

If you have a family office, make sure that you provide direction to the family office staff based on your discussions in the family council meetings. And assign them tasks that help provide follow-up to family council deliberations, plans, and decisions.

It is fascinating: key nonfamily managers follow these meetings with keen interest. They know that we are meeting. They have learned to appreciate the value to them of the meetings. The family council increases the confidence that key nonfamily managers have in the owning family and in its ability to address and resolve whatever comes its way. In that sense, it is a great investment in creating confidence, a sense of stability, and even retaining top nonfamily talent in the family companies for the long run.

## The family council's contribution to family governance

Talk to any estate-planning attorney about trusts and estates, and she/he will tell you that restrictive trusts and complicated estate plans – ostensibly crafted to maintain business continuity and family unity – often fail to prevent next-generation members from doing with the company whatever they wish. While trusts and estate plans often do generate tax savings, and preserve the asset-based legacy for a time, family estrangement and asset sales often result unless a way is found to rediscover the intangible, value-based legacy of earlier generations.

Rediscovering the values and the legacy takes time and plenty of conversations. It takes candid discussions regarding the strategies and growth opportunities sought by the different generations. It means making history come alive again, sometimes through family history projects and centennial celebration books and events. In the case of a family-owned bank in the USA, the inaugural family meeting started with one of the daughters of the founder reading a letter, which she attributed to her deceased father-founder, the contents of which had come to her in a dream on the night before the meeting. The letter urged the two generations participating in the meeting to honor the founding vision. Her reading of the founder's letter kicked off the meeting with a sense of purpose and a deep sense of family identity.

This family's first family council meeting was launched with a tremendous sense of history and a personal challenge to the next generation to do the right thing as the family and the business moved forward. The letter called for preserving the spirit of service to each individual client, one client at a time. The dream, and the letter, became the guiding light for the strategy and succession planning discussions that followed.

The existence of ongoing family meetings or a family council reduces the likelihood that family concerns will be ignored or inappropriately exported to a board of directors or the top management team of a family enterprise. Attendance at these meetings represents a deposit in the family's emotional bank account – an investment in increasing trust and respect for all those working on behalf of continued family wealth and opportunity – while reducing the family's likelihood of becoming a **zero-sum entity**. (A zero-sum entity is one where there are winners and losers.) Zero-sum or **win-lose dynamics** are much more likely between different branches of the family, between direct descendants and in-laws, when there is little information, divergent individual goals, and little sense of opportunity due to limited growth of the business as the family grows in numbers.

*The existence of ongoing family meetings or a family council reduces the likelihood that family concerns will be ignored or*

Figure 8.1 illustrates the boundaries that should exist between family councils and boards of directors. Although family councils and boards have different missions, they are also well served by some degree of integration. Having two members of the family council serve as at-large representatives of the family on the board, for example, will help to ensure

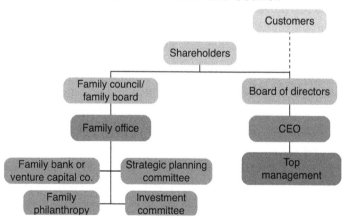

**Contributions of Board and Council**

FIG 8.1 **The different contributions made by a board of directors and a family council**

*Source*: Adapted from E. Poza & M. Daugherty, *Family Business*, 4th edn., 2014.

that family strategy and family preferences are known and considered by the board. Nonfamily, independent directors can also be added to the family council in order to enable it to go into **family board or executive committee** sessions as a separate part of its family council meeting. When in session as a family board or executive committee, this family body takes up ownership, business, investment, and wealth issues across all of its enterprises, including operating companies and family office investments and activities. (The alternative, as described by Julio Cazorla of the Grupo Landon in Chapter 3, is to create an ownership council, in parallel to the family council, to address these issues.)

## The family council as a strategic body

The family council is a governance body that focuses on family and ownership matters. It is to the family what the board of directors is to the business. The family council represents an institutionalized way to hold family meetings periodically. This formal approach ensures that meetings are held, even when they appear not to be needed. Family councils promote communication, provide a safe harbor for the resolution of family conflicts, and support the education of next-generation family members in responsible ownership, family dynamics, financial, and philanthropic issues.

Family councils frequently develop **family-participation policies** and deal with family member concerns regarding liquidity, diversification of the estate, and estate planning. The business/ownership education of family members not active in the management of the business is also an important agenda item. The interview with Bruce Halle, chairman of Discount Tire (Chapter 2) shows how he implemented a family council soon after the estate-planning work was done, precisely to educate and build family bonds that would result in next-generation members becoming responsible owners. He wanted that next generation to share in the responsibility of providing continuity to the founding dream of Discount Tire. He knew he could not rely on the language of the trusts to influence the behavior of next-generation members to this end. The family council became the chief venue for writing family policies into the family constitution, and for deliberations on succession, family member service on the board of directors, and the design of a family office specifically tailored to their needs.

The family council is **responsible** for ensuring that the **noneconomic goals** and **values** of the family are **articulated**, sometimes via a family constitution or charter. It is an advocate for the noneconomic goals; giving them the attention they deserve in the context of the owning family's strategy. A family council may be the vehicle for carrying out the family's philanthropic initiatives. Or it may oversee the creation of a family office to oversee trusts and other financial matters of the owning family. It gives family members, whether or not they are active in the management of the business, a voice in the business. It relieves the pressure to appoint all family members to the board.

A cautionary comment is in order here. Family councils, in the absence of boards with independent outsiders, have been known to present their own set of problems. Over time, some owning families have experienced a propensity for family members who are not active in the business to second-guess company management. In the absence of a board with truly independent outsiders, family members who do not fully understand the difference between owning and running a family company may meddle inappropriately in the management of the business.

CEO leadership in setting the boundary of what remains within the purview of management after adding a family council is essential in keeping responsibility and authority where it belongs. Gerry Conway, founder, retired chairman, and CEO of Fasteners for Retail, for example, considers the ground rule he set in his family's first family council meeting to have made all the difference. As he told us: "At the first meeting, there was a critical point where I had to remind my family that while this was a family business, I had to make the final operating decisions." While the comment may have reflected some natural anxiety at opening up for discussion decisions that had previously been made entirely by him in his role of founding entrepreneur, it also served notice that the management of the company was not the purview of the newly formed family council.

## Ownership and family policy-making[1]

First and foremost, family meetings should be about education and communication. Over time, if the education and communication tasks have been properly carried out, family meetings will become effective planning, policy-making, and decision-making bodies.

Open and safe processes for sharing information among family members in family meetings are prerequisites for effective planning, policy-making, and decision-making. Because many family-controlled companies decide to have family meetings to dismantle the culture of secrecy established by the previous generation, a slow, developmental process is best. Decisions regarding management and even some ownership issues are not the function of a family meeting or family council. Most decisions regarding ownership and management of the firm will be made in other forums: the board, the top management team, the ownership council, and the annual shareholder meeting. The **focus of the family council meeting agendas** should be on improving communication, educating particularly those who are not well-versed in the language of business, promoting open deliberations, policy-making, and, much less frequently, decision-making.

Family councils can also assist in developing a succession process. The succession plan developed by the two Peterson brothers, sibling partners of Mobility Systems, a plastic implements firm in the USA, was released just prior to the first of a series of twice-yearly family council meetings. The two brothers used this first meeting as their platform to communicate to shareholders the plans they shared for the future of the family company. Estate plans also represent a very appropriate type of plan for discussion by an owning family in their family council meeting.[2]

Several types of policies related to ownership and the family's relationship to the firm stand out in their usefulness to families in business. These include the following.

1. **A family strategy statement** in which the family's goals – required input for effective board leadership – are presented. The family strategy could include:

   - **Expectations for returns on equity** or invested capital by shareholders.

   - A **liquidity policy** that includes principles supporting the desired relationship between the controlling family and the company. This policy recognizes that individuals or family branches may have cash-flow needs or may prefer to allocate their capital to alternative uses. This policy usually differentiates between small transactions and the sale of large blocks of stock within the family or back to the company, and references the legal documents in effect (such as buy–sell agreements).

   - A **dividend policy** (not to specify the amount of dividends to be paid, which is a company decision, but rather to discuss family needs); to balance those needs against reinvestment in the business; and to inform the board and management of the general sentiments of family members.

2. An **employment policy** that outlines the prerequisites for employment in the business. Education, experience, and the expectations that the company has of family members seeking full-time employment in the firm are spelled out. Employment opportunity should be based on merit.

3. A **board-service policy** that includes criteria for the selection of family members to serve as at-large representatives of the owning family on the board. The system should provide a link between family strategy and company strategy without giving undue influence to family members.

4. A **family constitution**. This document usually includes a family mission statement, a list of values that are important to the family enterprise

and that the earlier generation wishes to pass on to the next, a collection of the policies listed above, a list of governance bodies and their function, and a statement of family history, family commitment, and the desired relationship between the company and the owning family going forward.

## Family dynamics

Family life and the analysis of family behavior is not the central focus of this book. But family dynamics and a family's emotional intelligence are important subjects for students of family business governance. Multigenerational family-controlled businesses, even those with some exposure to public markets, are largely illiquid enterprises. This lack of liquidity and need for selfless interest can be a burden for family members operating in a society that tends to focus on the short term, the last quarter, the fast trade. They will bear this responsibility willingly only if there are enough opportunities to acquire information, to be educated, to experience extended family identity and to engage with important family values of stewardship. Inclusion, affection, and mutual influence across generations and between active and inactive shareholders are a must.

Secrecy, lack of information, low levels of family emotional intelligence, and little knowledge of the business all threaten commitment by the family to the continuity of a family-controlled corporation. These deficits may be the result of a founding culture that supported autocratic leadership and control, or a reincarnation of this culture in a later generation. Or they may arise from the family's belief in the many espoused benefits of privacy: flexibility and stealth in relation to competitors, minimization of tax liabilities, and management of expectations of relatives, nonfamily employees, and even unionized workers.

After years of the current generation not communicating and hiding financial statements, profit margins, cash flows, and market share information, the **ability of younger family managers** to assist in the management of the enterprise and become capable successors is eroded. Similarly, family members who are not active in the business – but constitute its single most important resource, patient family capital along with a long-term orientation – can unintentionally be sidelined. Their positive engagement in continuity efforts can then become a significant challenge.

Family members who do not participate in the management of the business often have significant influence on the deliberations, decisions, and long-term processes of the family-owned or family-controlled corporation.[3] And when these members' perspectives and contributions are not considered, not deemed legitimate, or are undervalued, they may experience a sense of inequity.[4] This sense of injustice can lead to family conflict.

## Conflict resolution and the family council

Conflict is inevitable in families, and more so in families that live, work, and control assets together. Nevertheless, the very success of a multigenerational family-owned company is evidence of historic good management of the family's relationship with the business, even if problems or crises later ensue.

One of the benefits of family council meetings is the forum they provide to discuss issues as they arise, thus minimizing the potential for conflict. Some of the problems that can be addressed in family council meetings include the following:

1. **Frustration over lack of inclusion.** This is a common source of conflict as a result of the emotional distance between family members who are active in management and those who are not; and between members of the powerful current generation and those of the significantly less powerful next generation. Living in different countries or cities, gender

differences, differences in level of wealth, and lack of frequent and consistent communication only heighten this conflict and often lead to mistrust and a propensity for zero-sum dynamics.

2. **Anger over the unfairness of hiring practices, promotions, family benefits, and other opportunities enjoyed by some, but not all, members of the family.** In many families, "fair" means "equal." But in multigenerational families where being fair means being equal, family leaders – and, often, the company – become paralyzed, unable to make a decision and move on.

3. **Frustration over distribution/dividend policies and lack of shareholder liquidity.** By the time a family-owned company has reached its third or fourth generation of family owners, the financial needs of the various branches and individuals have become very different. A third-generation owner-manager receiving a fair market salary as a manager or corporate officer faces a very different reality from that of a divorced cousin pursuing a doctoral degree in history and raising three children.

All of these problems can be addressed in family council meetings and resolved to the best of the family's ability. Active listening is at the heart of much family council meeting activity. It leads to two-way communication that addresses the sources of feelings and allows plans to be drafted or changed. Because some of these feelings are based on perceptions, the education mission of family meetings can go a long way in creating common ground and ameliorating conflicts rooted in misinformation or misunderstandings.

Conflict is not the enemy. And family council meetings are not about always having consensus, or speaking with one voice. But conflict is very often the wake-up call to family leaders, a board of directors, or an extended family about *Conflict is not the enemy.* the need to revisit the strategy of the firm and promote renewed growth, or to urgently address the absence of succession plans, or to invest more in the education and unity of the family through family council meetings.

## The chief family officer

The **chief family officer** performs the function of **chairperson of the family council** and provides the glue that keeps family members united through the challenges that they encounter. As well as his/her formal role as chairperson of the family council, he/she may often act as mediator, facilitator, and communication conduit for the families. Individuals performing this role are sometimes referred to as **trust catalysts**.[5]

Chief family officers (like Antonio Luis Ferré Rangel in the Grupo Ferré Rangel interview earlier in this chapter) also take responsibility for family initiatives, such as writing the family's history, hosting weekly or monthly family gatherings, or being the contact person for facilitators of twice-yearly family retreats. Sometimes the polar opposites of the CEO – who, understandably, has a business-first perspective – they try to balance family and business by advocating a family-first agenda.

Chief family officers play a fundamental role in the search for continuity, and often have a unique appreciation of family dynamics and the interpersonal and developmental challenges at play in the business-owning family. Their capacity to understand and articulate various family members' points of view enables them to broaden the dialogue from an exclusive focus on facts to a wider view, encompassing both facts and feelings, so that better decisions can be made.

## Boundaries between the board and the family council

Family-owned businesses tend to have boards that are made up entirely of family members. Family-controlled but publicly traded businesses sometimes hold on to this tradition, although they may allow an attorney and a couple of outsiders to serve alongside family members. For the most part, these boards remain slow to welcome independent directors. As a result, **keeping a healthy balance between family and business** remains a challenge for most family companies. An exception to the rule is evident at Cargill, the largest private corporation in the world, which is 85% owned by the Cargill-MacMillan family. The family holds only six of the board's 17 seats and gets an A–rating for board independence.[6]

As they become multigenerational enterprises, family companies with a tradition of family membership on the board face another challenge: **family members often expect to automatically become board members** because of their family and ownership status. Although it is true that families are well served by at-large representation by family members, overwhelming the board with family influences is seldom in either the best short- or long-term interests of the company, the shareholders, or even the family. A line has to be drawn between family membership and board duty. Family councils derive some of their ability to contribute to family-controlled companies precisely because they help families draw this line and establish a system of governance that both differentiates and integrates family and business agendas. When it is perceived as an entitlement, family membership on the board, unrestrained by the input of family councils or independent directors, often leads to a board that is incapable of successfully handling the immensity and intensity of family dynamics. As illustrated by the situation at the *Louisville Courier-Journal,* sold by the Bingham family to Gannett Publishing in 1986, when family members know very little about the business's strategy and finances, their service on the board does little to further the effective functioning of the board as a body of ultimate oversight and accountability.

Even in family businesses that do have independent board members, there are challenges involved in **keeping family issues out of the boardroom.** The transition from an all-family board to a truly functioning professional board with a mix of family and independent directors is often difficult. Unless the board size is expanded significantly, family members may have to step aside to make room for independent members. Many family members don't accept this new order, or simply believe that they are entitled to attend board meetings. The best way to navigate this challenge is through a family council, which defines the relationship between the family and the board.

Figure 8.2 illustrates the **boundaries** that should exist **between family councils and boards of directors or advisory boards**. Although family councils and boards have different missions, they are also well served by some degree of integration. For example, having two members of the family council serve as at-large representatives of the family on the board will help to ensure that family strategy and family preferences are appropriately considered by the board. Should a holding company structure be in place to consolidate the various businesses, a holding company board is often used. In that case, the holding company board sits, structurally, between the shareholders and the family council (see Figure 8.2). In other family enterprises, the family council meets separately in executive sessions, with independent directors in attendance. When in executive session, the family council functions as the family board.

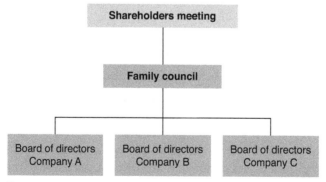

**In later generations...**

FIG 8.2 / In later generations a family council's role is that of a "supra board" or family board in a holding company structure

*Source:* Adapted from E. Poza & M. Daugherty, *Family Business*, 4th edn., 2014.

*Structures for the Family: Family Governance*

**1** Recognize that family unity is not just good for the family, but a unique resource for a business that thrives on a pool of patient family capital.

**2** Family councils represent proven best practice in addressing the challenges posed by family dynamics to a family enterprise, especially during the very vulnerable succession period.

**3** Start a family council. But proceed carefully – perhaps only involving direct descendants, not their spouses, to begin with. Then slowly incorporate larger segments of the extended family into parts of the family council meeting, for example in the parts of the agenda where education is provided, information is shared, or a family-bonding experience is created.

**4** Do not start a family council when the family is in serious conflict or family members have cut themselves off from the family. Paradoxically, family councils are best launched when they are least needed; when everybody is getting along and trust is high. But they represent a great investment in family unity and patient family capital over the long term.

**5** Select a chief family officer and have him/her assume primary responsibility for chairing the family council and maintaining a regular schedule of meetings.

**6** Use your family council as a launching pad for a variety of new initiatives or change efforts needed on the family or ownership front. Family councils (as seen in the interview in Chapter 2 with Bruce Halle, chairman of Discount Tire, and this chapter's interview with Maria Luisa Ferré Rangel, chairman of Grupo Ferré Rangel) can be to an owning family what a board of directors is to an enterprise.

# 9

# Family Philanthropy and the Family Philanthropic Foundation

**"The values passed on by my family and how they conducted their business pushed me to listen to and respond to the inner calling of helping others."**

Interview with Rina Lopez Bautista, the Knowledge Channel, the Philippines

In this interview, Rina Lopez Bautista tells us about the Knowledge Channel, a philanthropic foundation at the heart of her family's many philanthropic endeavors. Rina is passionate about her work and believes that education helps build strong people who can become agents of economic development and peace.

Rina Lopez Bautista is the founder, president, and executive director of the Knowledge Channel Foundation. She believes that the Knowledge Channel is more than a medium for academic instruction and learning, and that it truly empowers people, and helps build peace

and social justice in the world. A member of the third generation of the Lopez family, Rina is married and has two children.

The Knowledge Channel Foundation Inc. (KCFI) is a not-for-profit organization (http://kchonline.ph) that operates the Knowledge Channel (K Channel) and Kchonline, the first and only TV and online media tandem primarily focused on the Philippines' basic education curriculum. Following the Department of Education curriculum as a guide, KCFI brings online learning from kindergarten to Year 12 (K-12) and alternative learning subjects and concepts to life on TV, the internet, and video on demand in the classrooms, learning centers, and homes. It employs some 50 people and has trained about 30,000 teachers over the years.

*Denise Kenyon-Rouvinez:* **Can you tell us about the background and mission of the Knowledge Channel?**
*Rina Lopez Bautista:* The Knowledge Channel Foundation Inc. was founded in 1999. It envisions a world that is just and peaceful, where all live in dignity. It exists to empower children and other learners, especially the underserved and marginalized, through educational media and advocacy, that they be the best they can be, create the best communities, and help build a better world.

**Can you tell us what the program has delivered, and how it has evolved?**
Part of our family business is SkyCable, a cable TV network, and ABS-CBN, a broadcast network. We believed that these networks had the resources that could be used to set up an educational TV channel for use in public schools within SkyCable's franchise areas.

We later moved [to extend] our cable TV network to one that could be used by all public schools around the Philippines, either through partnering with other cable TV operators around the country or installing satellite dishes in the schools. K Channel programs, games, and activities are also available online (at kchonline.ph) and on demand.

KCFI has also expanded its reach to the out-of-school youth and adult learners though our Out of School and Mature Learners Alternative Learning Institute (OMLALI). This is a program that addresses the educational needs of a big sector of our population, the youth and adults, aged from 15 to over 80, who have not finished high school, that is, people in the streets, people in jails, people in the mountains, people in the islands. We produce content based on the DepEd Alternative Learning System (ALS) curriculum and distribute it to the teachers who reach and teach them, thus giving them an opportunity to learn better and, hopefully, graduate from high school.

Additionally, we have taken on the challenge of our Department of Social Welfare and Development (DSWD) to support the 50,000 daycare centers around the country. These centers are attached to local government and provide the service for children ages three to four years old. We continue to produce video learning materials to be used in these daycare centers, so that the kids get excited and interested and learn from them.

**Can you describe the geographic realities of the Philippines?**
Being an archipelago of more than 7,000 islands, transportation and

the communication infrastructure is a challenge. And so bringing ourselves, the TV sets, and satellite dishes to the schools, especially in the more remote islands and mountains, is difficult and sometimes dangerous. Rarely, but at times, we need the support of the army or the local government to ensure our safety. In spite of the difficulties, we continue to do what we do because these are the more resource-poor areas. An intervention such as this is embraced very warmly.

**You could have joined one of the businesses in your family's large, diversified group. Why did you choose to start up a charity? And why this one?**
I was actually already working in SkyCable. But it was a persistent inner calling that led me to set up Sky Foundation. Initially the CSR [corporate social responsibility] of the SkyCable company, we later changed the name to KCFI so that other people could help support it. I believe that the values passed on by my family and how they conducted their business pushed me to listen to and to respond to the inner calling. My family was

always big on education, so this was a natural initiative.

**How is KCFI linked to the family business and to the other philanthropic activities of your family? How is your family connected to KCFI?**

KCFI is a member of the Lopez Group Foundation (LGFI), which was established to coordinate all the different philanthropic and nonprofit work connected to the family businesses. Some of the businesses support KCFI in different ways. My dad chairs the foundation and my cousin, who runs ABS-CBN, is the vice-chairman.

**Few family foundations receive funds from outside the family. What made you decide to open up your foundation, and how has this helped you?**

In the first few years of the foundation we made a decision to go beyond bringing the K Channel to just the public schools within our cable TV networks' franchise area. This necessitated partnering with donors and other cable TV companies to reach more schools. These partnerships have enriched the work that we do and have allowed us to provide more learning materials and reach more learners and teachers.

**What has been KCFI's social impact during its 13 years of activity?**

With its relevant, dynamic, and engaging content, K Channel has become the foremost source of educational video materials in the Philippines. K Channel television alone is viewed by more than three million school children in more than 2,500 public schools in 62 provinces in the Philippines. It has an expanded household viewership all over the country. However, out of almost 42,000 public schools throughout the country, only 4.7% so far have access to K Channel. Still a long way to go. Schools that have used K Channel programs regularly have reported increased scores in national achievement tests, lower dropout rates, and increased participation rates.

**Is there anything you would like to add?**

KCFI is now also involved in educational leadership and management, as a result of my father, Oscar M. Lopez's desire to help the Department of Education and its current Secretary. This is in the form of a 15-month doctorate degree program on educational leadership for Schools Division Superintendents (SDS) of the Department of Education (DepEd). K Channel's role is to represent the Lopez Group Foundation and ourselves, as we host the superintendents one week a month at the Eugenio Lopez Center (ELC) in Antipolo. Because of the many shifts in education, globally with twenty-first-century education, and locally as we move from a ten year basic education cycle to a 13-year cycle (K-12), this is a timely program. We are now six months into training the first batch of 50 superintendents. Facilitators and participants alike say that the program is groundbreaking and transformative.

KCFI is also a partner in the Excellence in Educational Transformation Awards (EETA), which awards prizes to schools that have demonstrated excellence in various categories, such as curriculum design, administrative processes, learning spaces, etc. In its second year, I can say that the awards served not just to give recognition to these schools, but as inspiration to many other schools to strive for excellence.

The last thing I want to add is about the field of philanthropy, the field of giving. Each person has his/her own set of unique talents and gifts, which can be shared with others. Families and businesses are the same. They too have their unique talents and gifts, which can be shared with others. Given the multitude of pressing social issues and the fact that resources are finite and limited, it is important to find the best use of those talents. An industry leader in business develops leadership capital and thus the capacity to do and be much more than its smaller counterparts. Its philanthropic interventions, as they are more strategic, can and will have just as big an impact on society as in business. I believe that education and building the capacity of human capital is the most strategic intervention to bring about social justice.

*Each person has his/her own set of unique talents and gifts, which can be shared with others. Families and businesses are the same. They too have their unique talents and gifts which can be shared with others*

## The benefits of family philanthropy

Many families from around the world are generous givers. They are often deeply involved in their local communities as well as the world around them, leading to natural concern for others and a desire to make a difference. Business families often have a vested interest in bettering their environment; by improving social, environmental, cultural, medical, or other factors affecting the local community, they improve things for their own descendants. The Mercier family illustrates this perfectly. The Merciers were a family of French Protestants who fled persecution in their home country in 1740 and found refuge in Lausanne and Sierre, Switzerland. They established a prosperous tannery business and built hotels; and with the wealth generated they were able to donate to schools, hospitals, and churches, support the arts and the start-up of other businesses. Through their actions they created employment and helped an entire community reach higher levels of development.

The community development model used by the Merciers is a traditional model of family philanthropy. It is still very popular worldwide. The possibilities for philanthropy have multiplied, however, making the choices more complex, and families often struggle to know where to start when they want to begin giving. In this chapter we seek to describe some fundamental principles and practices to help families begin that journey:

1. Giving: an act of generosity that needs a vision, a strategy, and businesslike execution.
2. The structure and organization needed for effective giving.
3. The people involved in giving.

## Giving

In the USA alone, family foundations gave a total of $20.6 billion[1] in 2010. The USA has been at the forefront of shaping family philanthropy, but there, and even more so elsewhere, many families still struggle to identify a key cause with which to launch their philanthropy, and then to understand how to make the best impact with what they give. It sometimes helps to return to basics and ask questions such as, how often, or how much, should we give? How can we give? Or even, *why* should we give as a family? This can help families clarify their philanthropic mission.

## Why give?

The reasons why families give are often rooted in their fundamental values, or may stem from an unexpected event that has directly affected them or their community, altering the way they see the world around them, such as an illness, an accident, a natural disaster, or a war.

The main reasons why families give are as follows:

1. **To give something back to society**. Families feel blessed by the success the family business has achieved and the wealth it has created, and they want to share it.
2. **The feel-good factor**. Helping others can be a pleasure in itself. The experience of giving can also make us better people.
3. **Social values**. There is so much suffering in the world that many people feel a responsibility to step in and help within his/her means.
4. **Religious beliefs**. Most religions and spiritual philosophies have clear precepts on giving. Providing food to Buddhist monks or building a temple are natural acts of redemption in many places in Asia. The *zakat* (charitable giving) is one of the five pillars of Islam; giving assistance to the poor and the needy and other worthy causes is a duty in Judaism; and Christian teachings contain many references to the need to give and help others.
5. **Involving the next generation**. A philanthropic initiative is an excellent opportunity to involve children, even from a young age. It can be a powerful way to transmit values. Feeling part of something bigger than their usual daily experience can also be very instructive for the young.
6. **A way to reconcile family members**. Working on a common cause to help others can help distract family members from family disputes

and tensions, and may well help them find joy in a shared – and neutral – project.

Any of these reasons, or indeed a combination of them, may provide the basis for a family decision to embark on a philanthropic initiative (Figure 9.1).

## How to approach giving

Reasons for giving can be multiple and profound. The exhilaration generated by commercial success does not last forever, and the desire to make a difference to the world soon manifests itself.[2] Giving has the power to make social changes happen when root causes are addressed strategically. John D. Rockefeller, for instance, the US oil magnate, created the General Education Board, which revolutionized – in a lasting way – higher and public education in the USA.

*Giving has the power to make social changes happen when root causes are addressed strategically*

Givers who transform society usually don't start by asking, "Why should I give?" or "What motivates me?," but rather, **"What is needed?," "What**

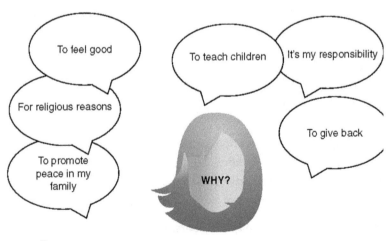

FIG 9.1 / **Why give?**

**is the issue?,"** and **"What can we do to bring about radical change?"** Making a real difference does not necessarily require a lot of money: it mainly requires an awareness that things can be done differently, as well as focusing on a need, and identifying the solutions most likely to have significant impact.

## The transformative impact of giving

While the straightforward action of giving to an established cause can have a rapid effect – such as **giving grants** to a school to hire better or more teachers – this may only result in superficial, localized, or temporary improvements and thus is not always the way to address root causes or bring about a deep societal change.

*address root causes or bring about a deep societal change*

For example, a study in the UK revealed that children of low-income single mothers performed poorly in class and were more likely to drop out of school too early or with insufficient skills or qualifications to enable them to move out of poverty and economic vulnerability. Further studies found that children raised by lone mothers were likely to have less economic security, less parental attention and guidance, and more likely to live in deprived areas.[3] The combination of these two studies indicates that while it is always good to give to schools to support children of single mothers, the way to achieve radical change is by addressing the mothers' needs. Helping single mothers to increase their skills to gain access to a better job will provide better housing and food, more security and warmth, and a healthier environment for their children. In turn, this helps those children perform better at school.

Similarly, a family who gave money and time to build a school in Africa were distraught to see that only few children attended classes. After an investigation in neighboring villages, they soon identified an additional need: they established a grant to provide lunches and uniforms. Once parents knew that the children would have food, clothes, and shoes, they immediately sent all the children to school. Today the school has progressed a step further as it has its own little farm and garden and produces enough food to provide lunches while teaching agronomy to the children, as they are in charge of tending the garden and the animals.

## A holistic approach

Some interventions help in many complementary ways, leading to a transformative impact on communities. The mission of Hand in Hand International,[4] for example, is to reduce poverty through job creation. It provides micro-credits to female entrepreneurs. In its "upstream" initiative, before the micro-credit stage, it provides training and education so that women first acquire a skill and then set up a business. Downstream, it provides the infrastructure so that the goods produced in a village can find their way to a market. In parallel it also offers gender-awareness courses to men so that they understand why micro-credits are given to women, and will support it.

An alternative holistic approach is demonstrated by Cordaid[5] in its work creating partnerships between the public and private sector. It is involved in numerous actions in 36 different countries, and wherever it operates it makes sure that the projects it launches are supported by local communities and local governments to ensure that they feel responsible for the projects, protect them, and are committed to making them work.

## Measuring the impact of giving

Measurements are useful. They can provide invaluable information, help **monitor projects**, ensure they are on track, or **warn when an adjustment is needed**. Just as businesses need to measure their key performance indicators (KPIs), measuring the impact and the efficiency of a philanthropic initiative is important, to ensure that everyone remains focused on the main objectives.

A first step in the measurement of charitable activity is to ensure that the money donated supports the causes and the people as intended. It is important to ensure that it is not used for something else: money given to develop a specific region must not be used to arm rebels, for example, nor diverted by "administration offices," which could indicate corruption.

There are many ways to measure impact. They range from **simple measurements** to **very complex mechanisms**. Measuring **quantitative achievements** is relatively easy, in particular after a few years of activity: the example of KCFI offered in the interview at the beginning of this chapter is a good illustration: the foundation trained 30,000 teachers. Measuring **qualitative achievements** is more difficult and may need access to broader data: KCFI was able to measure the quality of its education programs and their impact on students by accessing data that indicated their students regularly scored more highly in exams.

Measurement always has a cost and it is important to remain realistic about what can be achieved without becoming obsessed with measuring it. The 2013 Code of Good Impact Practice[6] developed in the UK offers some simple and insightful reflections on ways of measuring impact. It recommends applying time, effort, and methods that are proportionate and appropriate to the scale and scope of the work. It also advises that, if complexity or resources are a concern, the answer is to keep things simple. Following these recommendations should help focus precious time and resources where they are most needed – and may prevent projects from being abandoned too soon because feedback or measurements are not available.

## Being involved

Above all, as described by Charles and Elizabeth Handy,[7] for many people, giving is not only a matter of how much money, and to whom it is gifted. It is also about personal commitment and active involvement, working with those in need, and making sure that initiatives are sustainable.

For many families, giving is as much about spending time as spending money; dedicating personal effort and motivation, and bringing their wealth of management experience to the causes they support. There are opportunities for personal involvement, whether the family has its own foundation or gives to a public charity.

*For many families, giving is as much about spending time as spending money*

## The structure and organization needed for effective giving

There are many ways to give, and not all of them require setting up a specific structure. For example, families can:

- Give a set amount of money to an organization such as MSF[8] (Médecins sans Frontières/Doctors without Borders) for instance; or the Red Cross,[9] or a local orphanage.
- Decide to give a significant or regular amount to a philanthropic fund that invests in different causes in different countries, such funds set up by financial institutions or other initiatives such as the King Baudouin Foundation.[10]
- Join other philanthropists. Warren Buffett decided to join forces with the Bill & Melinda Gates Foundation to improve the impact and sustainability of his own giving. Reasons for joining others could be that the money available is not sufficient on its own to have a transformational impact, or that others have a depth of experience the family does not possess. In joining others it is important to make sure there is a shared vision and common values.

Any of the above actions can be organized within the family, or through the family council, or even through the family office (Figure 9.2).

### Family philanthropy or corporate social responsibility

Often, philanthropic initiatives occur both within the family – by itself or through its foundation – and within the business, the latter being carried out under the banner of **corporate social responsibility** (CSR). Just as the borderline between family and business is not always clear, the line between the different philanthropic activities of the business and the family can often

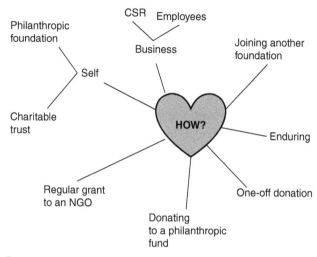

FIG 9.2 / **How best to give?**

also become blurred. While a clear separation is recommended, the most important point is to ensure that the actions are aligned, and that what is done at the business level cannot prejudice the family, and vice versa.

## Family foundations

Some families prefer to set up their own family foundation or their own family trust (also known as a **charitable trust** or **charitable foundation**; for simplicity we refer here to a "family foundation" to cover these types of entity). In doing so they probably gain more significance in their giving and more control of it, but to do this also requires a proper structure with its own management, governance, and control, just like any business, as described in the different chapters of this book. We will therefore not describe these structures in great depth in this chapter, but would like to highlight a few specific points that are particular to the governance and the management of family philanthropic foundations.

## The foundation board

The foundation needs a board that includes **independent directors**, who are aligned with its vision and capable of ensuring it has appropriate structures and management to achieve its vision – much as described for a business in Chapter 5. The board of a foundation has some particular tasks, such as:

- Providing values and **guiding principles** (particularly for family directors).
- Making sure that the causes supported and the results are aligned with those values and principles.
- Establishing a **time horizon**: the foundation can have a defined life, as long as capital is available; or the lifetime of the founder, or have an indefinite lifetime. Its strategy and operations will differ significantly, depending on duration.
- Periodically revisiting the question of whether the foundation is closed (funded by the family only), or open (also funded by **third parties**).
- Expecting similar professionalism from the family foundation as compared with the family business in terms of organization, plans, leadership, management, and control.
- Creating a reserve fund to help the foundation continue its activities through tough economic times when fundraising is difficult. Foundations should ideally have a reserve fund that enables them to run for two or three lean years without being forced to change course.
- Preparing a **contingency plan** of action for times of crisis.
- Controlling and **protecting the image of the family** and of the foundation.

## Management of a charitable foundation

*Foundations should ideally have a reserve fund*

Resources will always be scarce; the larger the foundation's resources, the broader its horizons and the greater its ambitions. It is therefore essential to organize and optimize management in a way that maximizes the efficacy and efficiency of the foundation. It helps to:

- Develop a strategic plan, including an estimation of the intended impact of each project, to enable measurement at a later stage.
- Propose a clear investment model.
- Have a system for identifying and **hiring talent**.

- Remunerate talent well, as this will add value to the work of the foundation.
- Evaluate projects strictly.
- Evaluate **tax efficiency**.
- Screen nongovernmental organizations (NGOs) and other institutions, and seek the assistance of organizations who can help do this when necessary.
- Have **clear processes** for selecting and following up projects.
- Measure impact and reorient a project where necessary.
- Organize **communication** in a way that is congruent with the values and guiding principles of the family and the philanthropic initiative.

## The people involved in giving

Families form wonderful and complex systems, which make working together at times challenging and at other times thrilling and highly motivating. Giving as a family is in no way different, except that negative and positive emotions may be exacerbated because of the importance of the task, because of the way people commit themselves to the causes, and because of the high emotional importance of their achievements.

Giving as an individual is challenging enough, but giving as a family brings added layers of difficulty and needs to be planned carefully. Family giving requires consideration of the **hopes and dreams** of all the people involved. For successful family giving, it is therefore important to acknowledge the aspirations and challenges of the different members of the family as well as their very special contribution to the **vision and mission** of the family's philanthropic initiatives.

*giving as a family brings added layers of difficulty and needs to be planned carefully*

## The family

The family sets the vision and mission for its giving and the values that support it. No matter what the mission is – protecting the environment, teaching every child to read, eradicating malaria, protecting the African elephant, finding a cure for autism, or providing access to fresh water to every village in Ethiopia – the more all family members are united behind it, the more it will be a binding force for family cohesion. This is not easy. As the family grows in number, branches, and generations, differences are likely to appear and at times they can be devastating. Some families even prefer not to have a common giving project because they cannot identify a single cause they all want to support.

*the more all family members are united behind it, the more it will be a binding force for family cohesion*

The vision set by the founding generation of the family business often helps to unify a family behind a foundation and its purpose. An example is the Murugappa family in India where the founder, four generations ago, indicated that the family was to work in two fields: education and health. These fields are broad enough to enable work on many different causes and in multiple ways.

## The individual

While a family has a mission for its giving, any individual in the family may have a different one. There are many ways to organize giving so that the family and individuals complement one another. This can be set within the foundation itself where different projects are supported by different groups or individual members: one family in Singapore has a foundation that supports wildlife in Southeast Asia and a general hospital. One of the daughters runs the wildlife efforts while the son devotes time and energy to the hospital, a cause close to his heart. Sometimes family members start their own individual foundations in addition to the family foundation. The structure chosen in each case is less relevant than the **degree of liberty** given to each individual to be involved.

## Women

Women often play a particularly important role in philanthropy. They often lead the family foundation. In some countries, such as India, men tend to have responsibility for the family business, while women are in charge of philanthropy, often leading significant institutions.

Women are involved at all levels of philanthropic activities:

- Providing time and money.
- Providing leadership – such as Rina Lopez (interviewed at the beginning of this chapter).
- Providing technical skills: for instance, a doctor offering his/her time to work in the family hospital in a developing country.
- Receiving money: as recipients of grants and micro-credit.
- Helping social entrepreneurs.

## The next generation

Philanthropy is a very good way of engaging the next generation early. There is no prescribed starting age, as it depends on each child, but from the age of six or seven most children are happy to join in and work on causes they can connect with: saving giant pandas in China, joining an association that protects animals, giving toys to orphans or baby clothes to single mums, and donating some of their savings to help sick children are just a few examples. And the best feature of this involvement is that when decisions are made on projects, when the time comes to chip in and **volunteer time**, there is **no hierarchy**, it is not about "adults and children," just about one big family ready to work together for a bigger cause. This is an effective way to transmit positive values to a new generation.

*Philanthropy is a very good way of engaging the next generation early*

In addition, the experience gained while managing philanthropic projects or by being involved as a trustee or foundation board member can provide useful experience for future careers in any segment of the family business or any outside career. Outside the family, some associations, such as Ashoka,[11] Wise,[12] and many others offer volunteer programs, an enriching experience from which many young adults benefit and are unlikely to forget. Early involvement in philanthropy can help to build strong and caring future leaders.

## BEST-PRACTICE RECOMMENDATIONS

1. Families are **generous givers**, yet family giving is not a simple affair. Going back to basics and asking the basic (but challenging) questions can help start meaningful discussions:

   a. Why should we give as a family?

   b. What is needed? And how can we best contribute to it?

   c. How? Is the best way to give money to an organization, join forces with other philanthropists, give through the business, or to form a family foundation?

   d. What are the important considerations for reaching a transformative impact? Is a holistic or a focused approach the best way to reach it?

2. If a family foundation or a charitable trust is the chosen vehicle, pay attention to the **special functions** of the board and of management in the philanthropic context.

3. Expect the same **professionalism** from the foundation as you expect from the family business.

4. Take care of the people involved in family giving, make sure it suits the whole family as much as the individuals, the senior generation as much as the next generation.

5. When working on giving, the stakes are high; make sure people's **emotions** are properly considered, and remember that philanthropy can be a wonderful way to bring peace within the family, if handled properly.

6. It is also an excellent way to transmit values to the next generation and to give them early **leadership responsibility**.

# 10

# The Family Office, Wealth, and Wealth Management

**"We care about professional excellence, continuity and succession."**

Interview with Dirk Jungé, Pitcairn (USA) and Alex Scott, SandAire (UK)

In this interview, Dirk Jungé (pictured left) and Alex Scott (pictured right) discuss the evolution of their respective family-owned multifamily offices.

Dirk Jungé is a member of the fourth generation of the Pitcairn family, former chief executive officer (CEO), and now chairman of Pitcairn (www. pitcairn.com). Pitcairn is an award-winning multifamily

office, dedicated to helping families protect and grow their financial assets and preserve their heritage across generations (40 of Pitcairn's 100 family clients are multigenerational). Pitcairn has been recognized as an innovator since its inception in 1923, when it was established to preserve the wealth and values of the descendants of nineteenth-century glass-manufacturing entrepreneur John Pitcairn, co-founder of what is now PPG Industries. The firm evolved into a multifamily office in 1987.

Alex Scott is executive chairman of SandAire (www.sandaire.com). Alex is a member of the fourth generation of his family, which owned Provincial Insurance until it was sold to UAP (AXA) in 1994. He subsequently led his family in the creation of SandAire in 1996. SandAire is a family-owned multifamily office that manages clients' assets and risks. It takes a long-term view and tailors investment strategies to preserve and grow wealth. It has offices in London and Singapore.

*Denise Kenyon-Rouvinez:* **Alex, Dirk; you both run your own family multifamily office (MFO). Could you describe the pros of having a family at the helm of a MFO?**

*Alex Scott:* Let's take a step back and see what a multifamily office is. It is a professionally run organization delivering financial services to a select group of wealthy families. What the owning family brings is extraordinary alignment of interests – exemplified by the probability that the family will have a great majority of its assets managed in the same way, with the same fees and with the same output as the client. In addition, the owning family is probably more focused on the performance of all of our clients' assets rather than necessarily the bottom line. As an example: we have invested significantly in systems to enhance client reporting. It is a major investment, but we felt it was appropriate, as we could take a long-term perspective on amortization.

*Dirk Jungé:* I agree with Alex. Aligned interests and shared values are critical to the success of any family office. We call it the "3Cs" – culture, collaboration, and continuity. Everything we stand for – our reputation, the people with whom we associate, the way in which we cultivate our talent – must be consistent with these basic principles of success. It also explains the success of our recent leadership

*Aligned interests and shared values are critical to the success of any family office*

transition in which Leslie Voth, a non-Pitcairn family member, so ably assumed the responsibility of CEO. We are one team. And in a business where generational family transition is a critical component, our ability to personally demonstrate the importance of *shared culture, collaboration,* and *continuity* is a must-have. After all, it is something that our client families understand to a far greater extent than most.

**How would you compare your business, your family office, to other family businesses?**
*Alex*: One of the competitive advantages of family businesses is their capacity to plan for longevity and represent stability, in contrast to a financial services partnership, which tends to be relatively unstable. What we are seeking to fulfill with our own multifamily office is to align the *longevity and stability* of a family business alongside the professional excellence of a financial services partnership, and doing that is...tricky, because we are dealing with a business that has as its core asset intellectual capital. Businesses that have intellectual capital at their core must attract, retain, incentivize top talent. As a family business

it creates an interesting dynamic because you need to ensure that you can mix the stability that the family ownership brings with the professionalism and dynamism of a financial services partnership. Well done, it is an extremely powerful combination.

**Do you think that the fact that a family that is at the helm of the family office, invests its own assets, and has to preserve its own capital makes your MFO invest in a different way?**
*Dirk*: Definitely. The fact that family members lead and/or manage the MFO is fundamental to its success. It speaks to people, process, and passion. It is vital for the longevity of the founding family that it continues to examine best practices, and share that knowledge with the other families that comprise the MFO. It means we are on the same side of the table. We eat our own cooking. Yet, like any business, it also requires that we remain open to change. Our move from single-family office (SFO) to multifamily office (MFO) 25 years ago enabled us to expand our business model as well as create new opportunities

for both new and existing clients. Similarly, our bold move to an *open architecture investment platform* five years ago was also consistent with the alignment of interest between the Pitcairn family and our clients.

**Dirk, I know you have had a nonfamily CEO at the helm of your MFO for a few months now, but you still have family members in the management of the family offices (FO), don't you?**

*Dirk*: In addition to my leadership role as chairman of the board, we have three family members involved in the day-to-day management of the business. My cousins Rick Pitcairn, chief investment officer (CIO), and Clark Pitcairn, who serves as the Pitcairn family's ombudsman, like me, represent the fourth generation (G4) of the Pitcairn family. In addition, Dain Kistner, my nephew and fifth-generation family member, heads strategic planning. Each of us sits on the board of directors, together with another five family members representing three generations of the family, our nonfamily CEO, plus four independent directors. The family leadership has a very strong relationship with our nonfamily CEO.

**Alex, how about your family governance, and how do you plan for succession?**

*Alex*: We have several family investments and operational entities, one of which is SandAire. This gives us the latitude to provide governance opportunities as competent and interested family candidates emerge. At the moment the two main boards we operate are: investment board, a mix of two family members (one G4, one G5 chairman) plus four nonfamily; and operations board, a mix of two G4 family members plus four nonfamily. We have one next-generation family member on the investment board, but otherwise we expect the family to pursue careers elsewhere until or unless they are either interested or qualified to contribute. We have a family constitution to manage expectations. The MFO is a blend of family ownership with the standards and mindset of a professional partnership: the latter implies a strictly meritocratic selection process.

**Your own families are clients of your own respective firms. Have your families established a risk**

**profile for their investments? How often do they monitor performance?**

*Alex*: We do have a *family risk profile* – as do all our clients. The family investment board meets quarterly. This board receives monthly updates. It meets with the manager to discuss investment and, like any client, can express its views.

*Dirk*: Our risk profile is part of setting our *strategic investment allocation*. It is set at three levels: Enterprise, Trusts, and Household. Reviews are made quarterly or more frequently as the situation dictates. In addition, we have a robust performance measurement process.

**Going back to the family-owned MFO model, we looked at the pros, but do you see any cons of having a family at the helm?**

*Dirk*: In the USA only 11% of MFOs were launched by families. It is a difficult assignment, and there are no free rides. Nevertheless, oftentimes family members and outside professionals are viewed differently – as if family members are not "real" professionals. So you need to have a bit of a thick skin and be willing to prove yourself. Family members who choose a career, in any business but particularly in the advising of financial assets, need to be qualified and wherever possible overqualified. For example, as a young investment professional, I recognized this importance. I became the first Chartered Financial Analyst (CFA®) at Pitcairn and the youngest member of its management team.

*Alex*: Also, one of the critics that the other model, the partnership MFO, would talk about is the possibility that the founding family gets the better deal. I think that is only a con if the founding family allows that to happen. I always told my family from day one that SandAire would be an MFO, and therefore they were just another client. I suspect that there are plenty of SFOs that would find it extremely difficult to convert to MFOs, because of that requirement, not because the family wants a better deal, but simply that it is a difficult shift in mindset – that change from being the foremost centre of your

FO's focus to being one of many. I think it is a remarkable transition that Dirk and his family managed to achieve.

**In a trendsetting move, you both recently joined forces with other family offices in an association called Wigmore. What led to this decision, and how did you select your partners?**

*Alex:* Wigmore is an association of seven heavyweight family offices, from Australia, the UK, Germany, USA, Brazil, and Canada, that teamed up to achieve greater impact on investment research and manager selection. It opens up possibilities about the way family offices from different countries could work together. Most are family-owned offices.

*Dirk:* We clearly share an understanding that economies and markets are increasingly global. Events in one region, as we have seen across Europe, Asia, and the Americas, have the potential to generate multiple impacts. Wigmore enables us to share and combine intellectual property on a peer-to-peer basis. The insights spawned by this collaboration broaden our perspective, enhance our counsel, and benefit each of our clients in the manner most suited to their particular situation.

# The family office

In 2005, the richest man in Ireland had a fortune estimated at €4 billion. Seven years later, in 2012, he was declared bankrupt in the Republic of Ireland and sentenced to nine weeks in jail.[1] Families of wealth often think that the wealth they have will last forever, no matter how they look after it. Yet history is full of examples like this where, within months or a few years, a family loses vast fortunes. There are few families who have kept their wealth throughout generations. To blossom, wealth needs to be nurtured with care and strong values, appropriate **knowledge and skills**, and the wisdom of long-term planning. Managing, growing, and preserving wealth is one of the essential tasks of family governance.

*Families of wealth often think that the wealth they have will last forever, no matter how they look after it*

# Understanding wealth and the impact of wealth

"I am grateful for the blessings of wealth, but it hasn't changed who I am. My feet are still on the ground. I'm just wearing better shoes," said talk-show host Oprah Winfrey. True, wealth comes with many blessings: access to better health systems, comfortable housing, entrance to select schools and expensive higher education, not having to worry about financial security, an active social life, the resources to care for family members, and the opportunity to help the community and the world at large.

Many people overlook the fact that wealth is a mixed blessing. It can also bring negative attitudes and emotions, such as:

*It can also bring negative attitudes and emotions*

- *Fear* of losing everything, which can turn into anxiety and sometimes into miserliness, due to the fear of overspending and the fear that someday nothing will be left.
- *Isolation* stems from the belief or societal attitude that wealthy people belong to a different class. When that notion is instilled

at an early age, young people feel disconnected and isolated – a painful experience.
- *Guilt and shame* at having so much when others have so little.[2]
- *"Affluenza"* and *entitlement*, also called "silver-spoon syndrome," when a young heir is perceived to display attitudes of impatience and arrogance.

Like the yin and yang philosophy, the positive and negative emotional impacts of wealth come together and influence one another: most wealthy people have a mix of both. A feeling of guilt, for instance, can lead to an initiative to support the community and charitable causes, and help establish a social role and a deeper meaning to life (Figure 10.1).

The most important issue for the wealthy is learning to live with wealth, to feel content, to be oneself, and to use that wealth as **a springboard for further achievement**. To do that, families need to start by opening up and breaking the **taboo** about discussing wealth and its responsibilities. This can help create a forum and become a basis for identifying solutions.

Health
Education
Social status
Pride
Stability
Comfort

**FIG 10.1** Some positive and negative feelings about wealth

## Wealth management

Wealth management is a delicate and important subject, to which families need to pay considered attention. A healthy start is understanding that wealth is much more than money, and that taking care of financial capital alone is not enough. To be preserved over a long period of time, the three forms of capital[3] that constitute wealth need care and attention:

1. *Human capital*: family members, education and health, history, experience, family values. The primary responsibility for human capital rests in the hands of the family council.
2. *Financial capital*: investments, properties, and cash. The primary responsibility for financial capital rests with the family office.
3. *Social capital*: community and philanthropic activities. The primary responsibility for social capital rests with the family foundation.

Strong family governance and coordination are needed to master harmonious management and development of these three aspects of wealth.

Financial wealth is often created when the business is sold, listed on the stock exchange, when a division is sold, or through having **strong cash-flow**. In such cases, families have to question whether they want to split the money and go their separate ways, or stay together and manage their wealth together. In the latter case, there is a larger pool of financial wealth that provides **wider investment opportunities**, while a smaller amount from split wealth may not. A larger fund also offers economies of scale in the cost of running an office, in commissions and financial charges, and gives more freedom of choice and diversity of investments, and thus a greater opportunity to spread risks.

## The family office

Once a family has made the decision, depending on the amount of financial wealth available, the degree of control they want to have and the trust they have in the service providers, they will either organize their own financial asset management (usually through their own family office/SFO) or subcontract that management to third parties.

## A typology of family offices

As their financial wealth grows, families often start organizing wealth management through the finance department of their business; then, as it grows, they dedicate one person to it; and later they organize it in a more structured way, using one of the following models:

**The office** is a dedicated space – an office, a floor, a building – within the business, which has one or two dedicated people who handle all financial, legal, and tax matters related to family owners and their wealth.

**The single family office (SFO)** is a separate legal entity, often geographically separate, dedicated to the management of the financial wealth of one specific family. People working at the SFO are greatly trusted, and are often considered almost as extended family members. The SFO offers a range of services that often go significantly beyond financial, legal, and tax management. For example, it may become involved in more personal matters, such as mentoring the next generation, or organizing holidays, family events, and education programs. SFOs are expensive but offer a high level of control to the owning family.

**The multifamily office (MFO)** offers predominantly bespoke financial, tax, and legal services to a select number of ultra high net worth (UHNW) families. Families who, for some reason – usually lack of specific skills or motivation, or cost considerations – decide not to run their own SFO usually join one form or another of MFO, such as one of the following:

- **Association of professionals**: usually former private bankers and investment specialists who pool their skills to offer a platform dedicated to a few close family clients.
- **Banks and financial institutions**: most private banks have a department dedicated to the wealth management of their family clients.
- **Family-owned**: some families decide to open up their own SFO to other families, turning it into an MFO. The interview with Dirk Jungé

of Pitcairn and Alex Scott of SandAire in this chapter offers a good overview of family-owned family offices and contains some points of comparison with other forms of MFOs.

- **Association of family offices**: in possible anticipation of a consolidation in that market segment, a handful of MFOs have joined forces to offer increased global services to their family clients (see the interview in this chapter).

One important aspect to consider is the family's need for privacy and discretion. This aspect needs to be discussed openly, especially when considering moving to using an MFO, and the family needs to assure itself of the discretion of the managers of the office, and of their ability to keep all matters – not just financial information – confidential.

*One important aspect to consider is the family's need for privacy and discretion*

## Structuring and managing the family office

Like any other structure in the governance system, the family office has its own governance and management.[4]

### The family office board

"Money is only a tool. It will take you wherever you wish, but it will not replace you as the driver."[5] This quote is a great metaphor for the role families have to play in governance as well as for identifying what they can and cannot delegate. No matter how skilled and talented family officers are, the family needs to be in the driver's seat to set the general direction of wealth management, ensure that the family values are built into the chosen investment strategy, set investment objectives, and check that the family office performs adequately and has control systems in place to ensure that the FO complies with the **demanding regulations** imposed by the sector. While they can delegate some of these responsibilities to the family office board and to management, they need to remain on top of strategic decisions.

*Money is only a tool*

The office and SFO are predominantly led by families, even if their board is open to outsiders – but they are more remote from decisions when their financial wealth is invested in a MFO. In that instance, an external board or family investment committee can supervise the actions and decisions of the MFO.

The main roles of the family office board are to:

- Establish the financial needs of the family and its expected growth in order to estimate the return needed on investments to cover for those needs and grow the financial capital.
- Clarify family values, principles, and desired investment risk profile.
- Build a long-term family wealth strategy.
- Design incentive structures to support long-term investment thinking;[6]
- Select key managers.
- Ensure that proper controls are in place to meet compliance standards and to prevent fraud.
- Monitor investments and benchmark results.

## The family office charter

The board also needs to make sure that the role, attributes, and tasks of the family office are clearly described in a family office charter. The charter describes the governance structure of the family office, as well as the family values and guiding principles.

## The management of the family office

The CEO of the family office takes care of wealth management planning, oversees the good functioning of the office, and is overall responsible for regulatory compliance and compliance with the owners' (or the clients') guiding principles.

The main tasks of the family office are as follows:

1. Investments and portfolio management: a department led by the chief investment officer (CIO). Investments cover items such as shares,

bonds, participation in financial funds, **hedge funds**, and passive investments (buy and hold). While portfolio strategy is not the topic of this book, it is still interesting to note that more and more families wish to invest in funds that provide steady financial returns and are close to their philanthropic principles: for instance, **"green" funds** that invest in companies involved with environment preservation (such as Virgin Green Fund[7]), or **"impact finance funds"** (private equity funds that invest in companies led by social entrepreneurs, such as Alterra Impact Finance).[8] In an SFO the CIO often has the responsibility to manage the financial capital of the family foundation as well.

2. Private equity, **new ventures** and acquisitions.
3. Tax, legal, and **estate planning**.
4. Real estate and property management.
5. "Concierge" services to shareholders.
6. Administration.

Family offices vary considerably from one country to another. They may be small or large, and may not carry out all of the above functions; at times they may have fewer responsibilities, and at times more. In addition, SFOs may place a strong emphasis on **financial education** for family members and set up a number of in-house educational programs or select a number of business schools' programs for family members to attend (Figure 10.2).

## Grooming the next generation of responsible stewards of wealth

A survey undertaken by Wharton and IESE business schools on the performance of SFOs highlighted that the more the SFO focuses on quality of items outside portfolio management – governance, human resources, etc. – the stronger the financial performance is. The same conclusions were drawn for education and succession planning.[9]

the more the SFO focuses on quality of items outside portfolio management – governance, human resources, etc. – the stronger the financial performance is

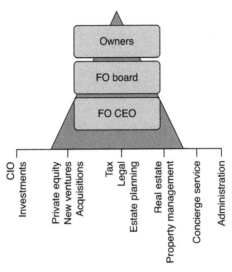

FIG 10.2 **Example of a family office organizational structure**

In order to preserve wealth over generations and to transmit it in a meaningful way, it is important to transmit it with values and to pay particular attention to education programs. Family members do not all perceive wealth in the same way, and each family member may be affected differently by it.[10] **Wealth creators** generally develop a strong feeling of pride and a sense of achievement for having built the wealth. **Inheritors** may feel unworthy of the wealth they receive, feeling they have done nothing to deserve it. As a result, as noted earlier, they may develop negative emotional reactions, and self-destructive behaviors such as substance abuse may become a way to compensate. The more that wealth inheritors develop a sense of responsibility and stewardship for the family wealth, the more they see how much wealth can enable them to grow their business, develop new businesses, create employment, support their community, and support other charitable interests, the more they will feel worthy of that wealth. They will then feel proud of carrying the flag for the family and transmitting the family values *the more they will feel worthy of that wealth* and wealth to their own children.

Families often ask, "How early can we start educating the children about wealth?" It is difficult to answer that question, as every child is different, but in general it is much earlier than families think – a good rule is to be ready as soon as children start asking questions about money. Some even start with preschool programs,[11] but in a manner appropriate to their age and their stage of development.

**BEST-PRACTICE RECOMMENDATIONS**

**1** Recognize the issues with wealth:

    a. Wealth is volatile; it can be lost as quickly as it is created.

    b. Wealth needs to be nurtured with care and strong values.

    c. Just like yin and yang, wealth comes with many blessings and many negative attitudes and emotions; discussing them openly is a first step to identifying solutions.

**2** Three types of family capital create family wealth: human, financial, and social capital. Each needs to be addressed to preserve wealth over the long term.

**3** One of the first decisions families need to make about wealth is whether they will *invest together or not.*

**4** Once that decision is made, the family can choose the vehicle that will help them best manage their wealth: an office, a single-family office, a bank, or a multifamily office.

**5** The choice should be based on the amount of wealth available, the cost of running each vehicle, the level of control the family wants, and the trust they have in financial and investment managers.

**6** No matter how skilled and talented family officers are, the family has to play a role in the governance of the family office, set *primary strategic objectives*, define an investment risk profile, and check that the office performs adequately and is compliant with *rules and regulations*.

**7** A family office charter must offer a clear view of the role of the family office and detail its governance structure.

**8** Just as succession in the business takes a long time, so does *succession in wealth.* An important task of the family and the family office is to groom responsible future stewards of wealth.

# Documentation of Governance Structures: Constitution

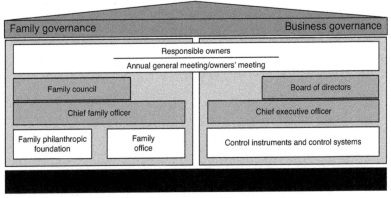

This figure highlights the family constitution in Part IV and acts as a navigational tool for the reader.

# Developing Governance with the Help of a Governance Code*

## "A family on bad terms is a disaster for a company."

Interview with Dr. Rheinhard Zinkann, managing director, Miele, Gütersloh, Germany

The family-firm specialist academy INTES and German Association of Family Enterprises ASU created a Commission comprising 27 family entrepreneurs and academics to write the German Governance Code for Family Enterprises, the second version of which was published in 2010. Dr. Reinhard Zinkann, managing director at Miele, representing the fourth generation of the Miele family business, was a member of the Commission. Miele has been a family enterprise for more than 100 years. It is a global brand manufacturing domestic appliances and commercial machines in the field of laundry care, dishwashing and disinfection. Today, more than 16,000 employees work for Miele worldwide, more than 10,000 of them in Germany. They generated sales of about

* Alexander Koeberle-Schmid kindly thanks Peter May as the initiator of the German Governance Code for Family Enterprises for his many contributions and personal help to developing our knowledge about governance in family enterprises. He also thanks Bernd Grottel for his support in developing this chapter from prior work on which they collaborated. Same applies to prior work with Peter May.

€3 billion in the fiscal year ending June 30, 2011. Miele's founding credo of being "forever better" remains the company motto.**

*Alexander Koeberle-Schmid:* **Dr. Zinkann, the Governance Code for Family Enterprises is a guideline for the responsible management of family businesses. What does it imply?**

*Reinhard Zinkann:* All companies need good leadership, no matter whether they are small or large, whether they are family-owned or publicly owned, whether they are managed by family members or third parties. There are certainly different opinions as to what good leadership means. The Governance Code was created in order to provide those in charge of family enterprises with guidance. It is intended to help owner families create optimum structures for leadership, control, and family governance. To that effect, it functions as a tool for establishing a good Memorandum of Association.

**Why did you participate in developing the Code?**

Talking to other family entrepreneurs, but also as a member of advisory and supervisory boards, it has repeatedly struck me how important these issues are. Unfortunately, I have encountered many examples of structures that were to the detriment of the companies concerned. Hence, I recognized the necessity to equip leaders of family enterprises with guidelines to help them establish better governance.

**In what specific way can the Governance Code be of support to owner families?**

In family enterprises, controversy often arises over issues such as succession, dividend payments, or long-term strategies. For this reason, the Code recommends developing comprehensive succession planning; it includes advice on what percentage of profit to pay out and how much to accumulate; and it recommends that ground rules are agreed for handling conflicts. This holds true for all family enterprises.

---

** This interview is translated from German, and has already been published in *Führung von Familienunternehmen* (*Leading the Family Enterprise*) by Alexander Koeberle-Schmid and Bernd Grottel, published by Erich Schmidt, Germany.

**What should an owner family do after having reflected on and developed solutions for all aspects of the Governance Code for Family Enterprises?**

The next step ought to be writing a family constitution. It should document everything that needs to be stipulated. It should then be implemented in company, family, and succession law contracts.

*The next step ought to be writing a family constitution*

**Some critics say that the Governance Code for Family Enterprises does not take the diversity and complexity of family enterprises into consideration sufficiently. Are they right?**

No, this criticism is unfounded. One detailed set of rules that does justice to all companies and constellations was neither intended, nor would it be practicable. What we intended, and what we were able to do and actually did, was to raise crucial points and define guidelines that would help find the best possible individual solutions to relevant issues. Therefore, the Code is not a comprehensive, detailed set of rules, but rather a manual which family shareholders and managing directors can use for orientation in their reflections on governance.

**The Code is a private initiative that was launched by entrepreneurs for entrepreneurs. Do you think that there is a risk of the Code being adopted by legislative authorities, and of this reducing the freedom enjoyed by family enterprises in developing their family business governance?**

No, I do not even believe that this risk exists. If legislative authorities were to adopt the Code they would need to limit themselves to certain company sizes and legal forms. And even if they did, such a legislative project would not be appropriate due to the fact that family enterprises come in so many different shapes and sizes. Politicians are also aware of this fact.

**If the legislator does not take up the Code, is it in danger of being just a trend that will pass eventually?**

No, I do not think that is true either. A lot of conversations with entrepreneurs have taught me that this Code serves a very real need which some owner families consider to be existential. This is why I am very confident that it will have become reality in, let's say, ten years, and that it will therefore have given itself credence in the process. It is clear, however, that over the years it needs to adapt to developments in the real world. For this reason, every five years, our commission will assess whether the currently valid Code needs to be updated to reflect new circumstances or findings.

**To sum up, why is good family business governance so important in family enterprises?** My father usually says: "Family is a company's greatest asset; it is also its greatest liability." A family on good terms is something wonderful. A family on bad terms is a disaster for a company. Good and appropriately laid-out family business governance can prevent conflicts before they arise, and ensure that the support which the family provides to the company can achieve its full potential.

## A governance code for family enterprises?

Family enterprises differ in their challenges, not only among themselves, but also from publicly-listed companies, companies owned by financial investors, and state-owned enterprises. Governance in family enterprises is therefore different to governance in other enterprises.[1]

Family firms cannot rely on the governance codes that have been developed for other enterprises. For instance, the typical governance problems of a publicly listed company, such as the risk of opportunistic directors acting primarily in their own interest, are less likely to occur in family enterprises (see Figure 11.1).[2] In addition, the shareholders in family enterprises are not anonymous. The family owners normally do not need to be protected from the misuse of power by opportunistic agents. Owners have to ensure that they act responsibly, and structure their company in a way that suits the context, and the challenges that the firm faces. Thus, the objective is to protect the owners from themselves; establishing **checks and balances** to prevent abuse of power or incompetence by owners. Examples include a long-established entrepreneur-founder who will not resign from his

| Aim of governance in publicly-listed companies | Aim of governance in family enterprises |
|---|---|
| • Increase trust of share- and stakeholders | • Increase responsibility of owners |
| • Protect shareholders against opportunistic behavior by managers who are pursuing their own agenda | • Reduce incompetence and misuse of power by owners |
| • Improve transparency and accountability towards stakeholders | • Assure responsible influence of owners |
| • Strengthen position of the company with regard to equity and debt | • Assure long-term success of the family enterprise for future generations |
| | • Reduce the potential for conflict |
| | • Establish family governance to assure cohesion and commitment of family members |

FIG 11.1 / **Goals of governance in publicly-listed companies vs. family enterprises**

position when it would be in the firm's best interests; or if information is shared unequally, for instance the CEO has more information about the financial situation of the firm than an owner who does not work in the business. Transparency and accountability should be encouraged. In addition, owners have to take into account cohesion within the family – a consideration that is not relevant for publicly listed companies. For all these reasons, there should be special codes for family enterprises.[3]

## Goals and functioning of governance codes for family enterprises

In publicly listed companies, the discussion about good governance began with the publication of the **Cadbury Report** in the UK in 1992, the first governance code internationally. In many countries, specific codes and regulations for governance followed. In the USA there was the **Sarbanes Oxley Act** (2002), in Germany the **German Governance Code** (revised 2013), in Brazil the **Code of Best Practice of Corporate Governance** (revised 2009), in China the **Provisional Code of Corporate Governance for Securities Companies** (2004), and in Ghana the **Corporate Governance Guidelines on Best Practices** (2010).[4] Nearly all countries have a governance code, but these are mainly for publicly listed companies.

By contrast, there are only about **12 codes internationally for family enterprises**. In Germany, the first governance code for family firms was developed in 2004. Six years later, under of the guidance of INTES (the German academy for family enterprises) and ASU (the Association for Family Enterprises) in Germany, a commission of family entrepreneurs and academics chaired by Professor Peter May has updated the code.[5]

The first German code served as a role model for codes in other countries, such as Belgium's **Buysse Code I** (2005) and **Buysse Code II** (2009), the **Austrian Governance Code for Family Enterprises** (2005, 2011), the Finnish code of **Improving Corporate Governance of Unlisted**

Companies (2006), the **Swiss Governance for Family Business Code** (2006) and the **Spanish Principles of Good Corporate Governance for Unlisted Companies** (2008). International initiatives include Corporate Governance Guidance and Principles for Unlisted Companies in Europe (2010) by the European Confederation of Directors' Associations and the IFC Family Business Governance Handbook (2008) by the World Bank.[6]

In general, governance codes for family enterprises serve as an instrument or checklist that allows owners to organize their **family business governance professionally and individually**, depending on the situation of family and business. The codes do not generally provide specific recommendations or general solutions that apply to all family enterprises. Because of the diversity of family firms, this is not possible. A governance code for a family business is not like programming code. The intention ought to be to clarify the questions that the owners of a family enterprise need to address to ensure an **individually tailored approach** to governance for the family firm. The primary target audience is the owner. To help owners, codes contain all the relevant governance issues that need to be addressed when drafting a family constitution.

**General Aspects**
1. Commitment to a Responsible Handling of Owners' Role
**Business Governance: Power Rights**
2. Owners
3. Board of Directors
4. Management Board
**Business Governance: Money Rights**
5. Determination and Distribution of Profits
6. Transferability of Ownership; Leaving the Owners' Circle
**Family Governance**
7. Family Governance

FIG 11.2 / Content of the German Governance Code for Family Enterprises (2010)

Good governance helps to create **economic value**, and assists the **emotional well-being** of the family, and others with a stake in the company. It demonstrates that the owners are taking responsibility for their employees and other stakeholders,[7] and helps to ensure the long-term survival of the family enterprise. Baron Buysse, the initiator of a governance code in Belgium, has declared: "This corporate governance code with recommendations for nonlisted enterprises is a professional collection of guidelines and recommendations which will help you, as an owner or manager, to optimize your future successes."[8]

The codes for family firms are voluntary, in contrast with most of the governance codes for publicly listed companies. Families can use the questions in the code (the content of the German Governance Code for Family Enterprises is shown in Figure 11.2 and follows at the end of this chapter) to develop their own family business governance, including a family constitution. The family constitution is, in turn, the basis for the articles of incorporation, inheritance documents, and other legal agreements (Figure 11.3).[9]

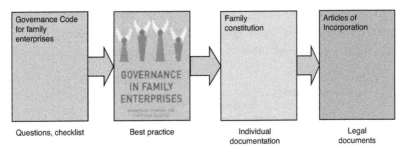

FIG 11.3 / **The process of developing a company's governance code**

## Quality requirements for codes for family enterprises

When a commission of family business experts develops a governance code for family enterprises it is helpful to consider four **quality requirements**, which are met by the German Governance Code for Family Enterprises. According to Professor Knut Werner Lange, governance codes must be:[10]

- Based on a broad consensus.
- Based on the specific circumstances and needs of the owner family.
- Flexible enough to respond to the heterogeneity of family enterprises.
- Clear and easy to understand (see Figure 11.4).

These four principles will now be discussed for the German Governance Code for Family Enterprises. This should help other commissions in other countries when developing governance code for their family firms.

## Broad consensus

The 27 members of the commission on the German Governance Code for Family Enterprises represent various owner families. They differ in legal form (non-incorporated firm, incorporated firm, etc.), financing arrangement (unlisted and listed), size (from 200 employees to about 84,000), and ownership structure (sole owner, sibling partnership, cousin consortium, family dynasty) as well as corporate structure (focused, diversified, national, international). Even the positions of the members in the family enterprise are different: family CEOs, nonfamily CEOs, chairman, board directors, juniors, and owners. In addition, specialists in the field of family business research also contributed. Thus, the Code is based on a broad consensus.

*governance codes must be clear and easy to understand*

## The circumstances and needs of the owner family

The German Code asks relevant questions that owners need to answer, and makes certain recommendations. For instance, it recommends that owners make special arrangements for making wills, and determining whether owners can work in the firm. In addition, it recommends that an age limit is implemented, especially for owners working in the business; that a long-term succession is established, and appropriate rules are set for determining and distributing profits. It also recommends that families should establish family governance to assure cohesion among the family members and engagement with the enterprise. The Code encourages an approach based on the specific circumstances and needs of the owner family.

| 1. Based on a broad consensus | ✓ | • 27 members with different backgrounds (family CEOs, nonfamily CEOs, chairman, board of directors, junior staff, owners only, researchers)<br>• Family enterprises differ in legal form, financing, size, and ownership structure as well as in corporate structure |
|---|---|---|
| 2. Based on the specific circumstances and needs of the owner family | ✓ | • Introductions before the checklist<br>• Owners as primary target group<br>• Specific family enterprise issues |
| 3. Flexible enough to respond to the variety of family enterprises | ✓ | • No single recommendations<br>• Owner can decide whether to answer the questions raised in the code or not |
| 4. Clear and easy to understand in order to be communicated to the various stakeholders | ✓ | • Uniform terminology; avoidance of technical terms<br>• Applicable to one-tier and two-tier countries |

FIG 11.4 Quality requirements of a governance code, applied to the German Governance Code for Family Enterprises (2010)

## Flexibility to respond to the heterogeneity of family enterprises

The German Governance Code for Family Enterprises recommends which aspects of family business governance should be regulated. The Code does not contain specific recommendations, because this is not possible due to the considerable heterogeneity of family enterprises. It is divided into two broad categories: first, it uses the term "shall" for those aspects that need to be answered by all family enterprises and "it is recommended" for those that are advisory. For instance, a small family enterprise does not need an auditor or a board of directors. The Code provides a checklist that owner families can use and apply to their particular context.

### Clarity and ease of understanding

The German Code has short introductions, uses uniform terminology, and avoids technical terms where possible. Where this is not possible, terms are explained. Synonymous terms are clearly defined. Furthermore, the

Code can be applied to countries with a one-tier (board with executives and nonexecutives) and with a two-tier (management and supervisory board) governance system.

## The development of governance in a family enterprise

Business-owning families can develop their family constitution with the help of a governance code (Figure 11.3). As stated in relation to the development of family enterprises and their challenges (see Chapters 1 and 2), owners need to update the constitution as the business and the family evolve.[11] The pace of evolution, and the need to adapt, may be gradual, however. Family owners should therefore attend to this on a continuous basis. For this reason, we recommend that **every family member reads the Code regularly** to recognize aspects that need to be adapted when there are changes in the family business.

## BEST-PRACTICE RECOMMENDATIONS

**1** Business-owning families can find the appropriate governance structures for their family and for the business with the help of a governance code. They should not apply governance codes intended for publicly listed companies unless their company is also listed.

**2** A governance code should meet certain quality criteria. The German Code, revised in 2010, provides a useful checklist.

**3** Business-owning families should decide whether they want to apply the different parts of the governance code or not. This decision should depend on the current situation of the family enterprise.

**4** Business-owning families should continuously develop their governance with the help of the governance code by regularly checking if changes are necessary.

**5** Business-owning families should develop a family constitution where they summarize all important governance aspects mentioned in the code and applicable to the family and its business.

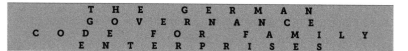

**THE GERMAN GOVERNANCE CODE FOR FAMILY ENTERPRISES**

**Guidelines for the responsible leadership of family enterprises**

*This excerpt from the publicly available German Governance Code for Family Enterprises has been translated from German with the support of the Arabian Chamber of Commerce in Amman and Andrea Prym-Bruck, a member of the German Commission for the Governance Code for Family Enterprises. This is the second version of the Code, dating from June 19, 2010. This is not an official translation authorized by the Commission. This translation has been carried out with care; however, the authors and the publisher accept no responsibility for losses arising from its use. As reference and for more information, please visit http:// www.kodex-fuer-familienunternehmen.de.*

## 1. Commitment to Responsible Stewardship by Owners

Family enterprises, where a family is the dominant shareholder, typically intend to sustain their businesses for at least another generation. In order both to compete in the market effectively, and to be a socially responsible corporate citizen, the owners shall make a commitment to responsible stewardship. This includes establishing appropriate governance structures. In this context the owners must take the following decisions and measures and must implement them into the business and into the owner family.

1.1 The owners shall decide to which values and goals they feel bound in view of their family ownership and their family enterprise.

They shall decide to what extent they want to take into consideration the interests of other stakeholders, in particular the employees and customers, in addition to the legitimate interests of the owner family, and thereby want to contribute to the development of the society.

The owner shall determine which stakeholder is to be given priority in the event of a clash of interest, in particular to what extent the business interests are placed above the individual interests of the owners.

1.2 The business and information structures shall be arranged to give the owners, the board of directors and the company's management an accurate assessment of the economic and financial situation of the business as well as compliance with the agreed values.

The owners shall decide whether and to what extent the internal transparency is also applied to the external stakeholders.

1.3 Businesses can be maintained as family enterprises only if they are able to sustain sufficient unity within the owner family and agree to maintain the firm as a family enterprise. Owners shall acknowledge explicitly the importance of management of the owner family's affairs, to the same level as management of the enterprise itself.

1.4 The owners shall ensure that family members who have recently joined, especially partners and members of the next generation, are given an introduction to their responsibilities as members of the owner family and/or owners of a family enterprise.

## 2. Owners

The owners constitute the highest decision-making authority in a family firm. Within the legal framework chosen by them, they have the authority to define the values and goals and to make the final decisions. If they delegate this authority to an independent board of directors, they are responsible for the effectiveness of this body. In the exercise of this responsibility, the following must be particularly considered.

## 2.1 Collective responsibilities of owners

2.1.1 The owners should define the values and goals of the business and the family ownership, and should make clear statements about keeping the business under family ownership, and about the role of owners in its management and supervision.

2.1.2 In addition, the owners shall formulate sufficiently clear expectations of the business model, especially their expectations as regards stability, profitability, and long-term growth.

2.1.3 Where a board of directors is not required by law, the owners shall decide whether and to what extent they want to delegate certain responsibilities to a voluntary body, especially relating to monitoring the company's management.

2.1.4 The owners shall organize themselves in such a way that guarantees their decision-making autonomy.

2.1.5 Voting rights shall be commensurate with equity holdings. Any other special rights that deviate from this right granted to individual owners or owner groups shall require clear rules and special justification, and it is recommended that such provisions are entered into with caution.

2.1.6 It is recommended that majority and minority rights are clearly defined, and appropriately balanced.

## 2.2 Individual owners

2.2.1 The owners' major participation rights are:

- The right to participate in the owners' assembly,
- The right to vote,
- Access and information rights.

In exercising these participation rights, it is recommended that all owners are treated equally and are allowed to exercise the participation rights personally. It is recommended that any deviations from the principle of equality are carefully regulated and clearly justified..

2.2.2 There should be guidance to determine who can represent an owner at the owners' assembly and how someone else can exercise his or her right to vote. For minors, or for those whose ownership rights are pending execution of a will, their authorized representatives should be able to participate in ownership decisions.

2.2.3 For designing the access and information policy of the business, it is recommended that it allows all owners:

- To get an accurate picture of the economic and financial situation of the enterprise and whether the values and goals of its owners are being maintained;

- To familiarize themselves with the most important aspects of the business activity of the company and to understand its strategy; and

- To strengthen the bond to the company.

2.2.4 The owners shall determine whether, how many, und under what conditions members of the owner family can work for the company and/or can receive benefits from the company.

In the event that members of the owner family work for the company, it is recommended that rules are established for the selection process and for who decides on the appointment.

2.2.5 The owners shall clearly define the rights and obligations for individual owners that arise from his ownership role. This particularly applies to

- Participating in the owners' assembly,

- Exercising voting rights,

- Secrecy of company internal issues,

- Ensuring no competition,
- Ensuring that the family enterprise will be affected as little as possible by consequences of divorce claims, entitlements to share of inheritance, and/or inheritance tax.

## 3. Board of Directors [this applies especially to nonexecutives]

As the size of the company and the complexity of ownership increase, it is recommended that family enterprises constitute a board of directors, even if not compelled to by law. Such a body can improve the quality and objectivity of advice and monitoring of the company's management. When constituting a voluntary board of directors, the following must be observed:

### 3.1 *Tasks of the board of directors*

3.1.1 The owners shall clearly define the tasks of the board of directors. The owners shall in particular determine whether and to what extent the board of directors is responsible for:

- Appointment and dismissal to the management board, and other personnel decisions.
- Decisions on a possible CEO or spokesman of the management board, rules of procedures and other internal decisions concerning the organization of the management board.
- Approval of business strategy, business planning, extraordinary management decisions, and
- Adoption of the annual financial statements and the distribution of profits,
- and to what extent the board of directors is included in decisions previously made by owners.

3.1.2 The content, extent, style, and frequency of management board reporting shall be clearly defined. The same applies to additional access and information rights that the owners may choose to delegate to the board of directors.

Reporting, and access and information rights, shall be arranged in such a way that the board of directors and its members are always able to carry out their tasks without restrictions.

3.1.3 The internal structures and decision processes shall be regulated in such a way that the board of directors can clearly understand the duties transferred to it and their contractual obligations. The board of directors should meet sufficiently frequently, and the effectiveness of its activity should be regularly evaluated.

### 3.2 Composition of the board of directors

3.2.1 The structure, size, and composition of the board of directors, and the capability of its members, shall be commensurate to the company's size and complexity of ownership structure and operations.

Owners should consider that the presence of nonfamily, nonexecutive individuals on the board of directors can improve the quality and objectivity of its work.

3.2.2 The owners shall determine in particular:

- To what extent the owner family can or shall be represented on the board of directors,
- How members of the board of directors are appointed and removed,
- Which majorities are required in an election,
- Which personal requirements for membership must be met,

- For which term of office the members of the board of directors will be appointed.

Attention shall be paid to ensure that members of the board of directors have the competences necessary for their duties at any time, and that the members of the board of directors act in the interest of the family enterprise and its owners.

3.2.3 The owners shall determine whether and under which conditions a member of the management board may be appointed as chairman of the board of directors after his or her retirement.

3.2.4 It is recommended that the owners set a retirement age for members of the board of directors.

3.2.5 When selecting the members of the board of directors, care should be taken to ensure that they are independent from the company and the management board, and that any conflicts of interest are avoided.

### 3.3 Compensation and liability

3.3.1 The activity of the members of the board of directors shall be adequately remunerated, with clearly defined criteria and transparent information on the amount and frequency of pay.

3.3.2 The basis and range of potential liability of the members of the board of directors shall be clearly defined.

### 4. Management Board [this applies especially to executives]

The management board manages the family enterprise, in compliance with statutory responsibilities, and in accordance with the values and goals defined by the owners. In addition, the remit and duties of the management board should be clearly defined. The following must be taken into consideration:

### 4.1 *The tasks of the management board*

4.1.1 The management board shall develop the strategic direction of the company, taking into consideration the values and goals of the owners, in coordination with the owners and/or the board of directors, and ensure its implementation.

The management board shall ensure compliance with statutory provisions and internal company policies, and shall ensure that an adequate management system to assess opportunity and risk is implemented, in accordance with the values and goals of the owners.

4.1.3 The management board shall report on its activities to the owners and/or the board of directors. The details are determined directly or in line with section 3.1.2.

### 4.2 *Composition of the management board*

4.2.1 The size and composition of the management board shall be based on the size of the company and the assigned responsibility.

If the management board consists of several members, it shall be decided whether there shall be a CEO or a spokesman of the management board. In addition, it is recommended that there are clear rules of procedure and an organizational structure to determine the CEO or spokesman.

4.2.2 The appointment of the members of the management board needs special care in the case of a family business. The owners shall determine clearly whether and under which circumstances members of the owner family can be appointed to and/or dismissed from the management board, and who decides this. These rules shall be clearly, transparently, and objectively verifiable.

The same applies to their dismissal, the determination of their employment contracts (including their compensation), and any other agreements with them.

Members of the owner family and independent members of the management board must be equally treated.

If the family enterprise has several owners, it is recommended, for reasons of objectivity, that nonfamily individuals take all decisions on family members.

4.2.3 Family enterprises need long-term succession planning. It is recommended that this includes a binding retirement age for management board members, and procedures for the preparation of potential successors, for the selection decision, and for the transition. In addition, there shall be an emergency plan that clarifies what will happen in the event of an unplanned succession.

### 4.3 Compensation and liability

4.3.1 The activity of the members of the management board shall be adequately remunerated. It shall be clearly defined:

- Who is responsible for taking decisions on remuneration,
- The principles according to which it shall be determined, and
- Who will be informed about the level of remuneration.

4.3.2 The basis and range of potential liability of the members of the management board shall be clearly defined.

### 5. Determination and Distribution of Profits

A family business should pay particular attention to securing its capital and liquidity base, since, due to its cross-generational orientation, it depends on the funds made available by owners, who have to balance the need to distribute profits and reinvest in the business. Upon determination and distribution of profits, the following must be taken into consideration:

### 5.1 Determination of profits

5.1.1 The owners shall determine clearly the principles of accounting and valuation during the preparation of annual financial statements. In particular, they shall in principle decide how any principles of accounting and valuation are exercised. It is recommended that a cautious approach to accounting and valuation is taken.

5.1.2 It is recommended that the annual financial statements of a family enterprise are audited, even if there is no legal obligation to do so.

5.1.3 Selection and appointment of the auditor shall be made by the owners and/or the board of directors.

5.1.4 Signing off the annual accounts shall be done by the owners and/or the board of directors.

5.1.5 Before deciding on the determination of the annual accounts, the owners and/or the board of directors shall have the opportunity to study the annual financial statements and the audit report.

It is recommended that the auditor takes part in consultations on the annual financial statements to give an oral overview of the audit, especially its conformity with the agreed principles of accounting and valuation.

### 5.2 Distribution of profits

5.2.1 The rules on the distribution of profits shall be designed in such a way that they align with the goals set by the owners regarding stability, profitability, and growth, and with a view to helping avoid disputes in the owner family.

5.2.2 The owners shall ensure that a sufficient part of the profits after tax remain in the company permanently to strengthen its equity base.

5.2.3 It is recommended that financial ratios for distribution and/ or profit retention are clearly established, to help achieve an appropriate balance between the financing interest of the company and the distribution interest of the owners.

5.2.4 In addition, how the profits are calculated and distributed shall be made transparent to all owners.

## 6. Transferability of Ownership; Leaving the Owners' Circle

The owners shall take precautions to ensure they maintain dominant ownership for the family over the long term. This implies limitations on the exchangeability of shares, while ensuring a reasonable balance of interest between the interests of the owner family and the individual owner. That being said, in the interests of good governance, the following principles must be considered.

6.1 The owners shall clearly specify to whom the ownership of business may be transferred without further restriction.

They should also clearly define the conditions under which a transfer to other persons is permitted, and what the legal consequences might be of a distorting transfer – that is, a transfer to persons who are not allowed to become owners.

The rules shall apply both to transfers between living persons and transfers as a result of death.

It is recommended that the owners make a last will and testament, and that this is in line with the requirements of the articles of association.

6.2 As compensation for limitation of exchangeability, according to section 6.1, the owners shall be given an appropriate right of notice of ceasing ownership. The owners shall in particular clearly define the following, relating to an owner resigning from the jointly held family enterprise:

- Under what conditions,
- At which time intervals,

- According to what valuation rules,
- According to which payment methods.

## 7. Family Governance

In order to maintain family ownership of a firm over the long term, those concerned must focus not only on corporate interests, but must also take the family into account and establish independent family governance in addition to business governance. The aim of this family governance is to strengthen cohesion within the members of the owner family and their engagement with the company, and to strengthen long-term commitment. It is recommended that the owner family maintain these disciplines for future generations.

Family enterprises and their owner families are so diverse that there can be no prescriptive recommendations for good family governance. The right solution must be worked out individually. Thereby, the following must be taken into consideration in detail:

7.1 In addition to the rules of business governance (see section 6.1), rules shall be defined in family governance concerning:

- Who belongs to the owner family;
- Under which conditions new family members would be admitted to the owner family; and
- Under which conditions membership of the owner family can be terminated.

7.2 The owner family shall provide values and goals for the family, as well as those for the company, and have them written down in a coherent mission statement.

7.3 It is recommended that guidelines for communication are established within the owner family and between the business and the family, for dealing with each other and for external communications.

7.4 It is recommended that companies establish a process for managing conflicts, so that the interests of the company will not be affected by conflicts within the owner family.

7.5 The bigger the owner family becomes, the more strongly it is recommended that it holds joint activities, and that responsibilities for their implementation are defined. This includes ensuring that the owners have sufficient competence.

7.6 It is recommended that each family individually promises to comply with the components of this code. The owner family shall adopt these regulations together and shall agree on a duration of validity – for example, a five-year period, subject to renewal. It is recommended that all regulations can only be amended before the expiration date by an agreed qualified majority.

## chapter 12

# A Family Constitution for Business-Owning Families – Process and Document\*

**"The constitution brings more discipline to the family, and fairness too."**

Interview with Dania Besher, Mac Investments, Cairo, Egypt

Dania Besher is an architect by profession. Her projects include both residential and commercial developments. She has just finished renovating her family business's headquarters in Cairo, Egypt. Dania is one of 37 cousins in the third generation of the family firm, and has been one of the leaders of the governance process begun by her family in 2010. She is a member of the family council, and recently became a member of the board of Mac Investments, a holding company of the family businesses in Egypt.

The family business was started in the 1950s by Dania's grandfather Abdulhak and his brother. In 1963,

---

\* The author would like to thank Arno Lehmann-Tolkmitt, Peter May, Catharina Prym, and Karsten Schween from INTES for jointly developing the knowledge of family constitutions.

one of Abdulhak's sons, Shaher, founded the family's trading company in Yemen. In the 1970s other sons gradually joined the business, as it expanded into industrial fields, then beverages, first in Egypt, later in Yemen, and recently in South Sudan. The group has since then seen a major diversification in different sectors and countries.

*Denise Kenyon-Rouvinez:* **Dania, what was the trigger that initiated the discussion on family constitutions?**

*Dania Besher:* As the family has been blessed with many children and has grown steadily we realized that there were a lot of issues we were facing every day that we didn't know how to deal with, without being emotionally involved or biased towards our own family branch. We decided we needed a constitution to keep family unity. We started in June 2011 and we signed it exactly a year later in June 2012. But we had established the family council in 2010 because we wanted to set the vision and common objective for the family, both inside and outside the family business. We also introduced a family office

in 2012 to help us centralize the organization and needs of an ever-growing family.

How did we start? We had been talking about governance for the family business since the mid 1990s, but nobody really followed through. Later, when we realized that we had many members joining the business, we felt it was time to have a proper organization. So, in 2007, I went to the Family Business Network summit in Berlin with my father. That was an eye-opening experience. I listened to and met other families, and realized we were not alone in our situation. In 2010, I also attended seminars on succession and governance and started initiating the process. I felt it was urgent to start putting something in place before the family fell apart.

*I felt it was urgent to start putting something in place before the family fell apart.*

**How often did you meet to work on the constitution?**
We had five meetings. We met every second month, usually for two or three days. For the first three modules there were only cousins – 14 of us – plus my father. You had

to be either aged at least 25, or to have graduated from college, in order to join the group. We wanted a group that was dedicated to the process.

For the fourth meeting we invited all the seniors, six of them. We presented what we had done, welcomed their feedback, had more discussions. It was the first time we were all together dealing with such issues. After the fourth session we forwarded our constitution draft to our trusted company lawyer. He gave his own feedback, which we integrated. The fifth session was the last session. That's when we signed the constitution. It is 28 pages long, very comprehensive and professional.

**Were any topics more difficult to discuss, and did you have external help to ease the discussions?**
We had a facilitator leading the process. We started with a questionnaire to all the 14 cousins and all the seniors, followed by interviews to define what was important to us. Our first discussion was on the definition of the family to whom the constitution would apply, because my grandfather had

a second wife. That family branch is almost as large as we are; they are all in Yemen but were never part of the family business. Another big topic was the prerequisites to join the family business, as none were in place back then. The values of the family also turned into quite a discussion, as it was difficult to distil them down to a few. Those were the topics we discussed a lot, and where we had democratic votes to reach final decisions.

**Were the discussions easier as you went along?**
At the beginning, a lot of the cousins had no idea about what we were doing or why we needed a constitution. It was difficult to gather everyone and make them understand why it was important, and in particular why it was important that they carried their weight as well, because, too often in the Arab world, the next generation is not asked for an opinion. The seniors usually decide. But during the process, as the document started coming together, people started realizing that what they *people realized that they had a voice; it was a very interesting process*

had said was actually written into it, they realized that their opinion mattered. The discussions became not easier but more heated because people realized that they had a voice; it was a very interesting process.

**Now that your constitution is in place, do you feel it provides more objectivity and transparency among family members?**

It is difficult to say, because unfortunately we have not been able to have our first family assembly since the signature, due to the upheaval in our region. Everyone knows there is a constitution: not only the cousins who worked on it and the six seniors, but the whole family. But not everyone is yet familiar with the full content and what it implies. The most important thing for us right now is to organize our assembly. It is needed for a proper and more comprehensive implementation.

That said, the constitution already resonates very strongly with the younger members of the family who are studying abroad or are about to take the decision as to where to get their higher education. That is where we have started implementing the constitution, putting in place guidelines and rules for the students. We hired an HR (human resources) person in January 2012. She is doing a great job and has the full support of the family council to implement the policies. We have also created an education committee, consisting of three family council members, me included, who deal with student issues and who try to advise and guide the younger generation.

We are now also starting to apply the guidelines defined in the constitution to those family members who wish to join the family business. Our HR person now also oversees the hiring of family members in our various subsidiaries and helps them gain outside work experience after they graduate. It is no longer enough to just have graduated from university to secure a job in the company.

**In what way is the constitution particularly helpful for the next generation?**

I would say that the constitution has been very helpful to provide guidance and support for the next generation and it also gives them a platform to share experiences through the family council who represents them.

## Are you happy about the results?

What makes me happy is when I hear that some of the younger family members want to do a summer school, or study something extracurricular, or volunteer to do an internship. It makes me feel that we have succeeded. The constitution brings more discipline to the family, and fairness too.

## Is there anything in particular you recommend to other families?

Absolutely, I would recommend them to start early with the governance process, 20 years before we did. These guidelines should be in place before the next generation enters the business. In our case there were no rules in place for the third generation, which created some dilemmas. They are now in place for the fourth generation.

I would also advise families to select a group with good chemistry to work together on the constitution. It helps the process and gives the document authenticity and acceptance. In my cousins group, we all know each other well and love each other; we spend a lot of time together and it helped tremendously. During the process we had heated discussions, but always with positive energy and respect, and we always still had fun together. As a matter of fact, the whole process strengthened our family bonds.

*we had heated discussions, but always with positive energy and respect, and we always still had fun together*

## A family constitution: why? or why not?

A family constitution is a written document that lists the family mission, vision, and values as well as a number of rules and policies that describes the nature of the relationship between a family and the business it owns. The mission and vision statement, important issues about the business model, and all family business governance aspects, are normally, but not always, documented in a family constitution (which sometimes goes under another name, such as family charter). A family constitution can be an important instrument for ensuring cohesion, commitment, and internal harmony, as well as economic and emotional success, in family enterprises.

A family constitution is a document that sets out both **strategy** and **structure** for the owners.[1] In addition to strategy and structure, it sets out rules and procedures for owners, the business, and the family. The constitution is **bound by moral force**, rather than legal, although the rules may also be included in the articles of incorporation. The constitution is normally developed with the help of the family business governance principles of "responsible ownership" and "fair process" (see Chapter 1).[2] Typically, owners develop the family constitution through a series of joint workshops. It is important for all parties jointly to produce a document themselves and approve it through consensus. Through the development process, the owners get to know each other better and learn the strengths and weaknesses of the others. They learn together. They are more likely to understand, respect, and accept the rights and obligations of each role – owner, board, management – through this participative process. Thus, the payoff of a family constitution is twofold: the process and the document itself (see Figure 12.1).

*It is important for all parties jointly to produce a document themselves and approve it through consensus*

It is important to note that, while not all content of a family constitution has to be legally binding and included in the articles of incorporation, in many cases this is advisable. The principle is: the greater the potential

| Advantages | Limitations |
|---|---|
| • Increases trust and mutuality | • Does not solve all problems |
| • Assures the long-term success of the family enterprise | • Problems and issues need to be resolved separately before working on a constitution |
| • Increases transparency | • Does not avoid the need to address the real issues |
| • Leads to professionalism and fairness | • It is of little value if people don't voice their opinion |
| • Increases verifiability | • Sometimes it is easier to start by addressing one issue rather than trying to work on the whole constitution |
| • Increases commitment and cohesion | |
| • Supports family and firm pease | |

FIG 12.1  **Pros and cons of a family constitution**

for conflict concerning the issue at hand, the stronger the case for it to be included.[3] For instance, there are often conflicts about succession and dividends. Therefore, those issues should be clearly defined in the articles of incorporation.

## Limitations of family constitutions[4]

It is important to note that family constitutions are **not a cure for all problems**. If a family has a deep-rooted conflict, for instance, the family will need to work on the conflict before they sit down and work on the constitution. Failing to do so will only increase disagreement as soon as an item of the constitution raises a divergence of opinions.

In addition, family constitutions have **little value** when family members **don't voice their opinion** during the process of discussing and formulating the policies or other elements of a constitution. This is unfortunately often seen in families or cultures where respect for the elders is paramount. Family members will usually agree to whatever the elder generation or the patriarch says. For example, two brothers could say that family harmony is one of their key goals to please their father, when in fact they have a hard time working together. Being upfront about an issue can help identify the challenges and work on a solution. **Not voicing opinions**, to the contrary, only creates the illusion that rules and agreements are in place when in fact they are not.

Equally important is the fact that a good number of families **cannot work on the whole constitution in one go**. Often they start with one item that is:

- a pressing matter, such as roles for students, when many next-generation members are about to enter college, as illustrated in the Dania Besher interview,
- an opportunity that presents itself in a timely manner, such as an owners' education program, as illustrated in the interviews with Franz M. Haniel and Sophie Lammerant, or
- a regulatory need, such as opening up the board to independent directors when going public.

Families often initiate work in one area of the constitution, and then add another and another as the need arises. Over time they eventually complete the full circle and have a full constitution signed and approved.

## Family constitutions in family enterprises

In Germany, only about a quarter of business-owning families have a family constitution, according to a study on family constitutions by INTES (the German Academy for Family Enterprises) and PwC Germany.[5] However, about 70% of owner families currently without a constitution plan to create one. The owners have recognized that setting out the strategy and structure of the business-owning family and the family enterprises in a formal document can increase the long-term success of the family and the business.[6]

Developing a family constitution only leads to **lasting change** if all family owners have the same or similar expectations. If there are divergent interests and expectations, families will struggle to develop a family constitution and, if they do so, it will not be as good as it could be. In this case, especially if there are emotional conflicts within the family, the first step is to mediate the conflicts and then, together, develop a solution that might lead to a family constitution.

The main **expectations** when business-owning families decide to develop a family constitution are to achieve the above advantages (Figure 12.1). The study by INTES and PwC confirms that a family constitution leads to peace and stability within a family, as well as cohesion and identification with the business, and an improved family business governance. This indicates that a family constitution leads to higher emotional value. The study also found that 58% of those family enterprises with a family constitution have a **profit margin** of 6% or more, whereas only 45% of family firms without a constitution have such a high profit margin. This leads to the conclusion that business-owning families with a constitution are more satisfied with their rules and procedures than those without a family constitution. So, we can conclude that appropriate family business governance documented in a family constitution leads to higher economic and emotional value, as postulated in Chapter 1.

*family business governance documented in a family constitution leads to higher economic and emotional value*

## Developing a family constitution

A family constitution helps the owners of a family enterprise to document their strategy and structures.[7] During the development of a family constitution, owner families should talk about the owner family's vision of and mission for the family and the business, fundamental aspects of the business model of their company, and family business governance (Figure 12.2).[8]

| 3. Business governance | 4. Family governance | |
|---|---|---|
| • Membership as owners; ownership succession model<br>• Rights and duties of individual owners and the AGM<br>• Board of directors<br>• Management board and management succession<br>• Working in the business<br>• Remuneration and liability<br>• Dividend and fungibility | • Family council and family manager/chief family officer<br>• Family conflict management<br>• Family philanthropic foundation<br>• Family office<br>• Family meeting<br>• Family educational program<br>• Family bank<br>• Family domicile<br>• Family intranet<br>• Family contact with the press/media | III. Roles |
| 1. Vision and mission | 2. Business model | |
| • Values<br>• Goals<br>• History<br>• Culture<br>• Symbols | • Core competences<br>• Wealth distribution<br>• Goals concerning stability, profitability, growth, productivity<br>• Risk, control, compliance management system<br>• Strategic, organizational, and financial principles | |

*(Left margin: II. Structure / I. Strategy)*

FIG 12.2 / A suggested structure for a family constitution

## Content

First of all, business-owning families have to establish a **unique vision and mission**. This means that values and goals are established against a background of the firm's history and culture. Most of the time, those are the only things that continue for generations.

On the basis of the vision and the mission, the **business strategy** should be established. These include concrete goals for stability, profitability, growth, and productivity. In addition, families should establish whether their wealth is focused in a company or whether they diversify. This could be done by the firm acquiring companies from different industries, or with the help of a family office by investing the money in different assets (shares, bonds, natural resources, real estate, etc.). This decision depends on the core competences of the company, as well as the risk appetite of the business-owning family and the family enterprise. All this rests on the definition of strategic, organizational, and financing principles.

Having established the strategy, decisions about the **structure** need to follow. This is the core of family business governance. On the business governance side, the primary questions to answer concern the appropriate number of owners, who can become an owner, and what the owner succession model is. Then the organization of the family needs to be decided – for example, whether to organize the family in branches or consider it to be one family where qualifications, not affiliation to a branch, matter when deciding about family members on the board of directors, for instance. After that, relevant aspects include the annual general meeting (AGM) (see Chapter 4), the board of directors (see Chapter 5), the management board and management succession (see Chapter 6), which all need to be decided. In addition, families have to decide whether family members can work in the company and, if so, on which level. They also need to establish procedures for remuneration, liability, dividends, and the question of when, and under which conditions, an owner can sell his/her shares or be excluded from the owner family.

As well as business governance, a family constitution deals with **family governance**. Here, it is important to establish an institution that is responsible for assuring cohesion and peace like a **family council** (see Chapter 8); many families appoint a **family manager,** who is sometimes called a **chief family officer,** as well. Other common initiatives include a family philanthropic foundation (Chapter 9) and a family office (Chapter 10). Furthermore, a business-owning family should also think about establishing family weekends or family meetings and assemblies, family education measures *a family constitution deals with family governance* (especially for the younger generation), as well as a family bank or a family domicile. A family intranet can be very useful to facilitate communication. Finally, family conflict management procedures should be established to be used in times of conflict.

Through a sound family business governance, many roles have been established. A family member and owner can involve him/herself as a manager, a board member, a family council member, a family manager, a responsible person for the family office, or the manager of the family philanthropic foundation. Family weekends, education measures, running the intranet and so on require active support by family members who care about them. Setting up such initiatives, with the help of a family constitution, expands the ways in which family members can become involved, and hence increase their commitment to and identification with the family firm.

## Process

Business-owning families should be able to develop their constitution, depending on the complexity of the family and the business, and on the level of conflict between owners, in three to eight days of workshops. The development of the constitution should be supported by **external family business consultants**; the INTES study showed that this occurred in 68% of cases.[9] On the basis of the workshop results, the family itself can write the constitution. The next step is to add the relevant aspects into the articles of incorporation. The whole process can take between six and 18 months.

A family constitution does not last forever. Experience indicates that a constitution should be **revised after seven years**. Some families update the constitution each year, if necessary. At the very least, the family constitution should be revised if there is a change in the business or in the family.[10] For instance, if there is a change from a sibling partnership to a cousin consortium, family governance issues become more important. And if there is a change from family-managed to family-monitored, then the role of the nonexecutive members on the board of directors changes significantly. Similarly, changes in the family constitution are necessary in the cases of international expansion, acquisitions, mergers, or initial public offerings (IPOs).

**BEST - PRACTICE RECOMMENDATIONS**

**1** When developing a family constitution, all family owners should be involved – or representatives, in the case of large families.

**2** The main principles of family business governance ("responsible ownership" and "fair process") should be considered when developing a family constitution.

**3** A family constitution should be developed in workshops with the help of family business experts.

**4** All conflicting issues should be discussed openly, preferably before developing a family constitution.

**5** Owner families should use the family constitution to prevent conflicts arising, which means that they should be developed in conflict-free periods.

**6** Owner families should establish a clear vision and mission, as well as develop a sound business strategy.

**7** Owner families should answer the relevant structural aspects in the field of family business governance.

**8** The family constitution should be written by the owners themselves based on the workshop results.

**9** If necessary, the family constitution should be included in the articles of incorporation and other contracts. The more prone an issue is to conflict, the more it should be legally binding.

**10** The family constitution should be revised when there are changes in the business or in the family, and at the very least after seven years.

## EXAMPLE OF A FAMILY CONSTITUTION

*This family constitution has been developed by the Schmidt + Clemens family and has been signed by all family members. We thank the family for giving us their permission to reproduce it here, as a constitution that shows an example of good governance in family enterprises.*

## 1. Preamble

As the S+C family, we stand by our employees, customers, sites, and products. We wish to preserve and continue our 130-year corporate history. We welcome innovation and continue tradition. We identify ourselves with Schmidt + Clemens at all times, and promise to be loyal to one another and treat each other fairly. We look forward to a future together! The family statutes form the basis for the legal contracts.

### 1.1 *Membership*

Owners may be the following
- Conjugal and hereditary descendants,
- Descendants who were adopted before the age of seven.

S+C family members are:
- The owners,

in addition to
- Their spouses (until a possible separation),
- Registered partners,
- And children who are not yet owners but will be entitled to owner status later on,
- And parents if they were formerly owners themselves and left the ownership voluntarily.

### 1.2 Values and objectives

**Values and objectives for the family ownership of S+C**

Principle

- We are S+C owners and wish to ensure that the company remains a family enterprise.

We give the company "professional ownership"

- Unity, loyalty, active participation, emotional identification, and recognition of and respect for our predecessors' achievements.

We expect the following from the company

- Long-term increase in and maintenance of value, appropriate dividends, information and transparency, respect.

**Values and objectives for the S+C family**

Principle

- The S+C family is a cousins' consortium.

We have the following values and objectives

- Openness and honesty, positive conflict culture, respect (including respect of foreign cultures), vitality, understanding ("understanding other people better"), tolerance.

**Values and objectives for the S+C enterprise**

Principle

- S+C is a focused family enterprise.

The following values and objectives are relevant

- Secure independence, lasting value-enhancement, satisfied employees, happy customers, partner-like relationships with suppliers, grateful S+C family.

**Multilingualism within the S+C family?**

Principle

- German is our main language, English is our second language.

Execution

- All corporate documentation for the owners is drawn up in two languages.

- We would like the children to be brought up bilingually (with German or English as their second language).

## 2. Business Governance

### 2.1 *Management (succession)*

The admission requirements for membership of the company management are as follows

- Professional qualification, personal qualification, and agreement with the values and objectives of the S+C family.

The decision regarding the above is made by

- The advisory board.

Special features in the case of family members

- Admitted if deemed suitable.

- Expressly approved of, "because a symbiosis of family membership and suitability creates the best basis for successful corporate positioning in the German, European, and international markets."

- Decisions regarding the admission of family members to the company management shall be taken solely by nonfamily members of the advisory board.

### 2.2 *Advisory Board*

Principle

- The advisory board is responsible for monitoring management.

Structure and Qualifications

- The advisory board consists of five members.

- In the event that family members are simultaneously members of the management, the latter must be chaired and the majority held by someone outside the family.
- Maximum age: 70 years.
- Term of office: three years, re-election possible.
- Vote with a qualified majority (75%).
- Fixed remuneration.
- Personal and specialist skills.

*Note:* It shall not be assumed that family members must have the same specialist skills as nonfamily members.

Tasks

- Appointment and dismissal of the management, drawing up employment contracts for the same (including remuneration).
- Advising and controlling the management in accordance with the family statutes.
- Responsible for transactions subject to approval.
- Approving the annual financial statements.
- Selecting the annual auditor.

**2.3 Working in the business below management, and business relations of an owner with the company**

- Not permitted.
- Exception: in order to induct future managing directors. The following rules apply in this instance:
  - Career outside the company, fixed career path, up-or-out rule.

**2.4 Rights and obligations of the S+C family**

Rights of the owners' meeting

- In principle, owners' resolutions require a simple majority. Important decisions requiring a qualified majority include:
  - Amending the corporate structure and legal form, amending the articles of partnership, capital increases or reductions, admission of new owners, approval of share transfers, election and dismissal of advisory board members, discharging advisory board members, decisions regarding profit allocation deviating from the stipulations in the articles of partnership, all other cases involving amendments to the articles of partnership.

Individual owners have the following

- Rights of participation
  - Participation in the owners' meeting, candidacy rights in company bodies, voting rights, information rights, representation rights.

- Ownership rights
  - Regulation of profit distribution (see regulation in 2.6 and the articles of partnership), profit share and dividends, sale option, termination with severance agreement.

The owners shall be obliged to fulfill the following

- Expectations
  - Emotional identification, active participation, loyalty ("company comes first"; enterprise is no guarantee of livelihood), make provisions for inheritance tax (and other taxes).

- Legal obligations
  - Make marriage/inheritance arrangements in accordance with the articles of partnership and clarify these to the family office; treat all internal corporate issues with the strictest confidence, nondisclosure to third parties.

### 2.5 *Remuneration*

Remuneration principles regarding owners/family members active within the company

- The level of remuneration paid to family members who play an active role in the company must be in line with market standards.
- This will be established by the advisory board (or, more precisely, by nonfamilial members of the latter).
- The salary components and their method of calculation must be announced to all family members at the annual owners' meeting.

### 2.6 *Profit allocation, withdrawals*

Profit allocation

- The decision regarding profit allocation is the responsibility of the owners' meeting.
- The assessment basis is the consolidated result after tax.
- The owners initially receive a tax payout.
- The residual profit will be allocated as follows:

| | Family = payout | Company = reinvestment |
|---|---|---|
| Rule (equity ratio 30 –50%) | ⅓ | ⅔ |
| Equity ratio <30% | ¼ | ¾ |
| Equity ratio >50% | ½ | ½ |

### 2.7 *Participation transferability*

- In principle, participation in the company may only be transferred with approval at the owners' meeting.
- This approval requires a qualified majority in order to be deemed valid.

- Participation may be transferred to those who can become owner without owner approval (see section on membership).

### 2.8 *Renouncing owner status*

- Exclusion on the grounds of just cause (e.g. a blatant contravention of legal corporate obligations).

- Resignation is possible (subsequent resignations by other owners possible within three months), every five years (from 2015 onwards), notice period: 24 months.

- The calculation basis is the "true value."

- Deduction: in the case of voluntary resignation: ⅓, in the case of involuntary resignation: ½.

- Payout in five equal annual installments (earlier payout possible in the case of high liquidity, delay possible in the event of liquidity shortages).

### 3. **Family Governance**

### 3.1 *Interactions with one another*

| Values | Attainment guidelines |
|---|---|
| Openness and honesty | Discussing problems, issues, praising, criticizing |
| | Raising issues promptly and clearly |
| Positive conflict culture and respect | Refrain from personal criticisms |
| | Refrain from putting others in a bad light |
| | Refrain from making negative comments about others |
| Vitality | "We can laugh at ourselves." |
| | Proactive communication |
| Understanding | Put yourselves in the position of others |
| | Active listening (listening, hearing others out, demonstrating interest, asking questions) |

### 3.2 *Dealing with conflicts*

|  | Process | Content (dos and don'ts) |
|---|---|---|
| Start | Raise the issue of the conflict with the conflict partner or family manager<br>Do this promptly, otherwise it will be too late | Choose direct route<br>Do not go behind conflict partner's back |
| During | Sit down with conflict partner.<br>Clarify conflict between conflict partners<br>Appoint an internal arbitrator (e.g. family manager)<br>Appoint an external arbitrator (e.g. mediator) | Ensure that the conflict remains within the family<br>Leave no conflict unresolved<br>Keep uninvolved parties out of the conflict<br>Call in a moderator or mediator, but no lawyers |
| Afterwards | All involved agree that the conflict has been resolved<br>Tell the others that the conflict has been resolved | Do not go over old ground<br>Do not bear a grudge |

### 3.3 *Family Activities*

Joint activities designed to promote solidarity and commitment.

What?

- Owners' meeting with supporting program (e.g. department visit and social activities) – annually.

- Family event/trip to countries with S+C sites or where owners live (South Africa, Israel, USA) – every two years.

How?

- Family event led by different S+C family members in turn, voluntary participation, coordination via family office, costs met by S+C.

### 3.4 *Family Education*

We expect the owners and members of the S+C family to participate in family education, regardless of age.

What?

- Practical experience in the form of internships or similar.
- Company and family history/culture/structure.
- Corporate tools/"owner driving license" (module content to be established).

How?

- Internally at S+C as far as possible, if not possible, internally: use of external options (including individual residential locations).

### 3.5 Family Office

What?

- General support regarding all legal and fiscal issues relating to the company shares (standard advice for owners residing in Germany).
- Asset management.
- Use of the company's purchasing conditions (including insurance policies).

How?

- Full-time family office, to be run separately from the company in the mid-/long term, costs covered by the company.

### 3.6 Family Manager [Chief Family Officer]

- The family manager coordinates all family-related activities (family activity, family education, family office) and may consult members of management who are also partners in the process.
- He/she shall be nominated by all the owners.

## chapter 13

# The Future of Family Business Governance

"In Chinese the same word means both 'crisis' and 'opportunity' ... a crisis always brings opportunities. For a family business like ours, I believe that it means that new energies and success will come from the current challenging times."

Interview with Sophie Lammerant, director of the Bekaert AK family council, Bekaert, Belgium

Sophie Lammerant (née Velge) discusses the implementation of "the Bekaert Academy," a bespoke training program for the fifth generation of the Bekaert family business. She unveils some of the content of the program, how it came to life, and tells why it is so important to train future owners.

A member of the fourth generation, Sophie Lammerant is director of

the Bekaert AK family council, director of FBNet Belgium in charge of the NxGen program, and director of the board of the Family Business Network International.

Bekaert is a world market and technology leader in steel wire transformation and coatings.

It was founded in 1880 in Belgium (Europe), where it is still headquartered. It has customers in over 120 countries and in all markets and sectors. A workforce of 27,000 employees helped reach combined sales in 2012 of €4.4 billion. Bekaert is listed on Euronext® Brussels (BEKB).

*Denise Kenyon-Rouvinez*: **Sophie, a number of years ago your family decided to set up a specific in-house program – the Bekaert Academy – for your next-generation members and future owners of the family business. Could you explain this program ?**

*Sophie Lammerant*: What we call the Bekaert Academy is an ownership education program for all the youngsters of the fifth generation (G5) who are over 18 years old. It is not a leadership program for future executives, nor a training program to become a board member.

The first objective is to enhance the G5 general knowledge about the family business, but we also strive to reinforce their feeling of pride and bonding, their "emotional ownership." Our purpose is to teach them how to become "responsible," and not "entitled" owners. By that, I mean owners who feel committed, who keep informed, who try to understand the business and learn how to analyze its performance; owners who identify with the family values, who try to be good stewards. Owners who aim to protect the business's future and the family wealth in the broader sense: the family assets but also the family unity, its values and culture.

If you don't have a thriving business, you are in trouble, but if you don't have a strong and united family you are also at risk, especially in turbulent times such as now, where the long-term view of stable family ownership is reassuring for the business.

*If you don't have a thriving business, you are in trouble, but if you don't have a strong and united family you are also at risk*

**What made you decide to set up such a program, where did the decision come from, and how long did it take you to set it up?**

We had a first trial when the G5 were too young and not sufficiently involved in the process. It did not work. In the meantime, we continued holding regular informational meetings, sometimes with company visits and family weekends. We created a comprehensive DVD containing Bekaert history and family testimonies, an interactive website, etc. We had an active communication program but nothing special for the next generation.

Ten years later, in 2006, at a family dinner, I was in conversation with some cousins, one of whom was the chairman of our family council, and together we re-launched the idea of an academy. We formed a committee with three members of the fourth generation and three members of the fifth. We discussed the program objectives, core content, and scheduling. We then tested the new proposal and found out that the G5 were interested in the whole program.

**Can you describe the program in more depth?**
We meet two or three times a year in the evening for a formal presentation followed by an informal/interactive session, accompanied by a buffet. So far the Bekaert Academy has covered various topics presented by our chairman, CEO, family directors and even now G5 themselves:

The Bekaert range of products, markets, clients, suppliers, competition, etc.

Strategy and SWOT (Strengths, Weaknesses, Opportunities, Threats) analysis.

Corporate and family governance: the general assembly, the interaction between the business board, the executive committee, and the family council.

Finance: two sessions on balance sheet, P&L statements, key financial ratios. The G5 also analyzed these figures in small groups in order to apply the theory to Bekaert. This was a particularly successful session.

Managing wealth: a next-generation member discussed his own experience in asset management and private equity. And we still have a lot of topics we want to introduce, such as entrepreneurship, as some are interested in starting their own ventures, corporate social responsibility, and Bekaert beliefs and values.

Discussing personal development might be an option at this stage (or even a mentoring program) but now it is the fifth generation that progressively takes the lead.

**How many members do you have in your fifth generation, and how many of them have already gone through the training?**
We have 180 members in the fifth generation among whom 135 [are] over 18 years old. Not all of them have done the training. We have had between 15 and 40 participants per session but not always the same individuals. There is probably a need to repeat parts of the program as some were too young to participate, and others could not attend due to prior commitments.

**What are the requirements for a next-generation member to be involved at the governance level of your family business?**
Up to now there is no member of the fifth generation in the governance of the family business, but this will change. As a matter of fact, only a few family members are involved in the governance. For the moment, the rule is that each family block with a given number of shares is entitled to name two directors at our family council (Bekaert Administratie Kantoor) and one director of the board at the business level.

At the *family council* level, the branches select their representative, paying attention to their family leadership skills, as we need directors with good listening and communication skills who can unite the family behind them.

At the *business board*, we have both family and independent directors who must be at least 35 years old – the reason why there is no fifth gen now. There is a strong focus on competences, experience and commitment, as well as the professional expertise that might be lacking at a particular moment.

*At the business board, we have both family and independent directors who must be at least 35 years old*

The new *legal constraints* in Belgium asking for publicly listed business boards to have 30% of women directors before the end of 2016 will necessitate further steps. This implies deep reflection on our governance system, branch representation, and future role of our next generation. Maybe we'll have to adapt our next-generation educational program to include coaching or induction for future board members. We expect new directors to be able to move up the learning curve quickly.

**What impact has the program had so far, and are you happy about the results?**
The second trial of this program is definitely a success as there is increased motivation, deeper knowledge, more respect, and trust.

Thanks to this Bekaert Academy, G5 are willing to see each other more often. On top of organizing their own events, they massively participated in a family trip to China where 50 of us visited Bekaert operations. The G5 also come more frequently to Family Business Network (FBN) events where they can exchange experiences and best practice with other families in Belgium or abroad.

More importantly, they have become proactive. They initiated a survey to evaluate their generation's willingness to maintain family cohesion and even family control. They tested the satisfaction regarding the current governance structure. At present they are taking charge of the Bekaert Academy program and have created four taskforces to deepen knowledge on the subjects of governance, communication, education, and family. They might soon be integrated in a few committees comprising the two generations, in order to tackle our next challenges. It is time to create new roles for them and to empower them progressively. We are rethinking our governance in order to prepare new family leaders and perhaps take the business into new directions, in order to continue developing family assets.

**Is there anything you would like to add?**
In Chinese the same word means both "crisis" and "opportunity." The yin and yang thinking is that worlds do not oppose but reconcile: a crisis always brings opportunities. For a family business like ours, I believe that it means that new energies and success will come from the current challenging times.

# Future challenges for family businesses

The family firm Zildjian, which began making gongs in the Ottoman Empire in the seventeenth century, is now the preferred maker of cymbals for the world's leading rock drummers. It is a typical example of the themes we have sought to explore and support in this book: how a family enterprise often blends timeless values with adaptation to new markets. Combining tradition with innovation is a paradox, but not a contradiction, and leaders of successful family firms understand this perfectly, as they open in new markets, adopt new technology, but resist short-lived business fashions.

To maintain this, it helps enormously to have **strong family business governance**; which means the right disciplines and strong emotional engagement, as well as reporting structures and constitutions, as defined in Chapter 1 and discussed in subsequent chapters. We hope that this book extends and deepens the knowledge around governance for family-owned firms, enabling them to be economically and emotionally successful and resilient, serving the interests of customers, employees, wider society, and, of course, the families who set up and continue to own or part-own the enterprise. Our recommendations are based on considerable research, and the authors' combined experience, which illustrates the disciplines and strategies most likely to help the family enterprise survive and thrive. A structure for family business governance is neatly captured in Figure 13.1, which is described in more depth in Chapter 1.

In this final chapter, we would like to highlight some of the **emerging challenges** faced by family enterprises during periods of rapid economic development and seismic demographic and cultural changes. First of all, however, we ought to pay tribute to the many responsible and enterprising families with whom we have worked over the years – plus, of course, many others – and pause to acknowledge their wider contribution to economic stability. During a period of immense upheaval, it is striking just how few of the firms to have hit a crisis in recent years have been family-owned.

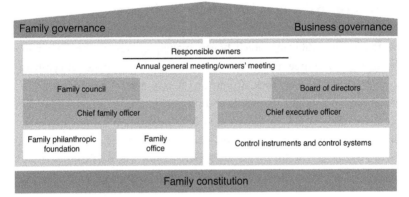

FIG 13.1 **Family business governance**

This is worthy of note. In the West, in particular, the term "nepotism" remains pejorative, yet the commitment to the next generation, and not just the next quarterly results, encourages a focus on the long term that some in the wider corporate world have overlooked. Many family enterprises have succeeded, and remained innovative as well as resilient, not just for decades but for centuries.

A major study in 2012 by the Boston Consulting Group, with the Center for Management and Economic Research at the École Polytechnique, found family-owned firms to be significantly more resilient and successful than a comparative group, certainly when judged over longer time horizons. The researchers identified **seven key characteristics** of the family enterprise:

- They are frugal in good times and bad.
- They set a high bar for capital expenditures.
- They carry little debt.
- They acquire fewer (and smaller) companies.
- They're more diversified.
- They're more international.
- They retain talent better than their competitors do.[1]

The study also found that family firms account for around 30% of all companies with sales in excess of US$1 billion. This is not obvious when one reads the business pages of newspapers. Many family firms have a low profile, not for reasons of secrecy but because they are successful: moreover, they are successful in a quiet, professional way that is based upon authentic service and integrity, building market share through a reputation for honesty and excellence, sustained by word-of-mouth recommendations. This type of business success is far more sustainable than those based upon profits from an asset bubble or temporary fad, and is exemplified in the beautiful testimonies that families agreed to give for this book to illustrate the different parts of family business governance. The best family firms have outlived business fads, economic theories, and entire nation states; there may be much in this book that nonfamily firms can learn from too.

## Governance as evolution

Governance in a family enterprise is evolution, not prescription: it requires consistent discipline, and strategies and structures have to be adapted not only as the business and the family change and grow, but also as the world changes economically, commercially, and demographically. Family enterprises should always know what type of enterprise they are, which challenges they face at each stage, and which structures and decisions they need to work. Governance is always a work in progress, never a completed project.

*Governance in a family enterprise is evolution, not prescription*

Inevitably, family enterprises will have to confront **challenges in the coming years**. Some of the significant emerging issues that have to be faced are:

1. Cultural change and globalization.
2. Demographic change.

3. An increasing role for women, both as owners and executives.
4. Rights of minority shareholders.
5. Transparency, communication, and a professionalized board.

## Cultural change and globalization

A cultural trend that we have begun to detect as advisers in the world of family business is that the generation that is starting to inherit now is less naturally obedient, **more short-term oriented, and more individualistic** than previous ones. Society and corporate culture have become **less patriarchal**, and families will eventually also have to evolve towards that new paradigm. Ironically, this can sometimes be caused by the generosity of the family in funding the best education that money can buy: their offspring, educated in a foreign country and fluent in two or three languages, may not wish to return to their home country to follow in their father's (or, increasingly, their mother's) footsteps. The younger generation appears to be more individualistic, with respect to the clan, but also highly collaborative and internationally oriented, through connections made while studying abroad, and through internet-based social media such as Facebook, Twitter, and so on.

*What will they need to attract their talented next-generation members*

There is an obvious challenge for family enterprises here. What will they need to do to attract their talented next-generation members, keep them motivated, and retain them? This challenge will have a crucial impact on the survival and the growth of their businesses. The 350-year-old Van Eeghen Group, illustrated in Chapter 6, offers some possible insights.

If the direct influence of the patriarch on the clan appears to be diminishing with demographic and cultural changes, exercising influence is more likely to be through education than imposition of will. In many cases, the high educational standards of the younger generation will help this. The profile of Heraeus (Chapter 1) is a good example of a family that has set up a family constitution, encouraging active ownership, and numerous ways of engaging and educating the wider family, such as the young shareholders' meeting, family weekend, and education day.

In addition, the wealth generated by a successful family enterprise can lead to a **sense of entitlement among inheritors** – such is human nature. Education on values also plays an important role in lessening the impact of this phenomenon.

Retention of owners may prove to be a challenge, too, in an age of growing entrepreneurship and global capital. Will someone inheriting shares in the family firm be tempted to sell them to invest in a start-up founded by a fellow university student?

These retention challenges underline the **importance of emotional engagement**, as well as commercial and financial stewardship, for the family enterprise. The strategies and processes we have described are founded on many years of research and experience; they are proven methods that assist family enterprises to achieve cohesion and economic success. This is neatly summarized in Figure 13.2, which describes the strategic objective of "warm hearts, deep pockets."

## Demographic change

Across many parts of the world, human population and lifespan are rising markedly. It is estimated that the first person to live to be 150 has already been born. The trend towards increased longevity in some countries is not tapering off in the 70s and 80s, as many actuaries and health professionals had expected, but is continuing to rise. For all businesses and governments, this creates immense opportunities and challenges, but there are naturally unique aspects for the family enterprise. **How will it affect the concept of succession**, if there are three or four generations of working age, many of whom wish to work in the business? As we saw in the interview with Bruce Halle, founder of Discount Tire (see Chapter 2), his enthusiasm for and involvement in the company did not diminish with age, nor did his energy or ability. He accepted the need to prepare for retirement and

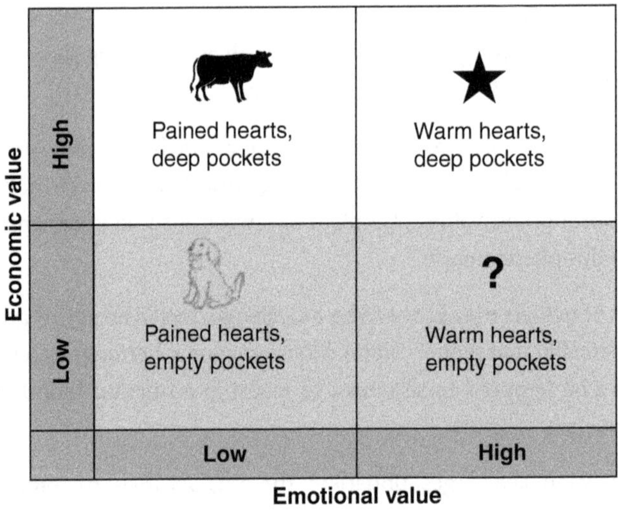

FIG 13.2 Striving for high economic and emotional value in family enterprises

Source: Sharma, P., "An Overview of the Field of Family Business Studies: Current Status and Directions for the Future," *Family Business Review*, 2004, vol. 17. With the kind authorization of Sage Publications, April 11, 2013, licence 3126051505600.

succession as a rational case, rather than an emotional desire to put his feet up.

Can family enterprises retain their talented and ambitious 30-somethings and 40-somethings, who have begun to acquire considerable executive experience, if the 75-year-old tennis-playing, highly active founder/CEO is still at his/her desk at eight o'clock every morning, showing no desire to make way for them? This situation could become more and more common. Older entrepreneur-founders may choose to set up a new business, handing over the established firm to daughters and sons, rather than retire. The choices will expand, but some will be difficult.

Another trend that follows reduced patriarchy is an increasing role for in-laws. Traditionally, those marrying into the business-owning family were held at arm's length from the business, and from formal family decision-making bodies such as the family council. This attitude is changing. Today, in-laws are more likely to be invited to annual general meetings (AGMs) as guests, or may be able to represent the rights of children aged under 18 after the death of the father or mother who had been the owner. Many families give an in-law a formal role, such as chief family officer or member of the family council, and find that this leads to a valuable infusion of new skills and different perspectives.

*Today, in-laws are more likely to be invited to annual general meetings*

## An increasing role for women, both as owners and executives

In Europe, the issue of female representation at a senior level in business has been a political issue that has built up over many years. It has culminated in a law that will require at least **30% of board directors** of listed companies to be women by 2016. This is a relatively short time-span; family enterprises will need to ensure that they are preparing. This will mean **promotion and development of women** who are willing and capable to operate at board level. In practice, the law may also lead to retirement or resignation of male board representatives, for which programs and help may have to be put in place. In many ways, it will be a significant change.

In the USA, Sheryl Sandberg, the chief operating officer of Facebook, has caused a storm with her book *Lean In: Women, Work and the Will to Lead*, which encourages ambitious women to take control of their career, become more assertive, and more comfortable with gaining promotion and exercising authority. Again, the impetus is towards more female presence in the corporate boardroom.

There are similar trends elsewhere. Asia has a high proportion of talented young women in business. **They are strong, motivated, and influential.** Some countries, such as Indonesia, are still influenced by old forms of matriarchy where estates are handed over from women to women. Even in the Middle East, where the role of women has not been prominent in most areas of life, least of all politically, in family enterprises they are key managers, CEOs, board members, and owners, and while their role is still somewhat less visible than the role of their male counterparts, they certainly are a growing force of the region.

## Rights of minority shareholders

A related issue is the question of rights of minority shareholders. In the USA rights have increased markedly in recent years; there has been a similar trend in Europe. Many active groups have emerged to **organize and protect minority owners** of publicly listed companies, and many laws would protect – or even rule in favor of – minority owners in a court battle.

In the Middle East, Asia, and to some extent in Latin America, this is only an emerging trend, but it is gaining ground rapidly. Wherever they are in the world, families need to be aware of these trends and **anticipate the tensions and frictions that may result**, as more and more minority owners will have a voice and have a right to fair and equal treatment.

## Transparency, communication, and a professionalized board

The modern business is more akin to a complex international network of teams than the monolithic structure of the twentieth century. Virtual, international teams and greater use of informal communication, in addition to formal face-to-face meetings, are natural consequences of globalization and internet-based technology. These changes call for a very different approach to communication. Engaging people – all stakeholders – remains of paramount importance, but can be a greater challenge for two reasons: people tend to be more geographically dispersed and, as noted above, they may be more mobile and ambitious. Owners also have high expectations of transparency and adherence to fair process. The Haniel family has, for example, established a family intranet (see profile,

*Engaging people – all stakeholders – remains of paramount importance*

Chapter 4) – an excellent initiative to maintain communication, engage the younger generation, and encourage cohesion in the family and in the enterprise. Successful families use technology to enhance their timeless family values.

As the preceding chapters emphasize, **professionalization of the board is increasingly recognized as essential** – not only for managing the business, but for safeguarding the family's interests. Collaboration between the board and the family council, which defines crucial matters such as risk appetite, investment strategies, long-term aims, and so on, is essential.

Professionalization should not be seen as a technocratic clamping down on the entrepreneurial spirit or the values and vision of the founder. On the contrary, it is a proven method to help safeguard these. A fully professional approach regards emotional engagement and retention of values as being of equal importance to shrewd investments and fiscal responsibility. They are complementary, not opposite, challenges.

## Generosity: an abiding characteristic

Finally, as authors we wish to pay tribute to the many inspiring leaders of family enterprises with whom we have worked over the years. We have concluded that one of their abiding qualities is generosity: **generosity of time, of money, of ideas, of services** – and, in the cases of the many companies with philanthropic foundations, generosity to society. For the most part, it is fine to be modest about such contributions, but occasionally it is necessary to recognize the achievements of family enterprises, not just for themselves, but for wider society.

# Notes and References

## Chapter 1

1. This chapter is based on the following articles as well as books and the literature mentioned there: Koeberle-Schmid, A., Fahrion, H.-J., & Witt, P. (eds.) (2012), *Family Business Governance – Erfolgreiche Führung von Familienunternehmen*, 2nd edn., Berlin: Erich Schmidt; Koeberle-Schmid, A., & Grottel, B. (eds.) (2013), *Familienunternehmen erfolgreich führen*, Berlin: Erich Schmidt; Koeberle-Schmid, A., Schween, K., & May, P. (2011), "Governance Kodex für Familienunternehmen in der Praxis – Ergebnisse einer Studie über Familienverfassungen," *Betriebs-Berater* 41, pp. 2499–2506; Koeberle-Schmid, A., & May, P. (2011), "Governance in Familienunternehmen – Führung und Kontrolle situationsadäquat regeln," *Zeitschrift Risk, Fraud & Compliance* 2, pp. 54–61; May, P. (2012), *Erfolgsmodell Familienunternehmen*, Hamburg: Murmann.

2. Chua, J., Chrisman, J., & Sharma, P. (1999), "Defining the family business by behavior," in *Entrepreneurship Theory and Practice* 23/4, pp. 19–39; May, P. (2009), "Familienunternehmen erfolgreich führen – Von der Inhaber-Strategie zur Unternehmens-Strategie," *Zeitschrift für Betreibswirtschaft Special Issue* 2, pp. 113–126.

3. May, P., & Koeberle-Schmid, A. (2011), "Die drei Dimensionen eines Familienunternehmens: Teil I," *Betriebswirtschaftliche Forschung und Praxis* 6, pp. 656–672; May, P., & Koeberle-Schmid, A. (2012), "Die drei Dimensionen eines Familienunternehmens: Teil II," *Betriebswirtschaftliche Forschung und Praxis* 1, pp. 52–72

4. Björnberg, A. (2010), "The critical pathway between the family business and the next generation: lessons in emotional ownership," *Family Firm Institute Practitioner* 6, p. 5.

5. Sharma, P. (2004), "An overview of the field of family business studies: Current status and directions for the future," *Family Business Review* 17, pp. 1–36; Chrisman, J., Chua, J., & Sharma, P. (2005), "Trends and directions in the development of a strategic management theory of the family firm," *Entrepreneurship Theory and Practice* 29, pp. 555–575; Debicki, B., Matherne, C., Kellermanns, F., & Chrisman, J. (2009), "Family business research in the new millennium: An overview of the who, the where, the what and the why," *Family

*Business Review* 22, pp. 151–166; Sharma, P., Chrisman, J., & Gersick, K. (2012), "25 years of *Family Business Review*: Reflections on the past and perspectives for the future," *Family Business Review* 25, pp. 5–15.

6. Aronoff, C., & Ward, J. (1996), *Family Business Governance: Maximizing Family and Business Potential*, 3rd edn., Marietta, GA: Family Business Publishers.

7. Sharma, P., Chrisman, J., & Gersick, K. (2012), "25 years of *Family Business Review*: Reflections on the past and perspectives for the future," *Family Business Review* 25, pp. 5–15.

8. Koeberle-Schmid, A., Fahrion, H.-J., & Witt, P. (2012), *Family Business Governance – Erfolgreiche Führung von Familienunternehmen*, 2nd edn., Berlin: Erich Schmidt.

9. Koeberle-Schmid, A., Schween, K., & May, P. (2011), "Governance Kodex für Familienunternehmen in der Praxis – Ergebnisse einer Studie über Familienverfassungen," *Betriebs-Berater* 41, pp. 2499–2506; May, P., Koeberle-Schmid, A., & Schnitzhofer, W. (2011), "Gutes Management sichern: Ein Kodex für Familienunternehmen," *Compliance-Praxis* 3, pp. 10–13; May, P., & Koeberle-Schmid, A. (2011), "Auf die Inhaber kommt es an," *Der Aufsichtsrat* 6, p. 81; Koeberle-Schmid, A., & May, P. (2011), "Governance in Familienunternehmen – Führung und Kontrolle situationsadäquat regeln," *Zeitschrift Risk, Fraud & Compliance* 2, pp. 54–61; May, P., & Koeberle-Schmid, A. (2011), "Governance Kodex als Leitlinie für die verantwortungsvolle Führung von Familienunternehmen," *Der Betrieb* 9, pp. 485–491.

10. Hack, A. (2009), "Governance Kodex für Familienunternehmen," *UnternehmberBrief* 3, p. 7.

11. Hack, A. (2009), "Sind Familienunternehmen anders? Eine kritische Bestandsaufnahme des aktuellen Forschungsstands," *Zeitschrift für Betriebswirtschaft Special Issue* 2, pp. 1–29; Björnberg, A., & Nicholson, N. (2008), *Emotional Ownership – The Critical Pathway Between the Next Generation and the Family Firm*, London: Institute for Family Business; Zellweger, T., & Astrachan, J (2008), "On the emotional value of owning a firm," *Family Business Review* 21, pp. 347–363; Zellweger, T., & Sieger, P. (2009), *Emotional Value – Der emotionale Wert, ein Unternehmen zu besitzen*, St. Gallen: Ernst & Young.

12. Zellweger, T., & Sieger, P. (2009), *Emotional Value – Der emotionale Wert, ein Unternehmen zu besitzen*, St. Gallen: Ernst & Young.

13. Björnberg, A., & Nicholson, N. (2008), *Emotional Ownership – The Critical Pathway Between the Next Generation and the Family Firm*, London: Institute for Family Business; Zellweger, T., & Sieger, P. (2009), *Emotional Value – Der emotionale Wert, ein Unternehmen zu besitzen*, St. Gallen: Ernst & Young.

14. Koeberle-Schmid, A., Fahrion, H.-J., & Witt, P. (2012), *Family Business Governance – Erfolgreiche Führung von Familienunternehmen*, 2nd edn., Berlin: Erich Schmidt; Aronoff, C., & Ward, J. (1996), *Family Business Governance: Maximizing Family and Business Potential*, 3rd edn., Marietta: Family Business Publishers; Koeberle-Schmid, A.

(2008), *Family Business Governance,* Wiesbaden: Gabler; Koeberle-Schmid, A., & May, P. (2011), "Governance in Familienunternehmen," *Zeitschrift Risk, Fraud & Compliance* 2, S. 54–61.

15. Lambrecht, J., & Lievens, J. (2009), *Responsible Ownership of the Family Business,* Brussels-Kortrijk: FBNet Belgium; Aronoff, C., & Ward, J. (2002), *Family Business Ownership – How to be an Effective Shareholder,* Marietta: Family Enterprise Publishers.

16. Heyden, V.d.L., Blondel, C., & Carlock, R. (2005), "Fair process: striving for justice in family businesses," *Family Business Review* 18, pp. 1–21.

17. Lambrecht, J., & Lievens, J. (2009), *Responsible Ownership of the Family Business,* Brussels-Kortrijk: FBNet Belgium; Koeberle-Schmid, A., & May, P. (2011), "Governance in Familienunternehmen," *Zeitschrift Risk, Fraud & Compliance* 2, pp. 54–61.

18. Heyden, V.d.L., Blondel, C., & Carlock, R. (2005), "Fair process: striving for justice in family businesses," *Family Business Review* 18, pp. 1–21.

19. Kenyon-Rouvinez, D., & Ward, J. (2005), *Family Business Key Issues,* Basingstoke: Palgrave.

## Chapter 2

1. Poza, E. (2012), adapted from *Family Governance: How Leading Families are Managing the Challenges of Wealth.* White paper published by Credit Suisse Private Banking and Thunderbird School of Global Management. June 26, 2012, Zurich, Switzerland. See adaptations of the material also in Poza, E., & Daugherty, M. (2014), *Family Business,* 4th edn., Mason, OH: South-Western/Cengage Learning.

2. Cadbury, A. (2000), *Family Firms and Their Governance: Creating Tomorrow's Company from Today's,* London: Egon Zehnder International.

3. Poza, E., & Daugherty, M. (2014), *Family Business,* 4th edn., Mason, OH: South-Western/Cengage Learning.

4. Molin, A. (2013) IKEA chief takes aim at red tape, *The Wall Street Journal,* p. B3, January 23.

5. Stewart, A., & Hitt, M. (2012), "Why can't a family business be more like a nonfamily business? Modes of professionalization in family firms," *Family Business Review* 25(1), pp. 58–86.

## Chapter 3

1. Some of the material in this section is adapted from Poza, E., & Daugherty, M. (2014), *Family Business,* 4th edn., Mason, OH: South-Western/Cengage Learning.

# Chapter 4

1. Waitley, D.E., American motivational speaker and writer.
2. Aronoff, C.E., & Ward, J.L. (2002), *Family Business Ownership: How to be an Effective Shareholder*, Basingstoke: Palgrave Macmillan.
3. Björnberg, Å., & Nicholson, N. (2008), *Emotional Ownership – The Critical Pathway Between the Next Generation and the Family Firm*, London: Institute for Family Business (IFB).
4. De Visscher, F., Aronoff, C.E., & Ward, J.L. (2010), *Financing Transitions: Managing Capital and Liquidity in the Family Business*, Family Business Leadership Series no. 7, 2nd edn., Basingstoke: Palgrave Macmillan.
5. Schwarz, N.E. (2004), *Family Business by the Numbers: How Financial Statements Impact Your Business*, Family Business Leadership Series, Basingstoke: Palgrave Macmillan.
6. Aronoff, C.E., & Ward, J.L. (2002), "Six kinds of owners," in *Family Business Ownership: How to be an Effective Shareholder*, Basingstoke, Palgrave Macmillan, pp. 7–9.
7. Kenyon-Rouvinez, D. (2011), *The Aftermath of an IPO – What families in Business Ought to Know Before they go Public*, Tharawat magazine, 9, January, pp. 60–65.

# Chapter 5

1. This chapter is based on the following articles and the literature mentioned in them: Koeberle-Schmid, A. (2008), *Family Business Governance: Aufsichtsgremium und Familienrepräsentanz*, Wiesbaden: Gabler; Koeberle-Schmid, A., Brockhoff, K., & Witt, P. (2009), "Performanceimplikationen von Aufsichtsgremien in deutschen Familienunternehmen," *Zeitschrift für Betriebswirtschaft Special Issue 2*, pp. 83–111; Koeberle-Schmid, A., Groß, J., & Lehmann-Tolkmitt, A. (2011), "Der Beirat als Garant guter Governance im Familienunternehmen," *Betriebs-Berater 15*, pp. 899–906; Koeberle-Schmid, A. (2012), "Professionelle Aufsichtsgremien: Aufgaben, Typen und Ausgestaltung," in Koeberle-Schmid, A., Fahrion, H.-J., & Witt, P. (eds.), *Family Business Governance – Erfolgreiche Führung von Familienunternehmen*, 2nd edn., Berlin: Erich Schmidt, pp. 120–154.
2. May, P. (2012), *Erfolgsmodell Familienunternehmen*, Hamburg: Murmann; May, P., & Koeberle-Schmid, A. (2011), "Die drei Dimensionen eines Familienunternehmens: Teil I," *Betriebswirtschaftliche Forschung und Praxis 6*, pp. 656–672 and May, P., & Koeberle-Schmid, A. (2012), "Die drei Dimensionen eines Familienunternehmens: Teil II," *Betriebswirtschaftliche Forschung und Praxis 1*, pp. 52–72.
3. Schweinsberg, K., & Laschet, C. (2010), *Haftung und Compliance in Familienunternehmen*, Bonn: INTES Akademie; Becker, W., Reker, J., & Ulrich, P. (2010), "Beiräte im Mittelstand – Ergebnis einer Unternehmensbefragung," *Der Aufsichtsrat 7*, pp. 154–155.

4. Zahra, S., & Pearce, J. (1989), "Boards of directors and corporate financial performance: a review and integrative model," *Journal of Management* 15, pp. 291–334; Ward, J. (1991), *Creating Effective Boards for Private Enterprises*, San Francisco: Jossey-Bass; Aronoff, C., & Ward, J. (1996), *Family Business Governance: Maximizing Family and Business Potential*, 3rd edn., Marietta: Family Business Publishers; Forbes, D., & Milliken, F. (1999), "Cognition and corporate governance: Understanding boards of directors as strategic decision-making groups," *Academy of Management Review* 24, pp. 489–505; Mustakallio, M., Autio, E., & Zahra, S. (2002), "Relational and contractual governance in family firms: effects on strategic decision making," *Family Business Review* 15, pp. 205–222; Heuvel, J. v. d., Gils, A. v., & Voordeckers, W. (2006), "Board roles in small and medium-sized family businesses: performance and importance," *Corporate Governance: An International Review* 14, pp. 467–485; Wiedemann, A., & Kögel, R. (2008), *Beirat und Aufsichtsrat im Familienunternehmen*, Munich: Beck; Koeberle-Schmid, A. (2008), *Family Business Governance: Aufsichtsgremium und Familienrepräsentanz*, Wiesbaden: Gabler; Koeberle-Schmid, A., Brockhoff, K., & Witt, P. (2009), "Performanceimplikationen von Aufsichtsgremien in deutschen Familienunternehmen," *Zeitschrift für Betriebswirtschaft Special Issue* 2, pp. 83–111.

5. Koeberle-Schmid, A., Groß, J., & Lehmann-Tolkmitt, A. (2011), "Der Beirat als Garant guter Governance im Familienunternehmen," *Betriebs-Berater* 15, pp. 899–906.

6. Lehmann-Tolkmitt, A. (2008), "Zehn Empfehlungen für einen effektiven Beirat im Familienunternehmen," *Der Aufsichtsrat* 1, pp. 6–8; Koeberle-Schmid, A., Groß, J., & Lehmann-Tolkmitt, A. (2011), "Der Beirat als Garant guter Governance im Familienunternehmen," *Betriebs-Berater* 15, pp. 899–906.

7. Aronoff, C., & Ward, J. (1996), *Family Business Governance: Maximizing Family and Business Potential*, 3rd edn., Marietta: Family Business Publishers; May, P., & Sieger, G. (2000), "Der Beirat im Familienunternehmen zwischen Beratung, Kontrolle, Ausgleich und Personalfindung – Eine kritische Bestandsaufnahme," in Jeschke, D., Kirchdörfer, R., & Lorz, R. (eds.), *Planung, Finanzierung und Kontrolle im Familienunternehmen*, Munich: Beck, pp. 245–255; Huse, M. (2005), "Accountability and creating accountability: a framework for exploring behavioural perspectives of corporate governance," *British Journal of Management* 16: pp. S65–S79; Lane, S., Astrachan, J., Keyt, A., & McMillan, K. (2006), "Guidelines for family business boards of directors," *Family Business Review* 19, pp. 147–167; Koeberle-Schmid, A. (2008), *Family Business Governance: Aufsichtsgremium und Familienrepräsentanz*, Wiesbaden: Gabler; Koeberle-Schmid, A. (2008), "Aufsichtsratsaufgaben in Familienunternehmen," *Der Aufsichtsrat* 7, pp. 101–103; Kormann, H. (2009), *Beiräte in der Verantwortung*, Berlin: Springer; Garratt, B. (2010), *The Fish Rots from the Head – Developing Effective Board Directors*, 3rd edn., London: Profile Books.

8. Schulze, W., Lubatkin, M., Dino, R., & Buchholtz, A. (2001), "Agency relationships in family firms: theory and evidence," *Organization Science* 12, pp. 99–116; Schulze, W., Lubatkin, M., & Dino, R. (2003), "Exploring the agency consequences of ownership dispersion among the directors of private family firms," *Academy of Management Journal* 46, pp. 179–194.

9. Karra, N., Tracey, P., & Phillips, N. (2006), "Altruism and agency in the family firm: exploring the role of family, kinship, and ethnicity," *Entrepreneurship Theory and Practice* 30, pp. 861–877.

10. Koeberle-Schmid, A., Groß, J., & Lehmann-Tolkmitt, A. (2011), "Der Beirat als Garant guter Governance im Familienunternehmen," *Betriebs-Berater* 15, pp. 899–906.

11. Sirmon, D., & Hitt, M. (2003), "Managing resources: linking unique resources, management, and wealth creation in family firms," *Entrepreneurship Theory and Practice* 27, pp. 339–358.

12. Kormann, H. (2009), *Beiräte in der Verantwortung*, Berlin: Springer.

13. Ward, J. (1991), *Creating Effective Boards for Private Enterprises*, San Francisco: Jossey-Bass.

14. Le Breton-Miller, I., Miller, D., & Steier, L. (2004), "Toward an integrative model of effective FOB succession," *Entrepreneurship Theory and Practice* 28, pp. 305–328.

15. Koeberle-Schmid, A., Lehmann-Tolkmitt, A., & Groß, J. (2012), "Der Nachfolge-Beirat im Familienunternehmen," *FuS* 4, pp. 135–141.

16. Arregle, J.-L., Hitt, M., Sirmon, D., & Very, P. (2007), "The development of organizational social capital: attributes of family firms," *Journal of Management Studies* 44, pp. 73–95.

17. Lane, S., Astrachan, J., Keyt, A., & McMillan, K. (2006), "Guidelines for family business boards of directors," *Family Business Review* 19, pp. 147–167.

18. For contingent factors, please refer to the following: Ward, J. (1991), *Creating Effective Boards for Private Enterprises*, San Francisco: Jossey-Bass; Aronoff, C., & Ward, J. (1996), *Family Business Governance: Maximizing Family and Business Potential*, 3rd edn., Marietta: Family Business Publishers; Lane, S., Astrachan, J., Keyt, A., & McMillan, K. (2006), "Guidelines for family business boards of directors," *Family Business Review* 19, pp. 147–167; Wiedemann, A., & Kögel, R. (2008), *Beirat und Aufsichtsrat im Familienunternehmen*, Munich: Beck; Kormann, H. (2009), *Beiräte in der Verantwortung*, Berlin: Springer; Koeberle-Schmid, A., Groß, J., & Lehmann-Tolkmitt, A. (2011), "Der Beirat als Garant guter Governance im Familienunternehmen," *Betriebs-Berater* 15, pp. 899–906; Garratt, B. (2010), *The Fish Rots from the Head – Developing Effective Board Directors*, 3rd edn., London: Profile Books.

19. Aronoff, C., & Ward, J. (2002), "Outside directors: how they help you," in Aronoff, C., Astrachan, J., & Ward, J. (eds.), *Family Business Sourcebook: A Guide for Families Who Own Businesses and the Professionals Who Serve Them*, vol. 3, Marietta: Family Enterprise Publishers, pp. 254–255.

20. Nicholson, G., & Kiel, G. (2004), "A framework for diagnosing board effectiveness," *Corporate Governance: An International Review* 12, pp. 442–460.

21. May, P., & Sieger, G. (2000), "Der Beirat im Familienunternehmen zwischen Beratung, Kontrolle, Ausgleich und Personalfindung – Eine kritische Bestandsaufnahme," in Jeschke, D., Kirchdörfer, R., & Lorz, R. (eds.), *Planung, Finanzierung und Kontrolle im Familienunternehmen*, Munich: Beck, pp. 245–255; Lehmann-Tolkmitt, A. (2008), "Zehn Empfehlungen für einen effektiven Beirat im Familienunternehmen," *Der Aufsichtsrat* 1, pp. 6–8.

22. Pohle, K., & Werder, A. v. (2005), "Leitfaden Best Practice von Bilanzprüfungsausschüssen (Audit Committees)," *Der Betrieb* 58, pp. 237–239.
23. Achenbach, C., May, P., Rieder, G., & Eiben, J. (2008), *Beiräte in Familienunternehmen*, Bonn: INTES Akademie.
24. Minichilli, A., Gabrielsson, J., & Huse, M. (2007), "Board evaluations: Making a fit between the purpose and the system," *Corporate Governance: An International Review* 15, pp. 609–622.

# Chapter 6

1. Based on a chapter written by Kenyon-Rouvinez, D. in *Family Business Governance, Erfolgreiche Führung von Familienunternehmen*, Erich Schmidt Verlag, 2010, with permission received from Erich Schmidt Verlag
2. Denison D., Leif C., & Ward J.L. (2004), "Culture in family-owned enterprises: recognizing and leveraging unique strengths," *Family Business Review* XVII(1), March.
3. Kenyon-Rouvinez D., Adler, G., Corbetta, G., & Cuneo, G. (2002), *Sharing Wisdom, Building Values – Letters from Family Business Owners to their Successors*, Basingstoke: Palgrave Macmillan, pp. 143–147.
4. Marcy Syms (2007), CEO, Syms Corp., interview with Patricia Olsen, "At the helm," *Family Business*, spring.
5. Ward, J.L. (1987), *Keeping the Family Business Healthy*, San Francisco: Jossey-Bass.
6. Howdy Holmes (2008), president, Chelsea Milling Co., "Shake-up at the baking mix company," *Family Business*, winter.
7. Schuman, A.M. (2006), *Nurturing the Talent to Nurture the Legacy: Career Development in the Family Business*, New York: Family Business Leadership Series, FBCG Publications/Palgrave Macmillan.
8. Kenyon-Rouvinez, D. (2006), *Who, Me? Family Business Succession. A Practical Guide for the Next Generation*, New York: Family Business Leadership Series, FBCG Publications/Palgrave Macmillan, Chapter 7.
9. Neubauer F., & Lank A.G. (1998), *The Family Business. Its Governance for Sustainability*, Basingstoke: Macmillan Business.

# Chapter 7

1. Institute of Internal Auditors: Standards, IPFF 2013, English, 1010, p. 6.
2. Forbes Insights, commissioned by Ernst & Young (2012), *Global Survey About the Evolving Role of Internal Audit*.
3. Definition of risk according to ISO 31000.
4. Definition according to businessdictionary.com.

# Chapter 8

1. Adapted from Chapter 9, "Family governance," in Poza, E., & Daugherty, M. (2014), *Family Business*, 4th edn., Mason, OH: South-Western/Cengage Learning.
2. The case is factually accurate. The names of the company and the family have been changed to protect the privacy of the family.
3. Heck, R. (2004), "A commentary on 'Entrepreneurship in family vs. non-family firms: a resource-based analysis of the effect of organizational culture'," by Zahara, S., Hayton, J.C., & Salvato, C., *Entrepreneurship Theory and Practice*, 28(4), pp. 383–389.
4. Stewart, A. (2003), "Help one another, use one another: toward an anthropology of family business," *Entrepreneurship Theory and Practice*, summer, pp. 383–396.
5. LaChapelle, K., & Barnes, L. (1998), "The trust catalyst in family-owned businesses," *Family Business Review* 11(1), pp. 1–17.
6. Hoover's Online & Orbis Database, Company Profiles, Cargill (2013). See http://www.hoovers.com and https://orbis.bvdinfo.com/version-201372/home.serv?product=orbisneo.

# Chapter 9

1. The Foundation Center, *Key Facts on Family Foundations 2010*, February 2012.
2. Skloot, E. (2007), *Beyond the Money – Reflections on Philanthropy, the Nonprofit Sector and Civic Life, 1999–2006*, New York: The Surdna Foundation, pp. 6–16.
3. *Telegraph* (2010), "Children in single parent families worse behaved," October 15.
4. Hand in Hand International; www.hihinternational.org.
5. Cordaid; http://www.cordaid.org/en/.
6. Inspiring Impact, *The Code of Good Impact Practice*, draft for consultation, UK, March 2013.
7. Handy, C., & Handy, E. (2007), *The New Philanthropists*, London: Heinemann.
8. Médecins sans Frontières (MSF)/Doctors without Borders; see www.msf.org.
9. Red Cross; http://www.icrc.org.
10. King Baudouin Foundation; http://www.kbs-frb.be.
11. Ashoka; http://www.ashoka.org.
12. Wise; http://www.wise.net.

# Chapter 10

1. BBC News, November 2, 2012.
2. Gibson, K., Blouin, B., & Kiersted, M. (1999), *The Inheritor's Inner Landscape: How Heirs Feel*, Sedalia, CO: Trio Press.

3. Hartley, B.B. (2006), *Unexpected Wealth – Fire Drill*, Venice, FL: Cambio Press. Based on Hughes, J.E., Jr. (2004), *Family Wealth – Keeping It in the Family*, New York: Bloomberg Press – Jay uses "intellectual capital" instead of "social capital" as a third form of capital.

4. Jaffe, D., & Roux, L. (2010), FFI Certificate Program of Family Wealth Advising (FWA); www.ffi.org.

5. Rand, A. (Russian-American novelist, 1905–1982), *Atlas Shrugged* (novel first published in 1957).

6. Family Office Exchange (FOX) (2012), *Developing a Long-Term View for Family Wealth Strategy*; www.familyoffice.com.

7. Virgin Green Fund; http://www.virgingreenfund.com.

8. Alterra Impact Finance; www.alterraimpactfinance.com.

9. Amit, R., & Liechtenstein, H. (2009), *Benchmarking the Single Family Office: Identifying the Performance Drivers*, Wharton Global Alliance.

10. Kenyon-Rouvinez, D., Riccard, M., Lombard, T., Ward J.L., & Gabs (2007), *Why Me? Wealth: Creating, Receiving and Passing it On*, Marietta: Family Enterprise Publishers.

11. Bodnar, J. (2005), *Raising Money Smart Kids*, Wokingham: Kaplan Publishing.

## Chapter 11

1. This chapter is based on the following articles, as well as books and the literature mentioned therein: Koeberle-Schmid, A., Fahrion, H.-J., & Witt, P. (eds.) (2012), *Family Business Governance – Erfolgreiche Führung von Familienunternehmen*, 2nd edn., Berlin: Erich Schmidt; Koeberle-Schmid, A., & Grottel, B. (eds.) (2013), *Familienunternehmen erfolgreich führen*, Berlin: Erich Schmidt; Koeberle-Schmid, A., Schween, K., & May, P. (2011), "Governance Kodex für Familienunternehmen in der Praxis – Ergebnisse einer Studie über Familienverfassungen," *Betriebs-Berater* 41, pp. 2499–2506; May, P., Koeberle-Schmid, A., & Schnitzhofer, W. (2011), "Gutes Management sichern: Ein Kodex für Familienunternehmen," *Compliance-Praxis* 3, pp. 10–13; May, P., & Koeberle-Schmid, A. (2011), "Auf die Inhaber kommt es an," *Der Aufsichtsrat* 6, p. 81; Koeberle-Schmid, A., & May, P. (2011), "Governance in Familienunternehmen – Führung und Kontrolle situationsadäquat regeln," *Zeitschrift Risk, Fraud & Compliance* 2, pp. 54–61; May, P., & Koeberle-Schmid, A. (2011), "Governance Kodex als Leitlinie für die verantwortungsvolle Führung von Familienunternehmen," *Der Betrieb* 9, pp. 485–491.

2. Witt, P. (2003), *Corporate Governance-Systeme im Wettbewerb*, Wiesbaden: Deutscher Universitäts-Verlag; Witt, P. (2008), "Corporate Governance in Familienunternehmen," *Zeitschrift für Betriebswirtschaft* 78, Ergänzungsheft 2, pp. 1–19.

3. May, P., & Koeberle-Schmid, A. (2011), "Governance Kodex als Leitlinie für die verantwortungsvolle Führung von Familienunternehmen," *Der Betrieb* 9, pp. 485–491.

4. For an overview of codes worldwide, see: http://www.ecgi.org/codes/all_codes.php

5. More information about the code can be found at: http://www.kodex-fuer-familienunterne hmen.de

6. May, P., & Koeberle-Schmid, A. (2011), "Governance Kodex als Leitlinie für die verantwortungsvolle Führung von Familienunternehmen," *Der Betrieb* 9, pp. 485–491.

7. Hack, A. (2009), "Sind Familienunternehmen anders? Eine kritische Bestandsaufnahme des aktuellen Forschungsstands," *Zeitschrift für Betriebswirtschaft Special Issue* 2, pp. 1–29; Koeberle-Schmid, A., Brockhoff, K., & Witt, P. (2009), "Performanceimpliktionen von Aufsichtsgremien in deutschen Familienunternehmen," *Zeitschrift für Betriebswirtschaft Special Issue* 2, pp. 83–111; Björnberg, A., & Nicholson, N. (2008), *Emotional Ownership – The Critical Pathway Between the Next Generation and the Family Firm*, London: Institute for Family Business; Zellweger, T., & Sieger, P. (2009), *Emotional Value – Der emotionale Wert, ein Unternehmen zu besitzen*, St. Gallen: Ernst & Young.

8. Baron Buysse (2009), Buysse Code II, Corporate Governance – Recommendations for nonlisted enterprises, p. 6.

9. See also http://www.kodex-fuer-familienunternehmen.de.

10. Lange, K. (2009), "Kodex und Familienverfassung als Mittel der Corporate Governance in Familienunternehmen," in Kirchdörfer, R., Lorz, R., Wiedemann, A., Kögel, R., & Frohnmayer, T. (eds.), *Familienunternehmen in Recht, Wirtschaft, Politik und Gesellschaft*, Munich: Beck, pp. 135–149; May, P., & Koeberle-Schmid, A. (2011), "Governance Kodex als Leitlinie für die verantwortungsvolle Führung von Familienunternehmen," *Der Betrieb* 9, pp. 485–491.

11. May, P., & Koeberle-Schmid, A. (2011), "Die drei Dimensionen eines Familienunternehmens: Teil I," *Betriebswirtschaftliche Forschung und Praxis* 6, pp. 656–672; May, P., & Koeberle-Schmid, A. (2012), "Die drei Dimensionen eines Familienunternehmens: Teil II," *Betriebswirtschaftliche Forschung und Praxis* 1, pp. 52–72; May, P. (2012), *Erfolgsmodell Familienunternehmen*, Hamburg: Murmann.

## Chapter 12

1. This chapter is partly based on the following articles and the titles mentioned there: May, P. (2008), "Leading the family business – Why creating an owner strategy must come first for family businesses," in Büchel, B., Read, S., Moncef, A., & Coughlan, S. (eds.) (2009), *Riding the Wings of Global Change*, Lausanne: IMG, pp. 83–89; May, P. (2009), "Familienunternehmen erfolgreich führen – Von der Inhaber-Strategie zur Unternehmens-Strategie," *Zeitschrift für Betriebswirtschaft Special Issue* 2, pp. 113–126; Schween, K., Koeberle-Schmid, A., Bartels, P., & Hack, A. (2011), *Die Familienverfassung – Zukunftssicherung für Familienunternehmen: Ergebnisse einer Studie*, Bonn: INTES Akademie; Koeberle-Schmid,

A., Schween, K., & May, P. (2011), "Governance Kodex für Familienunternehmen in der Praxis – Ergebnisse einer Studie über Familienverfassungen," *Betriebs-Berater* 41, pp. 2499–2506; May, P., Schween, K., & Koeberle-Schmid, A. (2011), "Inhaber-Strategie: Zukunftssicherung für Familie und Unternehmen," in Langenscheidt, F., & May, P. (eds.), *Aus Bester Familie*, 2nd edn., Cologne: Deutsche Standards EDITIONEN, pp. 16–21; May, P. (2012), *Erfolgsmodell Familienunternehmen*, Hamburg: Murmann; May, P., Schween, K., & Koeberle-Schmid, A. (2012), "Das Strategie-Konzept für Familienunternehmen – Mit einer Inhaber-Strategie zum langfristigen Erfolg über Generationen," in *Handbuch der Unternehmensberatung*, 18. *Erg.-Lfg.* X/12, 3190, pp. 1–25; Koeberle-Schmid, A., & Schween, K. (2012), "Familienverfassungen individuell erarbeiten – Hinweise für Unternehmerfamilien vor dem Hintergrund der Konfliktprävention," *KonfliktDynamik* 1/4, pp. 320–327; May, P., & Koeberle-Schmid, A. (2013), "Führungsstrukturen in einer Familienverfassung dokumentieren," in Koeberle-Schmid, A., & Grottel, B. (eds.), *Führung von Familienunternehmen*, Berlin: Erich Schmidt.

2. Lambrecht, J., & Lievens, J. (2009) *Responsible Ownership of the Family Business*, Brussels-Kortrijk: FBNet Belgium; Aronoff, C., & Ward, J. (2002), *Family Business Ownership – How To be an Effective Shareholder*, Marietta: Family Enterprise Publishers; Heyden, V.d.L., Blondel, C., & Carlock, R. (2005), "Fair process: striving for justice in family businesses," in *Family Business Review* 18, pp. 1–21.

3. Koeberle-Schmid, A., & Schween, K. (2012) "Familienverfassungen individuell erarbeiten – Hinweise für Unternehmerfamilien vor dem Hintergrund der Konfliktprävention," *KonfliktDynamik* 1/4, pp. 320–327.

4. Source: Kenyon-Rouvinez, D. (2007), *A Few Things that Truly Matter in Family Constitutions*, Marietta: Family Enterprise Publishers.

5. For the results of the INTES study, see: Schween, K., Koeberle-Schmid, A., Bartels, P., & Hack, A. (2011), *Die Familienverfassung – Zukunftssicherung für Familienunternehmen: Ergebnisse einer Studie*, Bonn: INTES Akademie; Koeberle-Schmid, A., Schween, K., & May, P. (2011), "Governance Kodex für Familienunternehmen in der Praxis – Ergebnisse einer Studie über Familienverfassungen," *Betriebs-Berater* 41, pp. 2499–2506.

6. May, P. (2012), *Erfolgsmodell Familienunternehmen*, Hamburg: Murmann; May, P., Schween, K., & Koeberle-Schmid, A. (2012), "Das Strategie-Konzept für Familienunternehmen – Mit einer Inhaber-Strategie zum langfristigen Erfolg über Generationen," in *Handbuch der Unternehmensberatung* 18, *Erg.-Lfg.* X/12, 3190, pp. 1–25.

7. May, P. (2008), "Leading the family business – Why creating an owner strategy must come first for family businesses," in Büchel, B., Read, S., Moncef, A., & Coughlan, S. (eds.), *Riding the Wings of Global Change*, Lausanne: IMG, pp. 83–89; May, P. (2009), "Familienunternehmen erfolgreich führen – Von der Inhaber-Strategie zur Unternehmens-Strategie," *Zeitschrift für Betriebswirtschaft Special Issue* 2, pp. 113–126;

May, P. (2012), *Erfolgsmodell Familienunternehmen*, Hamburg: Murmann; May, P., Schween, K., & Koeberle-Schmid, A. (2011) "Inhaber-Strategie: Zukunftssicherung für Familie und Unternehmen," in Langenscheidt, F., & May, P. (eds.), *Aus Bester Familie*, 2nd edn., Cologne: Deutsche Standards EDITIONEN, pp. 16–21; May, P., Schween, K., & Koeberle-Schmid, A. (2012), "Das Strategie-Konzept für Familienunternehmen - Mit einer Inhaber-Strategie zum langfristigen Erfolg über Generationen," in *Handbuch der Unternehmensberatung* 18, Erg.-Lfg. X/12, 3190, pp. 1–25; Koeberle-Schmid, A., Fahrion, H.J., & Witt, P. (2012), *Family Business Governance – Erfolgreiche Führung von Familienunternehmen*, Berlin: Erich Schmidt; Koeberle-Schmid, A., & Grottel, B. (2013), *Führung von Familienunternehmen*, Berlin: Erich Schmidt.

8.  An adaption of the model developed by May and discussed in: May, P. (2012), *Erfolgsmodell Familienunternehmen*, Hamburg: Murmann; May, P., Schween, K., & Koeberle-Schmid, A. (2011), "Inhaber-Strategie: Zukunftssicherung für Familie und Unternehmen," in Langenscheidt, F., & May, P. (eds.), *Aus Bester Familie*, 2nd edn., Cologne: Deutsche Standards EDITIONEN, pp. 16–21; May, P., Schween, K., & Koeberle-Schmid, A. (2012), "Das Strategie-Konzept für Familienunternehmen – Mit einer Inhaber-Strategie zum langfristigen Erfolg über Generationen," in *Handbuch der Unternehmensberatung* 18, Erg.-Lfg. X/12, 3190, pp. 1–25; Carlock, R., & Ward, J. (2001), *Strategic Planning for the Family Business*, Basingstoke: Palgrave; Montemerlo, D., & Ward, J. (2011), *The Family Constitution*, Basingstoke: Palgrave Macmillan.

9.  Schween, K., Koeberle-Schmid, A., Bartels, P., & Hack, A. (2011), *Die Familienverfassung – Zukunftssicherung für Familienunternehmen: Ergebnisse einer Studie*, Bonn: INTES Akademie.

10. May, P., & Koeberle-Schmid, A. (2011), "Die drei Dimensionen eines Familienunternehmens: Teil I," *Betriebswirtschaftliche Forschung und Praxis* 6, pp. 656–672; May, P., & Koeberle-Schmid, A. (2012), "Die drei Dimensionen eines Familienunternehmens: Teil II," *Betriebswirtschaftliche Forschung und Praxis* 1, pp. 52–72; May, P. (2012), *Erfolgsmodell Familienunternehmen*, Hamburg: Murmann.

## Chapter 13

1.  Kachaner, N., Stalk, G., & Bloch, A. (2012), "What you can learn from family business," *Harvard Business Review*, November. At http://hbr.org/2012/11/what-you-can-learn-from-family-business/ar/1, accessed July 8, 2013.

# About the Authors

**Dr Alexander Koeberle-Schmid** is an economist who comes from a business-owning family. His Ph.D was about boards of directors and family councils in family enterprises. Alexander is a family business advisor, who has worked for renowned consulting and family business advisory firms. He advises owner families of medium-sized to large multinational family enterprises in owner strategic issues such as governance structures, management succession, boards of directors, family councils, family offices, family philanthropy, and family constitutions. He has worked as a commercial mediator, was non-executive board member of a medium-sized family enterprise, and is in frequent demand as a speaker and lecturer.

**Denise Kenyon-Rouvinez**, Ph.D, is the Wild Group Professor of Family Business and co-director of the Global Family Business Center at IMD, Switzerland. For nearly 20 years Denise has worked extensively with very large family businesses in Asia, the Middle East, Europe, North and South America and is used to dealing with complex governance and wealth situations. Her key areas of expertise are governance, succession, liquidity events, ownership, wealth, and philanthropy.

Denise is also the founder and chairman of Gen[10] SA, an independent company providing high quality VIP Boutique services to HNW & UHNW entrepreneurial families and families of wealth around the globe; as well as a certified coach working with the Solution Focused Coaching approach (based on brief therapies and positive psychology), and an accredited Lifo® Licensee – a personal style survey which helps individuals reach their potential and improve their performance.

Author of numerous books and articles on family businesses, Denise has received several awards for her research work. Her books include: *A Woman's Place. The Crucial Roles of Women in Family Businesses* (2008, Palgrave Macmillan), *Why Me? Wealth: Creating, Having and Passing it on* (2007 Family Enterprise Publishers), *Who, Me? Family Business Succession – A practical Guide For The Next Generation* (2005 Family Enterprise Publishers), *Family Business – Key Issues* (2005 Palgrave Macmillan), and *Sharing Wisdom, Building Values – Letters From Family Business Owners To Their Successors* (2002 Palgrave Macmillan).

Denise is the founder and former president of the Family Business Network (FBN) chapter in French speaking Switzerland, and a Family Firm Institute (FFI) Fellow and mentor.

**Ernesto J. Poza** (BS Yale University; MBA, Sloan School of Management, Massachusetts Institute of Technology) is an internationally recognized, top-rated speaker and consultant to family-controlled and family-owned businesses. He is Clinical Professor of Global Entrepreneurship and Family Enterprise at Thunderbird's School of Global Management. As a speaker, consultant and board member he challenges business owners to revitalize mature businesses through strategic thinking, succession planning and change management. His work has been featured on CNN, NBC, and NPR, as well as in *The New York Times, The Wall Street Journal, Fortune, Business Week, Family Business Magazine, Inc., El Pais, Excelsior, Expansion, and El Nuevo Día*. Poza is on the editorial board of the *Family Business Review* and the *Journal of Family Business Strategy*.

Ernesto Poza has advised top managements of privately-held and Fortune 500 companies in strategic management, succession planning, growth, and governance. Among the firms served in the US, Latin America, and Europe are: Chiquita Brands, E. W. Scripps Company, Gonzalez Byass, S.A., Catalana de Occidente, and Almirall (wine, insurance, and pharmaceuticals respectively, Spain). Also Grupo Alfa and Grupo Femsa (conglomerates, Mexico), El Nuevo Dia (news media, Puerto Rico), Huber & Co, Mars Inc., and Simpson Investments in the US. Poza has also consulted with substantial family offices and smaller, yet equally wonderful, privately-held family firms and family offices in their efforts to keep the business successful and the family united during the often turbulent generational transition period.

In recognition of his contribution to the field of family business, the Family Firm Institute awarded him the third ever granted Richard Beckhard Practice Award in 1996 and its highly coveted International Award in 2010. His research interests are in the areas of family business continuity, global growth opportunities, family business governance, leadership of change, family offices, and family entrepreneurship. Poza is the author of *Family Business*, 4th edition, (2013, South-Western/Cengage Publishing) *Empresas Familiares* (2005, International Thomson Ed.), *Family Business* (2004, Thomson Publishing), and *Smart Growth: Critical Choices for Continuity and Prosperity* (1989).

He is a founding member and Fellow of the Family Firm Institute and serves on the boards of several family firms.

Lightning Source UK Ltd.
Milton Keynes UK
UKHW02f0003040418
320464UK00006B/460/P